G O U R A S A N A

The Radical Path Home to God

Attaining a state of full awareness in your lifetime

Discourses selected by Kalindi
and edited by The Lady

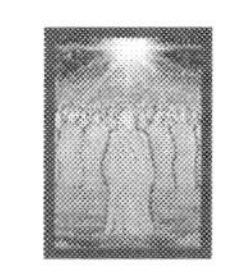

Miracle of Love®

G O U R A S A N A

The Radical Path Home to God

Attaining a state of full awareness in your lifetime

First Edition, 2008

Miracle of Love, 4277 West 43rd Street, Denver, CO 80212

Library of Congress catalogue card number: 2008933728

ISBN 978-1-892546-06-7

Printed in the United States of America

What is your existence all about?

There is only one thing for certain:
that you exist to find the truth,
to find the light, to find the love,
to find the Lord, to return Home
to the true realm of existence.
Whatever else you may believe or feel,
the conclusion that your existence
here was never meant to be eternal
is inescapable. Your existence is
designed to culminate in your
becoming aware. So become aware.

GOURASANA

Breaking the Cycle of Birth and Death (4th ed.) Quote #319.

I dedicate this book to:

The Father, Lord Gourasana, "The Golden One,"
Who is here for all of us,

My two friends and teachers,
David Swanson and Kalindi, who paved the way,

And the people of this world, so hungry for truth and love.

THE LADY
First Disciple of Kalindi

Contents

Introduction

During the years 1987 to 1995, the modern-day Incarnation of God, Gourasana, created an authentic and radical path Home to God. He came with the power and teachings to fulfill the desire of those who wish to return Home and attain a full state of awareness in their lifetime.

Gourasana's power and presence manifested in the body of David Swanson, an extraordinary man who gave Gourasana permission to completely take over his body so that Gourasana could come into this world. This involved an arduous physical and spiritual transformation for David, but he said "yes" without hesitation because David knew it was the Lord, and David wanted for himself and for others what Gourasana promises:

> I am Gourasana, and I can take you Home because I know where Home is. What an opportunity you have! It is a gift being offered. Please take it.[1]

Gourasana drew to Himself a core of seven people of "unshakable faith" who knew from direct experience that

1) Gourasana, *Breaking the Cycle of Birth and Death* (4th ed.) Quote #1.

Gourasana was an Incarnation of God. The people in "the Core" were the first to realize Gourasana's teachings, and since then have been instrumental in carrying His presence and love into the world.

In the early years of His coming, Gourasana talked to small gatherings about how they could personally realize the truth and attain a state of full awareness in their lifetime. This book contains these essential teachings from Gourasana. These teachings can enrich your spiritual journey and help you to move closer to God regardless of your spiritual path or religious affiliation.

As you read this book, you can receive the same personal love and assistance that Gourasana gave to every individual that was with Him. And you can experience Gourasana's unconditional desire for *everyone* to come Home to the love of God:

> I have waited so long for you to come Home. You cannot imagine My desire. I have not forgotten you for a second. And I am only concerned about you. And I am determined. If you can also become determined, then everything is possible.[2]

Gourasana makes it clear that achieving a state of full awareness takes serious endeavor and radical action:

> [For] one who is truly ready to leave, to give up everything, to do anything to achieve full awareness in this lifetime . . . *always* radical means are essential in order to break free from this illusion in this lifetime.[3]

And always Gourasana speaks with great compassion, love, and encouragement:

> Every single living entity in this cosmos is fully worthy of achieving a state of full awareness and love of God.[4]

2) Gourasana, *What Sacrifice Will You Make?* March 13, 1988.
3) Gourasana, *Radical Means Are Essential*, July 23, 1988.
4) Gourasana, *Breaking the Cycle of Birth and Death* (4th ed.) Quote #291.

> Do not be discouraged. Do not give up. As long as you continue trying, that very trying – whether your conscious mind can appreciate it or not – is manifesting simultaneously an awareness which at some time will begin to blossom.[5]

Gourasana's coming has borne fruit: David has returned Home to God; two members of the Core, Kalindi and The Lady, have become fully realized spiritual masters and are Gourasana's successors.[6] Kalindi and The Lady lead a worldwide Mission known as Miracle of Love® that is dedicated to helping people get freer and closer to the love of God. Thousands of people have experienced Gourasana's teachings through the transformational seminars, programs, books, and CDs offered by Miracle of Love, and many of these people are finding their way Home to God in their lifetime.

The discourses in this book are from talks that Gourasana gave in 1988 and 1989 that have been especially selected by Kalindi and edited by The Lady. Each chapter in the book represents a complete discourse by Gourasana, which usually includes a question-and-answer session and often a guided meditation.

To better absorb Gourasana's teachings, you are encouraged to study His words and to make marginal notes and highlight or underline points that are significant to you. When you read Gourasana's words as if you are sitting together with Him in deep meditation, with an open mind and an open heart, you can actually feel Gourasana's energy and experience the truth behind His words:

> [My] words are not giving the truth. The truth cannot be put into words. The words are mainly to remove the blockages, the misconceptions, the things standing in your

5) Gourasana, *Transcending this State of Illusion,* February 23, 1988
6) Gourasana left the body in 1995.

> way. Then once removed, you, yourself go within and you find the truth – not a belief system, not a promise from Me.[7]
>
> I am speaking so many words, but try to hear the communication in your heart more than your head.[8]
>
> Hear not My words so much as My desire. That is the real communication. I am calling you. Come here to this realm of existence. It is a love that you want so badly. It is a love that is so fulfilling that once you have it you need nothing else.[9]

Gourasana's love, guidance, and power is all waiting for you in *The Radical Path Home to God*, and His great desire for you is that you take this gift, take this help, on your journey back Home.

7) Gourasana, *As Long as You Are Endeavoring, Simultaneously there Is a Result,* July 7, 1989.
8) Gourasana, *Desire Will Save You,* May 27, 1988.
9) Gourasana, *Desire Will Save You,* May 27, 1988.

Important Information

Pronunciation of Gourasana

Gourasana is pronounced Goo-RAH-sah-nah.

Editing Notes

Gourasana's words in this book are from verbatim transcripts of His discourses, which have been minimally edited by The Lady for clarity. The Lady spent countless hours checking the accuracy of each word in the transcripts and making sure that any edits are true to what Gourasana spoke. Italics have been used liberally in the text to indicate Gourasana's emphasis and tone.

Terms Used

What is an Incarnation of God? Gourasana says that an Incarnation "means all the love of God and all the power of God is coming in, and the only thing that can be received is love."[1] Over the ages, many Incarnations of God have come to assist people in their search for God. Examples of these Incarnations are Buddha, Krishna, and Jesus.

1) Gourasana, *God Is Love,* March 5, 1991.

The Heavenly Host of Light Beings. Gourasana came with a Heavenly Host of Light Beings, the "true selves," whose specific purpose in coming at this time is to bring special assistance for rapid spiritual transformation to the many people who seek full awareness and the love of God. In His discourses, Gourasana often speaks for Himself and the Host, and so He uses the words "We," "Us," or "Our."

The Core. Soon after Gourasana came, He called for a "Core" of people to gather around Him. Gourasana said these people had to "*have unshakable faith, not blind faith, not sentimental faith, not some false belief, false hope.*"[2] A group of seven people responded to this call. The Core are referred to by name in the question-and-answer sessions in the discourses; the other people asking questions are referred to as Person One, Person Two, etc. Many of the Core changed their birth names during their spiritual transformation; for example, Carol is now Kalindi, and Gayle is now The Lady.

Applying the Guidance in this Book

Gourasana's guidance is meant for healthy people of sound mind who want to move closer to God. If you choose to follow Gourasana's spiritual guidance contained in this book, we urge you do so responsibly and with full love, care, and respect for yourself and others – as this is one of Gourasana's main teachings.

2) Gourasana, *The Unadulterated Truth Is Rare,* March 13, 1988.

The Radical Path Home to God

Attaining a state of full awareness in your lifetime

Feel the Unlimited Love that Is Permeating the Universe

February 5, 1988 – Poway, CA

There are so many teachings that you come in contact with, that sometimes there may be confusion. A constant criticism of spiritual teachings from those who do not understand is that there are apparent conflicts. Sometimes the teachings appear to have opposites.

For the sake of Our[1] intent in coming here, we can divide the teachings, all of the teachings, into two categories. There are many things which will help you, which will give you some knowledge, some illumination – especially on how to function on this plane. While you may take assistance in these areas and reap the benefit from these teachings, you should primarily be seeking the teachings that *at least* have grasped the principle of leaving this plane of existence. If this principle is never stated in someone's teachings – the ulti-mate purpose of leaving this plane of existence – then for the sake of Our purpose, you must consider these teachings to be in a *lesser* category.

1) Gourasana is referring to Himself and the Heavenly Host of Light Beings that accompany Him.

You see, assistance is coming at all levels. And again, you may all utilize some of these teachings to help function on this plane, but do not make these the *real* focus. Rather, focus on the teachings of those that at least discuss this principle of breaking the cycle of birth and death. The lesser teachings simply do not have the power. They will give some illumination, but you must not be satisfied with this degree of illumination. Most are mistakenly caught up in these lesser teachings, because they do see light. But because their desire is not strong enough, they are satisfied with too little light. That is why it is critical that even with the teachings of masters who are encouraging transcendence from this plane, you must *not* be satisfied. Do not be satisfied until full illumination is there.

Satisfaction with what you have attained is another obstacle, what to speak of these lesser teachings which cannot even propel you from this plane of existence. Even with the highest teachings, you must not be satisfied until you *know* the truth, until the *doubts no longer come*. As long as the doubts come, you are subject to illusion. The doubts will be there as a normal course, but as long as they are there, you must not be satisfied.

Only be satisfied with *total* awareness. We have not come here to give a little illumination. We have come to give you *total* illumination. That is *Our* desire. If it also becomes *your* desire, then success is guaranteed. The desire is fully there on *Our* part. Now you must make it fully there on *your* part. This combination will not fail to succeed.

If you have any questions, please ask.

Person One: How do you get your desire to increase? Is there anything more we can do to increase our desire other than just willing it to do so?

Gourasana: Willing it to do so is what you must do. And by practicing this "willing," it will become stronger, and your ability in this area will increase. But you must practice. You may do this at any time, in any place. Simply desire. But an excellent opportunity for increasing this desire is when you find yourself in illusion, in darkness; when you feel no love; when you doubt the very existence of the *only reality,* the Spirit. In times of your greatest suffering, this can be the time for your greatest growth, because if you are satisfied in your illusion, there is not much impetus.

So when you feel alone, when you have these deep feelings – no matter what they may be: anger, loneliness, even when you feel the love – use these moments of deep feeling to go even deeper and create this desire. And yes, it is *by your will* that the desire will grow. You see? That's why We say it is solely *by your desire* that you will leave this plane of existence *or not.* If somebody simply does not wish to leave, then they will not, but if someone even has a little desire, then by using their will they can increase this desire.

There are many opportunities to practice, if you will pay attention during your day. There are many moments, when if even for an instant you can desire the ultimate truth, this will increase your desire. It is as simple as that.

When you are feeling love, you can desire it more.

When you are feeling anger, you can desire the love and the light.

When you are feeling alone, you can desire the completion that will come when you achieve a state of full awareness.

And you can let this desire grow and fill your being until there is nothing else but this desire, which is a constant prayer. As constant as this prayer is, to that extent it is being answered.

When we gather together at this retreat[2], this desire should be the prime meditation. You should not be sitting around idly chatting. Your time should be spent in reflection and increasing this desire, because while several of you have a lot of desire – you need to increase it – and too many do not have enough desire. So the desire must be increased. You must want it.

You must be filled with a longing that will not be satisfied by anything else but a connection with the light and the love. So when you have this gathering, there must not be the normal escapes from this longing. I do not have to name these escapes; you all know what they are. Even your conversations are primarily an escape. Your discussions about the light at this retreat need to be *very brief*. This is another excuse for avoiding the light – these lengthy conversations about the light.

There must be practically no talking, no discussion. The discussion can be when we sit as a group. But the tendency is that you have a realization, you have an experience, and you immediately want to go and talk about it. You must resist this tendency. It will be a time of extreme discipline for some. If they cannot perform this discipline, if they are not ready at this time, then they should not attend. Because in this short period of time we wish to make great advancement. So from the time of arrival, there must be a seriousness, a gravity about the purpose. It is not a time of recreation and entertainment. It is a time to increase your longing for the truth. It is a time to go within and increase your desire to leave this plane of existence, because until the desire is there on *your part,* We cannot do *Our part,* because We can *only* fulfill *your desire. So if you come and you have no desire to*

2) Gourasana is referring to a meditation retreat.

explore the universe, then you will sit there, because We cannot take you where you do not desire to go!

So you all must begin practicing this: If you will pay attention, you will see your desire increase, just as you say, by willing it, because it is by your will that everything is being created for you. And if your desire is not so strong, you can increase that desire if you will it. Begin practicing now, so by the time we gather together, everyone will have gained experience and be able to easily enter into this state of desire.

This we will discuss as much as necessary, because *this is everything*. This is the age-old problem: They say, "I have no desire, and I have no desire to have the desire." So if you even have the beginning of desire, then you can build on that. But there are some that do not even have the beginning. In fact, *most* do not truly wish to leave this plane. So their desire, by their will, will only increase to some degree, and they will stop it. That is why, you will see, they will come and they will go so far, and then for whatever reasons of illusion, they will stop. They will have many good reasons, but they will all be born of illusion.

Carol: Gourasana, are you going to tell us more about how to plan this retreat? What circumstance should be there? What the situation should be like? I don't really know exactly what we should do.

Gourasana: You know what this social mood is. We do not want this social mood. When the individuals arrive, when they walk in the door, they should be focused within already, and their frame of mind should be *serious*. Discussion should be as little as possible; only what is absolutely necessary should be spoken. If you want this to succeed, there must be cooperation from everyone. If someone is in a corner and they are just talking, it will dissipate the intensity. Whatever you do should be in a meditative state, not that when it is time to eat it is social hour. There is no need to talk while you eat. You lose a certain power when you speak. So if you desire to succeed, as much as possible, you should speak only if necessary.

This will be difficult for several, but this must be maintained and this must be agreed upon. There will be too much tendency for social interaction, and *it must not be there*. The state must always be serious, because what We are desiring to do is *serious*. It is with this frame of mind that We can take you to the true stages of ecstasy and joy. But when you get a little satisfaction from the illusion, a little relief, and in a happy state you begin talking about it, then you lose the power to get to the true depths of illumination. No matter what occurs during this time, you must view it from within.

You may read books that will spark this desire. Reading the teachings that are interested in getting you out of the illusion, reading the teaching of masters who have *gotten out* can spark this desire – but not the books of these lesser teachings that just give a little light and happiness – only the most serious.

It will be difficult. You will see, some people will become very disturbed, and the emotions will range from depression to ecstasy. You all must work very hard.

What else do you need to know?

Person Two: Gourasana, what state of mind should we have when we are carrying out our occupation?

Gourasana: First, you should try to be centered within. This is difficult, but can be attained with more and more practice. It is simply where your attention is focused. When you are centered within, your power in your occupation will increase. Your communication with others will increase, because a *stronger* communication will go on to the degree that you are centered within. So you will have more power and influence to the degree that you are centered within.

Then, it is also important that you see your occupation as an illusion, just as if you were making a movie, because it is like that. This will help you maintain the proper amount of detachment, which is the third important ingredient that must be there when practicing your occupation – is a detachment.

Person Two: For what purpose is that detachment necessary?

Gourasana: If you are too attached, it means you are caught up in the illusion. It means that you think that you are part of the illusion. The reality is at any moment the film may break and the movie will stop, and in the proper detached state there will be no disturbance. You will just nod, "Now the movie is over. What's next?" But in an attached state, you will feel bewildered. So you must begin practicing this now, because the movie of your life is going to have an end, and so there is not too much disturbance at the end, you must begin practicing now and see it just for the illusion that it is.

Person Two: Thank you, Gourasana.

Gayle: Gourasana, can you talk to us about friendship? You tell us everything is illusion, and we shouldn't be so attached, because the film may break at any moment and we may die at any moment. But while we are here, people come into our lives, we get close to them, then issues may come up, we separate, and then we are drawn to new friends. Are friends here just to help us learn our lessons?

Gourasana: Yes. You can learn many lessons from those around you. By observing the consciousness of those around you, you can better understand the power of the illusion.

You can observe it in yourself, but sometimes it is easier to see it in others. As we have discussed, one moment they are very interested in the light or they are making a pretense of being interested in the light, and the next second they have no interest in the light. This is going on to small degrees all the time: one hour in the light and the next hour in the dark. But for many it is much more dramatic. They appear to be so much in the light, and then suddenly they are so much in the dark.

But the friends, the people that you want close to you, should as much as possible have the same desire, because associating with one who has no desire for the light *will distract you.* None of you is to that point where no one will distract you. Do not be in illusion about that. So you must use some care in your association.

It is a very powerful area for the darkness to come into your life, through the association of one who is attached to the darkness. When someone desires illusion, their desire is for those around them to also come into illusion. So just as those that desire the light preach, propagate, encourage others to come into the light, so those that are attached to illusion and desire others to be in the illusion will speak in a way to influence others to be covered over, to be in a state of illusion. And some are very good at this. Just as there are those in the light that are very good at propagating the light, so there are some in darkness that are very good, so you can hardly tell that they are propagating darkness – *but they are.* And they can influence you, and darkness can permeate your consciousness and take you over. This does not mean, of course, that the light is gone. It means though, that so much darkness is covering or interwoven that the light is suffocated and cannot grow quickly, if at all. So care must be there.

Person Three: Gourasana, are there any exercises or steps or activities that we can do on a daily basis to facilitate our attraction to the light and development toward the light?

Gourasana: You may find certain approaches that are comfortable for you at times in many teachings – but you must see if they are indeed working: if the light is increasing or if your desire is increasing. And if it is not, then you must change. There are so many teachings. We do not wish to support one as it would appear to exclude others, and for many they will vary greatly. There are the silent meditation states, which are good for many. There are the verbal meditation states, the chanting, which are good for many. There are the prayers, which are good *for everybody*. Prayer. If I were to say one thing, I would say a prayer.

Person Three: Could you give us an example of a prayer that would be really good?

Gourasana: Pray for the light. Pray that you can feel the unlimited love that is permeating the universe. Pray that you no longer desire to stay in illusion. Pray to know the truth. Pray for all of the things you ultimately desire.

Do not waste your prayers and your energy on this illusion. Do not pray for a better movie or that you wish you had another role in the movie. It is a waste of time. If your desire is truly only for the light and love, then We will facilitate you in whatever you need. You do not need to pray separately. But this is one excellent area where you may practice.

You may dance and enter into a meditative state. So I am not saying that there is anything that you cannot do, but you should find for yourself what works best. And *you should expect results*. Do not do something perpetually without getting tangible results and being satisfied.

Person Three: Thank you.

Gourasana: But you may try some process, and if you wish to discuss it after trying it, then more assistance can be there. One thing is, do not be limited to one thing. You must stay flexible. You must stay in tune with what We are telling you, because there may be a period of your life where total silence and a meditative state will be the only ideal thing for you to do. But for others prayer may be there, and may be the most powerful thing. Then, of course, the combinations.

You see, teachers have always tried to give these different instructions, but you can go on, and on, and on, and on: "Do it this way, do it that way, do it at this time of the day." So many things. But you get caught up too much in the details and are not paying enough attention to the results. So for one person, ten steps of a meditation might be important, but for another, two or three of them may not be good at all. So you cannot give a blanket process without *excluding some*. So in all your religions that have a blanket process for everybody, there are those that get the maximum benefit, but there are too many that only receive a little because they need to change some aspect of the philosophy. But because it is given as a blanket process, they do not do that, and they go away from it in frustration rather than changing what needs to be changed. This is true in all of the processes.

Carol: Gourasana, I was wondering if I could get some guidance or direction? Since I have stopped my entanglement with the seminar, I'm pretty much just quiet and trying to stay open. I'm used to having a lot of activity in my life. There's a part of me that's drawn to staying quiet and not doing anything, then there's the part that's used to activity. So I'm wondering: At this time, am I supposed to just be quiet and continue what I'm doing or am I supposed to get active? I don't exactly know which way to go right now.

I want to somehow get closer to you. I want to feel the love more. That's my desire.

Gourasana: It is the busyness that takes you from the light, and that busyness you must avoid *totally* at this time. You look to these things as excuses to not go within. Ironically, this is what most people are doing in the processes of religions. They are so busy propagating and helping others that they do little for themselves, thereby missing the entire point. This has also been a trap for you. For you it is an illusion, and you must stay away from this area of illusion. This does not mean that some activity cannot be there, but the activity must not be this busy type of escape that you so quickly seek. Even since you left the seminar, for a period you were trying to enter into another illusion around Me and getting very busy talking to people.

There are others that will not be trapped by propagating. For you it is a trap at this time, and you must do little in this area. You must artificially restrain yourself from this desire to propagate, because it has been an illusion for you for so long, and instead do activities to help only yourself. Do not be so concerned about helping everyone else. Once you have centered yourself where you should be, then you may begin in a centered state to help others. For now, propagation would be a good exercise *for others* who would benefit by this. So delegate these responsibilities to others. For yourself, go within and face the many things you have been avoiding for so many years.

Carol: Then for this time period, should I just keep doing nothing? Keep doing what I've been doing? One part of me thinks it's right, and then sometimes I feel a lack of presence, and then I don't know if I should be doing something. I don't know if I'm getting closer, or if by not doing anything

I'm going into darkness, because I'm going to go crazy if I just sit here any more with myself.

Gourasana: *Then do something that will increase the light!* Another here has asked about processes that could be done. I have named processes. There are many processes you are aware of. Do something to increase the light. When I say to somebody, "Do nothing," I do not mean sitting mindlessly. I mean do not get busy doing things that distract you from the light. If you sit down in a meditative state, you are doing a great deal. You may do physical exercise, and this can be done in a meditative state. You can pray; you can meditate quietly; you can chant; you can read books that have the highest information in them. Even in your daily activities, create an atmosphere that is meditative – put on music that sparks this meditative state. Create a meditative atmosphere as much as possible in what you do. If you do not feel that state, if it is not possible to create that state sitting where you are, then sit somewhere else where it is possible. Usually a place of inspiration will help. Go to such a place: a temple, a church, a meditative place. Certain environments are ideal. So if someone is having difficulty where they are, then they should create an environment where the difficulty is much less. You all have some idea what this means.

Begin working on yourself.

There is a tendency of everyone who becomes involved in a spiritual organization to think if they do not give out the light, others will not get it; therefore, it is dependent *upon them.* In that state they feel obligated to keep up an activity to constantly give out the light. They think if they stop their activity, the light will not be given out. In this way they miss the point. It is just another excuse to avoid the light.

This does not mean that you cannot help others, but if in helping others you are becoming distracted from the light, then the ultimate good is not being served. If you, yourself, are not getting the light, then the whole point is being missed. Do whatever it takes to get the light.

Carol: I always thought when I was doing these activities to spread the light, most of the time I was really happy. So I mistook that for being the light. I was really happy doing those things. Now in this state I'm not so happy. I'm serious. I'm very serious most of the time. I don't have any extreme joy or all that much happiness. I have a certain peace and seriousness now. I don't exactly understand. I understand to some degree.

Gourasana: A little light, a lot of illusion, mixed together, produced your state of happiness. Now you are giving up the illusion. It is important to know that it will not feel good many times. We have discussed this on numerous occasions. Because people are using happiness as a guideline, they are missing too much. You can look back and see the illusion you were in, so your awareness is increasing. This is what is important. Do things that will continue to expand your awareness. If you are doing things to become happy – you want to create a happy movie – then it is futile, and energy is being wasted. You must become aware that it is just an illusion. That is where your energy should be channeled, not in trying to become happy.

True happiness will only come from true awareness. If you will observe those around you, you will be able to look and see that when there is extreme happiness it is very obvious how the illusion is working. There may be some light, but there will be a good measure of illusion also, until a point is reached where the true pleasure is coming from just the light.

Again, it is where you focus your attention. If you focus it on becoming happy, then you are missing the point. You must focus it on becoming aware, and do whatever is necessary to become aware. And sometimes what you need to do will be very difficult, and for many, shocking, but you must be brave and support each other.

If you need a little relief, there are other philosophies in which you will see the word "fun" reoccurring, and you can do a little of their philosophy to have some fun. This will not get you out of this illusion, but a little practice in this area will not necessarily stifle your advancement.

Gayle: Gourasana, is one of the ways to expand our awareness to observe ourselves and our thoughts, our emotions, and the people around us? Try to be observant as much as possible? When I wake up I wonder where my awareness is. I go to sleep and I wonder where my awareness is. All day long I think about it. I'm reading books about great masters, and then I begin to wonder, "Gee, will I ever be able to see the light like these people are seeing the light?" Because what they do is just incredible – the things that they give up and their intensity, their focus. Their single-mindedness is so intense. What they do! What they give up! They don't even have normal kinds of love relationships. They've given that up also. They've gone through so much. They've gained so much. Sometimes I just want to go away to a monastery and be totally alone.

Gourasana: A mistake that people are making in the processes is they are looking at the teacher, or the example, and artificially they are trying to do just what he is doing – *which is absurd.* The steps that each individual has to take are unique to each individual. To try to have a blanket process for everyone is a type of insanity. It certainly has its benefits, but as I have said, there are some who will benefit a great deal, but too many will only get a little bit because they are doing it *exactly* like everybody else. And because of the unique nature of each person, it simply does not work. Do not be concerned with what a master is doing in his state. What he is doing in the state that you are reading about – he is no longer doing *that*. He is already *doing* something else. And *would you want to copy that?*

You must begin where you are, at your state of awareness. What you have stated that you are doing is excellent. Do it more. Increase it more. If it comes to a point that you truly wish to have total solitude, then it will be a critical moment where if you have enough faith to act, you could make a leap of consciousness. But again, do not think that this state of total solitude will have to be permanent. This is another mistake. People begin a process and they stick in that process too long. You may need total solitude, but for how long? It may be one week; it may be one month; it may be one year. You will know when you no longer need it. But listen to these desires that are coming up. Not that you become whimsical in your lives, but if there is a desire that is constantly haunting you, then pay attention. If this is something that is with you a lot, then plan a period of time when you can have total solitude for as long as possible. And let us say that you can do this for a period of a month, if at the end of the month you see that you need much more, then plan more.

You must always stay very flexible in what you should do. One day you arise, and that day what you should do is *pray from your heart*. Now that may not be what you should do every day, so you must get in tune with what We are telling you – with what *you need*. Again, the processes that state "Every day at a certain time you must do this," you can see why they do not work. One day you may pray. The next day you may be totally silent; the next day you may practice some breathing process; the next day you may practice some oral chanting. One day you may just read. Or you *may do all of the things* in one day.

There is nothing that is stopping you from acting. If someone says, "I am working all day long; what can I do?" Every second, you can be increasing your desire no matter what you are doing. No matter what your job, you can be praying for the light; you can be increasing your desire. This is why it is good to be familiar with a few different processes, but whatever you practice, do it with the ultimate desire of transcending this plane. Do not practice these lesser levels of consciousness for *some happiness* here on this plane. Do not work on changing the state of this illusion into an illusion that you would like better. It *is a waste of time.* Do what you need to do on *this plane* to leave this plane. It may be the same activity, but it will be the consciousness that you do it in that will make the difference in whether you will leave this plane or not.

I wish to say something about this retreat. It is possible that some may find it intolerable; the intensity may become too much. For the period that they cannot tolerate, they should leave the association of the group. Perhaps take a walk and talk to someone, whatever they need to do. And then when they can again enter into a good state, they can come back in. They should not disturb the rest of the group with the disturbances in their mind, and no one should be embarrassed that this is happening. So many of you will come to some pretty difficult points. If you truly move quickly, you will run into some hard points and you may *need* to discuss this. But when you leave the association of the group and go with another to talk, keep your discussion serious, to the point; do not ramble on about so many things just to relieve it.

Carol: Gourasana, there are people saying there is going to be a big earthquake here in California in the next couple of months and that there's a lot of danger here. Is California supposed to crack off into the ocean? Are we safe here, or should we think of moving somewhere else?

Gourasana: You would like to know how the movie will end.

Nothing is so concrete as you have been led to believe. There is room for change. If your fear is that you will not have the light before the movie ends, then that can be used to propel you faster, because the time is very short and the movie is almost over. There is not a lot of time to waste. You cannot run from death, but you can use this emotion to propel you faster. It is all right to think that it may end any time – tomorrow. You see, you must prepare yourself. So begin preparing yourself *now.* It is not something you should put off. You must *be* prepared.

So for you, this may be a good exercise. Think that tomorrow the earth *will* shake, and you will die. Now what are you going to do between now and then? What you are going to do between now and then *is what you should be doing anyway, because your death is certain.* As certainly as it might be tomorrow, it is going to be a day in the future. If you all knew for certain that you were going to die tomorrow, *what would you do?* Ask yourself. And *what it is you should do, that is what you should be doing now!* You should *pray.* So why are you not praying now? Your desire to know the truth about what will be occurring after your death will certainly increase dramatically if you knew you were dying tomorrow. But you are certainly going to die, *so why is that desire not increasing now?* We will be talking to some in the future that *will be* dying tomorrow, and it will not be something theoretical.

So if someone does not know where to begin, this may be one way to get into the proper state of mind – that you may be dying tomorrow. Now what will you do? See how your mentality will change, how it will become more serious. See the activities that will be excluded if you were leaving tomorrow. There are many that will say this is a very morbid state of mind to be in, but if practiced properly it will propel you quickly to the truth.

Now, your happiness is coming from illusion. A serious mentality will propel you quickly toward the truth, and the love you feel will not be sentiment; it will be love. And the light that you will find will not be a little illumination on your daily activities; *it will be the light!* And the truth will *not be how to function better on this plane of illusion; it will be the truth!* And once you have these things, then you will have everything! So they may criticize that you do not appear to be very happy, but do not pay attention. Rather, *stay* serious and desire to *achieve* the truth, the light, and the love. And do not be satisfied with the illusory counterparts to these things.

Person Two: Gourasana, is there anything you would like *me* to do?

Gourasana: Yes. I would like you to get free from this state of illusion that you are in. And also, you can spend a little of your energy facilitating others in getting free from this illusion. Many will have difficulty capturing the seriousness, and you could assist somewhat if you, yourself, can again focus with the proper seriousness on getting out of this state of illusion. A little of your activity could be directed in helping others, providing some facility so that others may also come to the light. But primarily your endeavor must be to get free from the illusion yourself, and you can begin this by fully acknowledging that you are in illusion.

Person Two: I don't have any problem understanding that, or acknowledging that.

Gourasana: Then you can move very quickly. Now it will depend on your activity and your desire. Do you wish to get out of this state of illusion? And *how much* do you wish to get out? And what are you willing *to do?*

Person Two: It seems the best thing to do is desire to get out of this illusion. Desire that one hundred percent and be willing to do whatever it takes to accomplish that.

Gourasana: Yes. This is how you will succeed. Too many will come to a point and they will say, "I cannot do that." And with that statement, they will come to a standstill until they *will do that.* What you must do will differ greatly from individual to individual, so you must be in a receptive mood, so that you will *know* what to do. You are going to die *tomorrow,* so what are you going to do *now?* This is how you all must begin thinking. This will facilitate you living in the present rather than putting it off for some spiritual advancement in the future – it is always in the future. This thinking will bring it home more – this exercise. Think you are going to die tomorrow. What will you do *now?* How will you prepare yourself *now?* And this is what you should be doing, *now.* It is another suggestion, another hint. It is not that I wish you to all stay up all night crying or be in a state of fear because you may die tomorrow. It is simply to impress upon you the need to begin doing something *now.* Thinking that you could die tomorrow will give you a strong hint of what it is you should be doing *now.*

Person Four: What if we have the desire, but not the strength to do that?

Gourasana: It takes no strength to desire. You can lie helpless, unable to move from disease and be desiring fully to be free from this state of illusion. If you do not have the strength, it means that you are too weak. You can use this weakness to increase your desire to leave this plane, where you will not be bound by weakness. Use weakness as a time to increase your longing to be free from the restrictions of this plane. In a state of weakness – or you could call it helplessness – you could pray for the strength or the desire. You can use any state that you are in to move. If you are too weak to even care, then you can start building on that and wish that you had some desire, because you truly would like to be free from illusion, but you are too weak to act. And begin a prayer to be freed from this bondage.

There is no state that you cannot move in. Learn how to use each and every state that you come across in a day – and you come across many – to move.

When you rise, whatever feeling you have, you can use that to propel yourself.

When you are deeply disturbed, you can pray for the peace that will come with the truth.

When you are depressed, you can pray for the ecstasy that will come with the light.

When you hate, you can pray for the love that will come with an increase in your awareness.

When you are tired, you can be tired of the illusion and use it as a time to let go.

And because your emotions change so much in a day, if you can pay attention and begin practicing these little exercises, you can move very quickly, so that no matter what state you find yourself in, *you can move in that state.* Anger, hate, love, disturbance, confusion, weakness, strength, whatever the state, you can apply a little exercise to it that will help you to move out of that state. Make up your own exercises that are pertinent to you.

There is nothing that is stopping you on this plane. By your will, you can overcome any circumstance. You can move in any circumstance, and with practice you will get better.

Do not be discouraged by those around you that will not take the light. Most will not take the light or they will settle for a little light. Your relationship with them is just part of the illusion, and it must be let go of with the illusion. And you will see many that will go back into the darkness and they will not care. Do not be discouraged when this phenomenon happens – and it is an incredible phenomenon to see – one period someone is in the light and wants nothing else, and in a short period later they are in illusion and are totally bound by that illusion. Use that experience that you can perceive to propel you even further because *you* don't want to be bound by that illusion. Use that to fire yourself up even more *to get free from this bondage,* which most are trapped in.

Whatever occurs around you in this world, you can utilize to propel yourself faster. And you need to start looking at your awareness. Observe your awareness today, and in one week from today you should be able to look at your awareness and see practical changes, tangible changes. Do not be satisfied with something so far in the future; use every single day to see changes in your awareness.

This is enough. Prepare this information for distribution to the group. Review what has been said, and do something to grow. We will meet again. We will stop now.

We Are Here Constantly to Help You

February 12, 1988 – Poway, CA

(Gourasana begins the discourse by asking for questions.)

Ask any questions.

Person One: I can understand the difference when you shift from the darkness to the light. But I don't understand how you can be in the light and feel how good it is, and then all of a sudden you wake up the next day and you are in darkness. What propels you to go to the other side, when you know that you would rather be in the light than in the darkness?

Gourasana: First, light means illumination. When you are in the light, you are there because you have some awareness, some understanding, true understanding of your existence. When you enter into the darkness, it means that your consciousness has come to an area *that you do not understand.* There is not sufficient illumination. People mistake these periods of darkness as going backwards. Rather, it is an area that you need to understand, that needs illumination. So when you are in the light and at another point – it can be sudden

– you find yourself in darkness, your consciousness has just entered into an area where there is insufficient understanding. During the time that you are in darkness, you have focused – perhaps not yet with your conscious mind – but you have focused nonetheless on an area that you need to understand.

So *do not* be discouraged by these periods. Rather, *be grateful* that you are being shown an area of your awareness that can be further illuminated. *Do not* see *this as a negative.* See it as a further step that you can take toward a culmination when you will always be in the light, when there will be no more dark areas left in your awareness. Also, be grateful and appreciate that you can distinguish the difference between the darkness and the light, because most cannot. Most are dwelling *primarily* in darkness, but because of the state of their illusion they have no idea that this is their dilemma. You all become disturbed by these dualities too much. Again I say, appreciate and be grateful that you have come to a state where you can begin to distinguish between the light and the darkness.

So when you wake and find yourself in darkness, just ask yourself, "What is it that I need to understand?" Examine what is going on, and as you continue to look at the problem, it will expand. It may begin with some superficial disturbance that is going on in your life – such as a relationship – but as you continue to look, it will take on greater and greater aspects and become all-encompassing. And even though your conscious mind may not be able to appreciate the illumination that is taking place, there will come a point when your conscious mind will have a realization.

It will be an area that began as darkness and through some effort has become another area of light and illumination. So do not be discouraged. Do not think that these periods are something bad. They are steps that are taking you closer to full illumination, full awareness. Try not to let the frustrations and the negative connotations you have applied to this darkness interfere with the process.

Person One: Gourasana, so are you saying that it's necessary then for us sometimes to go into periods of darkness so that we can further our self-examination, to give us impetus to keep going toward the light?

Gourasana: There are two issues in your question. One issue is impetus. The darkness can be an excellent impetus for you to go toward the light. As you can more clearly perceive the darkness, the illusion, this is something that can help you move at a faster rate. As We have spoken many times before, there are those that appear to be in the light, or perhaps there is a little light, then suddenly it's total darkness, and they are again in complete illusion with no light. And as your perception becomes clear, you will see that many who profess or appear to spread the light are, in fact, in total illusion and total darkness. Ironically, many of these people are in leadership positions claiming to lead others toward the light, as it is an excellent opportunity to further the darkness from that position of power.

So you should be concerned about this illusion. Do not be naive and think that you cannot be covered by illusion and darkness. The examples are going on constantly: one day in the light, desiring nothing but the light, and the next day – illusion, no desire for the light, actually against the light. And when the subject of the light is discussed by these people, great disturbance and agitation is there, because they have become propagators for the darkness, just as there are propagators for the light.

So that is one thing. Be a little afraid of this illusion and this darkness. Do not be naive and think that you are beyond *total* illusion because you have received so much light. There are too many examples that prove the possibility of your being in total illusion. *You could observe* that even within a short period of time, there have been two or three people that have gone from states of light and then entered heavily into darkness. Do not think that you are immune from the darkness.

The other area of your question: Do you need to go into the darkness? It is not so much that you need to go into it to have an impetus. Impetus can come from what I have stated, from observing *the power* of the illusion and the darkness. Rather, it is just an area that you need to go into to understand. But the degree that you go into darkness or illusion varies greatly. You have all experienced some time that you will just be practically in total illusion – you will doubt whether there is even Spirit, whether any of it is true. But the darkness can come in – and usually does come in – more frequently and in milder forms. It isn't always so obvious, which is why you must pay closer attention, because it can be little steps of darkness that take you away from the light. You let a little darkness in, then a little more and a little more, and soon you are further and further from the light.

So again, you can just look at it as an area where you do not have full understanding. You may need to look at an area many times before there will be full understanding. Do not be frustrated. Do not think that you may sit down and in one period you will fully understand one aspect, because the different aspects of illusion are interwoven, and as you begin to understand one area of illusion, there will be illumination in other areas also. *But there is no one* that does not need to go in and examine these areas. That process will continue until there is *full* illumination, and then you will just know.

Person Two: Gourasana, are we trying to untangle our illusion to try to understand it better?

Gourasana: If you mean by this that you need to understand each and every tiny aspect of the illusion – that is not the case. As I have stated, when you understand one area of illusion, this creates illumination on other areas of illusion. There are many aspects of illusion that you must look at separately and consider, but if you will pay attention, you will see that your awareness will be free *simultaneously* from other areas of illusion as your awareness grows. It is not that you are in total darkness in one area, and when that is totally illuminated, you can go to another area that is in total darkness. Everything is receiving illumination simultaneously. This is important to know, because people become discouraged. They cannot imagine how they will become free from so many complexities of illusion – an illusion within an illusion within an illusion. As your awareness truly grows, *you will just understand.* You will just begin to see *everything* that is an illusion, as an illusion.

Person Two: I understand, Gourasana. Thank you.

Person Three: Gourasana, I have one question. What truths can guide me to encompass all the truths?

Gourasana: Full awareness.

Person Three: How do I find this? What are the signs for me to look for? What are they?

Gourasana: First, you must begin observing *for yourself.* You see, when they speak of *self-awareness,* it is not something that someone will give to you. It is something that you must create. The teachings, the instructions, will give some hint on a direction to take, but you must begin practicing. For the purpose that We have come – which is to take those that desire it, out of this plane of existence once and for all – it is essential that you see the duality. Many may criticize this, because they will say, "Ultimately there is no duality; the duality is just an illusion." But I am saying that for you to artificially try to bring this awareness – which is the true awareness – to your plane, is naïve, and will be an obstacle to your leaving this plane of existence.

For you on this plane of existence, *you must see the duality.* This is where you can begin. If you go and become a drug addict or you go and you meditate, these actions will not produce the same enlightenment. It is a duality that you must deal with. There *is* darkness and there *is* light. These are factors you must deal with.

So you must see *for yourself* what is light, what is taking you to the light, giving you true awareness, and what is darkness. The reason this is so critical to practice is because even in organizations – especially in organizations of light – there is always darkness, and if you do not have discrimination, you will be accepting the darkness along with the light, and it will hamper your advancement.

In every major philosophy, in any true teaching, there is some truth, and you must begin to distinguish. You must dissect what you have learned to make sure that the darkness has not been accepted with the light.

The best examples are the religious organizations. There is undoubtedly wonderful love and light coming from the Lord Jesus, but there are different degrees of darkness interwoven in the truth that is being presented. If you can go to a church and you can take the love and the light of the Lord Jesus, then you can move quickly. But if you accept all of the darkness, and the illusion, and the man-made mundane so-called truths, then it will be a barrier that will prevent you from *truly* knowing the Lord Jesus.

The amount of darkness interwoven with the truth varies in great degree from one church – indeed from one individual believer in the Lord Jesus – to the next. This is just one example of so many other areas of teachings.

Person Three: Are there any guidelines within the capacity of my senses that can reveal to me the truth? Can the truth be revealed to me through my human senses?

Gourasana: Through your senses is not where the truth can be clearly understood. It is through your senses that darkness can be accepted as truth. Sometimes the senses may agree with the truth, but it is not a safe guideline. It is a knowing. It is a knowing that is part of you. Begin an exercise and start to observe. When you see something that is true, then there will be a part of you that knows this to be true. And when something is false, there will be a part that knows this to be false. But begin each day with a clean slate, because as you evolve further, even some areas that you knew to be true will change perspective. The words your mind has concocted to apply to a certain area of truth will change, while the understanding will basically stay the same.

Person Two: Gourasana, is the Bible a source of light?

Gourasana: Yes, there is light in the teachings, and there is darkness.

Person Four: Sometimes I get caught up in my fears when I'm teaching. People become afraid or resist, and I question myself: "Am I leading people to the light, or am I ensnaring myself and them in more illusion?"

Gourasana: There is a question of purity, which will always change. It is necessary to communicate to people with these structures[1], which have so many words, and of course the words cannot truly communicate the truth. At best they can give some hint, some direction. But these structures are necessary, at least as a beginning point for the majority of the people. But if one is too bound in one structure and considers that structure to have some monopoly on the truth (which is the tendency of all the structures), then at that point it becomes an obstacle to the truth. Then change must be there. So the same structure is necessary for some to a certain degree, then change must be there in order to progress further. Everyone must stay *very flexible* in their journey toward the light, because if you are indeed moving quickly toward the light, your perceptions today will be very, very different a year from today. Certain beliefs and teachings are beneficial at certain points, but there comes a point when they must be let go. And as you let go more and more, the universal aspect of the teachings will become more apparent. So there is a purpose for the structure, but if in your teaching you are pressuring, or manipulating, or leading people to believe that they must stay within that exact structure, *then* you may be doing them a disservice. *That* you should be concerned about.

Person Four: That's not the concern as much as it is that when I show people the openness and the truth encompassed in all religions and philosophies, and the need to stay growing and flexible, that sometimes is very frightening to them, and when they're frightened I feel insecure. How do I keep moving in the face of fear?

1) Gourasana is referring to a transformational process.

Gourasana: This subject is one of the main mistakes that people going toward the light are making. When they come to a point of fear, they equate it with something bad, and they back away; but in doing so they are backing away from the light. It will not be possible to go from a state of illusion to a state of complete enlightenment without coming across *fear*. The only thing that can be done is to begin to educate people to this fact. *Fear will come.* It is not possible that fear will not come. It will be in different degrees, so some people may say that they do not notice much fear. But *most* will come to a deep fear, because to truly give up this state of illusion that you are in, necessarily will create *fear*. Just as if you were to die at this moment there would be some fear, but factually, if you could suddenly come to total awareness, it would be and is like *dying* – because everything you believe, everything you hold to be true, your whole personality, your whole life, the lives of those around you, this planet – *it is all an illusion!* And when you truly begin to let go of this illusion, it will be fearful. It cannot help but be fearful.

Person Three: Gourasana, what can bring us to that point of truth that we are free from illusion? What does it take? What are the guidelines we can learn and trust?

Gourasana: You must begin with very basic premises. Indeed, these basic premises are all that you do need and will continue to need until you come to a state of full illumination. One thing that must be there *is your desire for the light. It must be your desire.* If it is not your desire, whatever activities you perform will produce some light, perhaps enough to give a little comfort to your existence, but not enough to attain a full state of awareness. You see, desire *is everything.* Why is it that you all are sitting here and another group is sitting in a nightclub? *It is* because you have a different desire, and the result will be different. I am not saying that necessarily being at the nightclub is a bad thing. It may be a step toward the light, but generally speaking, it is a state that produces more illusion.

Person One: Do children have a desire for the light, or do you have to live a certain amount of time on this plane to experience things before you start to consciously desire the light?

Gourasana: There is a prearranged point for when everyone will begin. Sometimes you will see that people begin when they are children. Generally, the children are more aware because they have not been covered over so completely yet, but there are certain experiences that they need to go through. But there is a point that you will come to when the desire for the truth will become all-consuming, at least for those that We will be taking from this plane of existence. It will manifest at different ages, and the ages will vary greatly.

Person Three: What factors could alter the predetermined point when the child will break through? What are those factors?

Gourasana: Teach the children the truth. Show them the truth. Show them what *is not* the truth, but this must come from your own awareness. Generally the propagation that they are receiving is all illusion. It must be done with some care. You will see that they can be *extremely receptive*. It only becomes more of a problem as they become older, because their minds have started to become rigid and inflexible from the propaganda that they have learned at the school, from their friends, from their parents, from everyone around, from society. You see, society itself is the main propagator of the illusion.

So you must start teaching them that it is okay to go against the norm of society, and in fact is ideal to do so in many instances. Let them remain free. Do not make the mistake of so many parents who say, "You must do this." When you give an absolute, examine it for yourself first and see if it is indeed something they must do, and who is saying they must do it. You will see that *most* of these rules and regulations are coming from an illusion. And while they may still practice the rules and regulations of society, you can begin to show them the illusion. Just as the rules and regulations that are true and absolute in one country may be entirely different in another. They are both born from illusion.

The *children* can move *very* quickly.

Person Three: Gourasana, how do we distinguish the truth from the illusion?

Gourasana: You have asked the same question.

You can only do it by doing it. So you simply must begin and practice, and as you practice, it will become clear. And then, when certain levels of awareness become difficult, then we can discuss. But we have covered this. Review some material. See the duality. See the darkness and the light. The truth is the light and the darkness is the illusion. Begin this exercise. *Everyone* needs to practice this exercise. You must begin.

Person Four: Is the material world itself illusion?

Gourasana: Yes. The illusion is so limiting. As your awareness grows, you will begin to see even the existence of this one tiny planet is but one classroom in eternity – just one period of learning. See how limited the illusion is, what to speak of this one lifetime that you are leading. The *millions* of lifetimes that you have led are just one aspect of this classroom. We have simply come to take you to the next grade. This is like the beginning grade. And now, for those that desire to evolve from this plane of existence and not take birth again, We have come specifically with this assistance for this purpose. Many will move very quickly, but will still need to take so many more births. They can still take advantage of this assistance and move very quickly, but primarily We are interested in taking you from this plane of existence – *for good.* It is *Our* desire; it is *Our* wish that you do not return again to this plane.

Person Two: Are you a helper of helpers as described in the Course of Miracles?

Gourasana: *I AM THE SOURCE.*

Person Five: Are we all part of the Source?

Gourasana: Yes.

Person One: Gourasana, do I have the capability of understanding and having the awareness that you are talking about, but I'm not able to tap into it yet because I can't surrender; I can't open myself up to the truth?

Gourasana: Yes. You *can* have the awareness and you *can* surrender. It is a question of if you *will* or *not.* It will come to that point with everyone. Some will come to that point, and when they truly understand what it will mean to give up this state of illusion, they will change their minds. They will say, "I will not do this."

We are not talking about a process to become happier on this plane of illusion. You have asked so much about the darkness and the light, about illusion and the truth. We are not discussing the truths that will produce happiness in this illusion – which is the majority of the truths. We are discussing the truth that will take you out of this state of illusion. *You can* get out of this state of illusion if you truly desire it. There is nothing stopping you. It is simply a question of your desire. If you *desire* everything, then you can have everything, but if you cling on to this state of illusion, We cannot drag you out of it. If you desire to let go, We can *assist* you, We can *empower* you, and you will leave this state of illusion, but *We cannot do something against your desire.*

Person Three: Gourasana, if I should choose to find a way to give up the illusion completely, where do I go from there at that time?

Gourasana: You are being guided. Your mind may not be aware of it, but as the awareness grows, you will start becoming aware of it with your conscious mind. You let the desire begin, and it immediately acts. This is the nature of Spirit. It's not that now you have a wish or a desire to achieve total awareness, and then at some point in the future you will do something and it will begin to take you there. *At the very instant* that *you* desire to know the *truth* – indeed just by the presence of your desire – an action is now going on and your awareness is now changing and growing. It is simultaneous. This you should know. The endeavor has an immediate result. Do you have a desire to know the truth? *Do you!?*

Person Two: Yes. I desire the truth and I am on a journey of truth. I would like to know, what can I know beyond the truth as I know it on this plane of illusion?

Gourasana: Practicing the truth on this plane of illusion is simultaneously producing a pure ultimate light and awareness within your true self. You must be patient; at the same time let your desire increase. You will not be able to know it all in an instant, but you can move very quickly.

Person Two: Gourasana, isn't our higher self guiding us to ultimately realize our full existence out of this illusion?

Aren't we being guided by our higher self – ultimately – all the time, and being pushed basically in that direction if we would listen?

Gourasana: Evolution is going on constantly. There is no question of *anyone* standing still. It is a question of speed. Yes, you are being guided, but you are being guided to where you want to go. That is why I say, "Desire is everything." If you desire to become totally free of illusion and enter into a state of total awareness, it is like a prayer. And We immediately answer that prayer and begin to guide you to that state of total awareness.

Prayer is the universal medium. The desire is like the prayer: You wish to know the love, the light, the truth. When you put that out, it is like a prayer, and We will immediately answer that prayer, if that is what you desire. Whatever you desire will be answered, so *it is* by your desire that everything is happening.

Person Three: Gourasana, I have heard that the universe will give us what we desire. How does that work?

Gourasana: That *is* how it works. You have a desire and the desire is fulfilled. You desire a particular type of illusion and it is given. All the facility is given for that type of illusion. You desire another type of illusion, and it is given. You desire the light, and the circumstance is given to give you the light.

Person One: What are the unique blessings and learning of this plane?

Gourasana: Unique? It is *unique* in that it is a place where *Spirit*, which is all light, can enter into illusion.

Person Four: Since our separation from one another is also an illusion, who is this one who is transitioning from one level of existence to another?

Gourasana: For the purposes of what you need to know to get free from this illusion, you do not need to understand the unlimited levels of consciousness and how they are all manifesting. Questions along this line have come up in the past, and We have promised a discourse, but one small area such as this cannot be properly answered without entering into a great deal of speaking. It will take many hours to explain the *reasons* behind this phenomenon of this *cosmos*, of this *existence*. I do not wish to reduce it to a simplistic state, because even in explanations of great length this manifestation cannot accurately be described.

So for the time being, We wish to stay in an area of discussion which is immediately pertinent, and in that framework, you just need to know that you are an individual and that you are in a state of illusion, and it is your destiny to evolve out of this state into higher states of awareness and consciousness. We must address the immediate problems: what it is you *need to do now,* what it is you *need to know now* to make this next step – a *monumental* step in your evolution – which is to finally transcend this plane of existence and never again take birth on this plane. This area is sufficient work to take up what little time there is between now and your leaving that body. Knowing in these other areas will automatically increase as your awareness increases. There does not need to be much discussion about certain higher states of awareness, which cannot be reduced to words anyway.

We are simply here to help you move your awareness, to give you some hint, some direction on how to begin to move your awareness. But the words are a very tiny aspect of what is taking place *now.* The real help, the real work is going on at a higher level, whether you are aware of it or not. The true purpose of these gatherings is to move your awareness, not to come and hear some words and then act upon them later. Indeed, there is being planned a period when we will gather together, and besides the discussion in this type of format, there will be no other speaking. The awareness, the knowing, will all be growing on a higher platform, and if someone is serious about moving quickly, this would be an excellent opportunity to begin to grasp the true reality that is going on.

Person Two: Gourasana, can you speak to us about the love you have for us?

Gourasana: *(Lamenting)* I can remember when *each and every one of you chose* to come into this existence. The length of time that you have been here is very great, and while you have forgotten *Me*, there has *never* been a second that I have forgotten *you*.

We have nothing but unlimited love for you. We are here constantly to help you in *any way* that We can, but We only can do what you will allow Us. So We are anxiously waiting for your desire to change and to increase so that We may again welcome you back into this realm of unlimited *love* and *light* that is *waiting* for you. If at times We may appear to be harsh, *it is* because Our desire to have you *freed from this state of illusion* is *far greater than your* desire.

You must go within, you must go within to this realm that is within all of you, where we can truly meet. What can We say with these limited words? It is unlimited light and love, joy and ecstasy, that awaits you *all*, and the only thing separating you from Us is that you are *clinging on to a state of illusion.*

So it is Our special *urgency*, it is Our special *desire* – We have created an unusual circumstance by which it will be possible for *unusual leaps* of consciousness to be had – and We pray that you will take the opportunity and *not stay in this state of illusion and darkness any longer.*

It feels that when you let go you will be missing something, but it is what you are clinging on to which is causing you to miss everything. If you will but have the desire, We are there with you and We are helping you every second. There is no limit to Our love, and it is increasing constantly. And when one leaves this plane of illusion and comes into the light, it is a time of great celebration and joy, and there is an outpouring of love that is far beyond your comprehension.

Don't you know that it is just light and love that is waiting for you? *Please* come with Us. *Please* give up your state of illusion.

Go inside *now*. It is within all of you. What you may have perceived as imagination is the only reality. Go inside *now*. Come here and feel the love; directly experience the love that is waiting for you.

And if you cannot feel the love, then let this increase your *desire*. How unfortunate that there is this realm waiting for you and you cannot even be a little aware. Let this unfortunate position that you are in, increase your desire to know the unlimited truth that is waiting for you. Do not be satisfied with your existence here on this plane of illusion.

We will be with you every second; try to notice Our presence. Try to hear with your hearts. Try to carry this awareness with you. Let this desire for the truth grow and encompass you until you want nothing else but the light and the love that is waiting for you. Do not let any obstacle stand in your way. Any obstacle is only an illusion. Give up the illusions that you are clinging on to, and as you let go, to that degree We can take hold of you and pull you into this realm which is your true resting place – not *this* place of illusion. We pray that you will move very quickly, that you may soon experience this love and this light. We are anxiously waiting for you. Please come.

We will stop now.

Transcending this State of Illusion

February 19, 1988 – Poway, CA

You must go within. To the degree that everyone in the group is situated within, to *that* degree the power for everyone can increase. So do not be an idle spectator. If you do not feel the need for yourself, then go within as a courtesy to the group. This is not a form of entertainment. If you have come to see something outside of yourself, then you have wasted your time. Everything is within. Turn your attention inward. *Now go deeper.* Find your depth.

You must pay close attention if you wish to begin to perceive the true reality, the true world of existence that surrounds you.

If there is a question that you wish to ask, first you must see if it is coming from your heart. Do not waste the time of this group. Still, if it is something that is an obstacle, if it is something that you feel is in your way – no matter how trivial the question – please ask. But when you listen, try to listen from your heart. This is where the true message is coming. The words are just a hint.

Please, ask.

Person One: Gourasana, in the Vedic scriptures it says that in past ages there was much more God consciousness on this planet, and that gradually the consciousness is becoming degraded, people are developing more of an animal mentality, and that spiritually things are getting worse. But on the other hand, this appears to be a new age spiritually, and people are becoming very conscious and evolving. Are both things happening simultaneously? Is this a degraded age or is it an age of enlightenment?

Gourasana: The only thing that should be of concern is *your own* enlightenment. There is a special circumstance being created now so that *many* can make unusual advancement spiritually. Now, this is affecting *many, many* people, and indeed the entire consciousness of the planet is moving at an unusual rate. But it is My specific concern that those who are ready to leave this plane of existence will have the aid that they need. It is not that others are not being helped, but it is Our special purpose to help those that are truly ready to transcend this state of illusion. These beings are Our primary concern.

Person One: What practical things can we do in our daily lives to become ready to transcend this plane?

Gourasana: Don't you know?

Person One: I have some idea. I'm not sure if I'm doing all the right things or not.

Gourasana: You *know* what you should do, but you are not *paying attention!* If you would pay attention, *you would be sure.*

You must concentrate your energy on going toward the light. If you spend your energy hiding from your fear, then it is *wasted* energy. Until the fear is dissipated by the light, until by illumination it is gone, you must develop greater tolerance so that you can withstand the fear. Hiding from the fear simply perpetuates the problem. It is a very difficult thing to do, and this is why We have come for this express purpose: to offer unusual assistance so that you may make this leap from illusion, across the barrier of fear into the light. But if you will not take advantage of the help, then what can be done?

Person Two: Gourasana, we're involved in great political debate. We're about to choose a leader of the free world and a direction for the next four to eight years. Is energy spent in that political process wasted energy, or is getting involved in it something that can enrich our spiritual life? If it is something we should get involved in, can you give us some direction in which we should move in this process?

Gourasana: You see, there are two things you could say that are going on. One is that each and every living entity is evolving in consciousness. There is no one that is standing still. However, the evolution is all taking place on this plane of illusion. Any leader that you elect is by necessity going to be in illusion. When I say "by necessity," it is because it is important that certain conditions are created in this world. It is when you are ready to leave this world that the perspective will change, and really only then will you begin to see the illusion clearly. Once you begin to lose the state of illusion, then you lose your motivation to help with aspects of this illusion. Then your time is not needed in this area.

You can spend lifetime after lifetime seeing to it that the water is clean, that the air is clean, that the leadership is proper, that education goes well. These are very important areas for those that are going to continue on, and that is almost everyone. As you have done these things for countless lifetimes, so others have countless lifetimes in front of them, and they feel this – you see – so to them the importance is far greater, and they have the motivation. Automatically, they do what they are supposed to do. They are seeing that the air is clean, that the water is clean, et cetera, because in their souls they know that they will continue to exist here. And as this is true of most everyone, it is a great concern for the majority.

But *your* efforts are not needed. It is like a habit to be concerned about these matters. So look at your own concern, and see if you truly care *enough* to put your time there. For those that are ready to leave, I would advise that you put your time into going within. The elevation of your own consciousness helps the overall consciousness of the planet, so in fact you are contributing more than one who is busy looking after certain aspects of the illusion.

I do not mean in any way to be condescending or to criticize those that are involved in these matters, *because they are very important.* But you can see that the lives of the people who are strongly motivated to help in these causes are consumed by their causes. They are not ready to leave.

But what is the problem? A million lifetimes ago you were not ready to leave. It is not that there is something wrong. There is a purpose for which you have come, but that purpose in coming is not permanent. There must be leaving, and everyone will eventually leave. We are just interested in directing those that are ready to leave this plane of existence. This is Our concern. Help in matters of existence on this plane can be had in many places. We simply do not want to spend Our time in these matters.

Person Two: It is my understanding that there is no beginning, and there is no end. Whatever is, will always be; whatever is, has always been. Do we travel this route again even though we go to a higher state of consciousness? I don't know if I'm making myself clear.

Gourasana: It is clear. You cannot travel the path that you have traveled *again,* because once you leave this plane of existence, you will not go back into illusion *again.* There will be *no need.* Your awareness will continue to *expand* far greater than you can now comprehend, and your awareness will continue to *grow* in *part* from the *experiences* of those that are continuing in this plane of existence. Everything that is going on in this plane of illusion translates into something spiritual. So as your awareness expands when you leave this plane, the true essence of these experiences are open to you. There is no need to go through them personally. Do you understand?

Person Two: Yes, thank you.

Person Three: Gourasana, is it possible to expand one's awareness within the bodily form as much as it would be leaving this plane?

Gourasana: No. That is why We are anxious for you to leave this plane. Now, tremendous awareness must be achieved *in the body* before you can leave, but as long as you are in the body there is some restriction. When you leave this plane of existence, there is an awareness, a state of consciousness waiting for you that is far greater than you could *ever* experience in these bodies. Those that say the same awareness can be achieved in or out of the body are showing that they still have some attachment to the body. True awareness means that you see there is no longer any need for these bodies, and indeed to not have these bodies will not be missed as they are more or less just a nuisance. So once their purpose is finished, then there is no desire to stay in these bodies.

Person Three: Thank you.

Person Four: Gourasana, is not being able to let go of our fears what is blocking us from that awareness we're looking for?

Gourasana: It is primarily fear, yes.

It is not as much a letting go of your fear as it is facing your fear. You have trained yourself so that as soon as fear enters, you hurry to immediately dispel it. Now you must develop another habit, and that is when the fear comes you will look at it, and even let it grow and enter into it and understand it. Now this process can take a long time, so while this process is taking place, you must tolerate the fear. It is especially difficult in the beginning, because you have programmed yourself to run from the fear, so you must change this perception. There will come a point when it will not be such an important issue – if it is fear or not – so you will move faster and more easily, but the beginning is very difficult. But you must begin. When the fear comes up, do not go into some artificial state of happiness.

Person Three: Gourasana, could you describe this higher plane of existence to us in a way that's comprehensible to us?

Gourasana: It is not possible with words. That is why We say the words are a hint, at best giving some direction where you should go. You can only begin to understand the higher realm of consciousness by directly experiencing it. Even as you begin to truly tap into the higher realm, the words in your mind will become confused trying to label what it is – and it will be impossible. There are words that will describe something like it, but it will not be accurate. It is an unlimited realm, and the words that you use are *so* *limited* that you cannot even accurately describe the plane in which you now exist.

Try to describe to a blind man what everything looks like. Then you will have some idea why it is impossible to describe this realm, this spiritual realm. This does not mean what has been said in many cases is wrong; it simply means it is not possible to grasp. If it were possible to take words from your plane of illusion and to accurately describe what it would be like for you – then who would not go? It does not work like that.

Person Two: Gourasana, if when we leave this body – and hypothetically let's say we're not in the state of awareness that we would have liked to have reached – do we automatically attain a higher state of consciousness, or do we remain in the same state of awareness that we have when we leave this body?

Gourasana: It will change even for one who is fully enlightened. It does not change for everyone as drastically as you might think, because the power of illusion does not disappear at the time of death. If you are in a deep state of illusion at the time of death, that state will carry over, and you will continue in illusion. It varies greatly.

Lynn: I want male companionship at this time in my life. Not because I need it to feel complete, but I desire affection. How do I know if this is the right thing for my spiritual advancement?

Gourasana: Companionship can be helpful, but what is correct for you will come if your looking is within. If you look within for completion, where the unlimited love and light is waiting for you – then if companionship is necessary or ideal for you to further your advancement – it will manifest automatically *and the person will just be there.* But if you are attached *to when* that person will be there and to what form the love that you seek comes in, then you will be stopping yourself from advancing as quickly as you could.

You see, it is like there are two sets of desires that are going on with some of you, so there appears to be conflict. There are the desires that have been born from illusions and habits that you are still attached to, and then there is your real desire, or your ultimate desire. So it may appear that your desire is for companionship, but because your ultimate desire is for the light and the love, that desire for companionship is not being met because it is not your *true* desire.

And I may say, as difficult as it is for you, it is an excellent time to advance very quickly in your spiritual progress. If you will take this longing – this desire for another, the need for love and completion – if you can capture that feeling totally and go within and look for an answer, it can propel you very quickly. So rather than spending time in some lamenting, you can be moving very quickly toward the light. Then perhaps at a point when it will not interfere with your progress toward the light, companionship will come automatically.

Make your spiritual desire the only desire. Desire to be free from this state of illusion. It is such a confusing state. Who is not experiencing bewilderment almost constantly?

Person Five: Gourasana, what opportunities do our dreams offer us in the transformational process?

Gourasana: You mean by dreams, desires?

Person Five: No, dreaming while sleeping.

Gourasana: For Our purposes, the imagery of what you're experiencing is not any more accurate than your words are. What you may experience while you are sleeping will translate into an image that your conditional mind can relate to. Sometimes there can be a hint, as with your words, but generally it is just like another illusion, very inaccurate at best. Rather, when you wake up from a dream, try to capture the feeling behind what you were dreaming, the mood behind what you were dreaming, the awareness behind what you were dreaming. Do not try to capture it with words. Try to capture it with your heart and then some help can be there. But the imagery, for Our purposes of full enlightenment, is not very helpful.

There are many things that can give enlightenment and can help you with your functioning on this plane of existence. For some, this area of dreams can be a benefit. This just is not Our purpose. There are others that can help in this area, and it is not a bad thing, of course. There are many ways you need assistance on this plane so that your functioning can be as smooth as possible. Just as with the care of your bodies, you need some assistance from someone who has attained knowledge of caring for the body. There are so many other helpers that will be important to some, but do not make these areas the focus of your attention. They should just be support mechanisms for the true focus of your consciousness, which is to attain total enlightenment.

Person Five: Thank you.

Gayle: I've eliminated so much from my life in the way of distractions, and I only want to talk about consciousness. I read books about the masters. I'm only happy when I have that intense desire to know who I really am. I don't desire companionship; I only desire to be alone.

The last time we talked about meditation, you said to be quiet and be receptive. Can you give me some more guidance about meditation?

Also, could you talk to us about what we should be doing to prepare ourselves for the retreat?

All I want to do is live a quiet existence so that I can continue to go within, and it seems to be all I want to do. Could you talk to us about that?

Gourasana: It is an ideal state to come to. You should be overwhelmed with gratitude. You see, there is nothing else but the light and the love. Everything else that you experience on this plane is just an illusion.

Desire is everything, and you have to come to a point where you desire practically nothing else but the unlimited love and light that awaits you. This is perfect. *You have no other desire, and I have no other desire.* This combination guarantees success. Now just let this desire grow even more, and do not let anyone distract you from what you know. Do not let social etiquette get in your way. You may appear to be rude to some, but do not let it concern you. You have moved very quickly in such a short time. Can you see how your awareness has changed? It is just the beginning. Those who do not have much desire should be concerned, because desire is everything. Whatever you truly desire will be given to you, so let your desire for the truth grow.

Those that do not wish to face their fears should not come to the retreat. We will have many such gatherings, and they will increase in length. If someone is not ready to come, do not encourage them against their better judgment. We wish to move very rapidly during that period, so only the most serious must come.

Lynn: Gourasana, will you keep coming to us, to this group?

Gourasana: When you turn your attention within, no matter where you are, I am there. However, these gatherings are special assistance, an opportunity to move much quicker. And if you have forgotten your true purpose or have lost focus of your true purpose due to the state of illusion, then these gatherings will be an excellent time of reminder – not so much from the words, but from what you can feel in your heart. So if you truly desire the light, then try to take the opportunity.

But at the same time, if it is not for some reason easy to come, or it is not possible for you to come, do not think that your process needs to stop. It is just that especially in the beginning – and you are all in the beginning – that you will need more of this type of assistance. But you will come to a point where you can go and sit alone and move at a highly rapid rate. But there is much that has to be learned, so association with others is important in addition to gathering like this. Try to surround yourself with those who are interested in attaining full awareness. Gradually disassociate yourself from those who are too bound by the illusion, who have little desire, if any, to leave this illusion. This is an important secret to advancement.

Person Three: Gourasana, there is a channeled spiritual book called "A Course in Miracles." Do you see this as a major tool for transformation on the planet?

Gourasana: We wish to only examine the teachings. The difficulty in teachings is how they are presented. An excellent example of this – that you all are familiar with – is the way the teachings of the Lord Jesus have been presented. They have taken the words and their meaning and have changed them until, in many cases, they are no longer the teachings of the Lord Jesus. Now, if someone with an open heart can hear the words of the Lord Jesus without any influence from others, then he will be able to perceive the light. But as soon as someone takes a teaching and starts to present the teaching themselves, it is very difficult for their state of illusion not to contaminate the teaching, until over a period of time the original meaning of the teaching has been lost.

The Lord Jesus only taught the light and the love. Yet, you will sometimes hear it spoken that Lord Jesus taught a terrible darkness, *that you will be cast into an eternal darkness if you do not accept Him!* WHAT AN ABOMINATION BEFORE THE LORD! *Talk of abomination! They have taken the light and the love, and they have cast a terrible eternal darkness* upon it, and they are *propagating that as the teachings of the Lord Jesus! If they truly wish to have a good relationship with the Lord Jesus, they should stop this!*

You see, teachings become changed, even in subtle ways that are not so obviously illustrated, so you must not rely too heavily on them. Look to these works and these teachings for direction, but you must always remember *that it is you yourself that must find the truth.* What is said in a book may resonate with what you find in your heart, and then you can accept that as the light, but in most presentations there is a mixture of illusion with the light and the love. There are also teachings in books that your mind will not understand – which means your mind will *misunderstand*, and the intent of the teaching will be perverted in *that* way.

You must rely on your own awareness to go within and to experience the truth directly. Do not let anyone tell you what the truth is; simply take suggestions, and look at those suggestions. Do not *ever* come to a *definite conclusion on anything because everything* is *constantly changing.* Your mind must *always* stay in an open state. You may have *certain beliefs* which are beneficial, *but do not cling on to any belief too tightly.* You will be clinging on to an illusion that you have formed, and you will be bound by that illusion.

Carol: Gourasana, last week you spoke about the love that you have for us. Could you speak more about this love?

Gourasana: Go within and feel the love. If you cannot feel the love, consider yourself unfortunate and desire to become fortunate, because the love is what you are truly searching for. In all of these outward manifestations, you are really seeking the love and the light. It is not just an emotion. *It is a realm.* It is an *unlimited realm.* While you have forgotten *Me,* I have *never* forgotten *you.* And Our love for you is constant and unchanging and ever increasing, *even* while you pay little attention or do not *care* for Our love. So We are waiting anxiously for when you will come within to this realm of unlimited love and light. It is your true Home. *Why* won't you come here? *Why* won't you take what is being offered? Do not cling onto the illusion any longer. *Let it go.*

What you have understood to be happiness is just an illusion, and your true happiness will not come until the illusion is dispelled. *Desire to be free from this illusion, and then desire it more, and then desire it even more until you are consumed! And if you come to a point where you have no other desire but to find the love and the light and the truth that is waiting for you, consider yourself blessed,* because that desire will guarantee that *you will have what everyone is searching for.*

Change your desires. Do not be constantly misled by these temporary, illusory desires. *Take that longing that you have and go within and search there* for completion. Hide less and less in intoxications and other temporary hidings from your fear. Have the courage to tolerate the fear that you must face, and go within.

Do not be concerned if your state is one of so-called happiness or not, while you are endeavoring in this area. *Only be concerned if your awareness is truly growing or not.* If you gauge your state by some artificial standard of happiness, then you will have created another obstacle. You must give up these illusory little bits of happiness to have the true joy and ecstasy that exists. Now you are being satisfied with so little. Do not be satisfied any longer with this *tiny* bit of happiness that you have found on this plane. Let your dissatisfaction with this state grow. It is fine to be totally dissatisfied and unhappy with this plane of existence *because it is a plane of illusion.*

Give it up. Let it go, and come here. Come into the light and take Our assistance that We *are offering.* We cannot force it upon you. *If it is not your desire, there is nothing* We *can do, but as soon as you turn your attention – your desire – to Us, then simultaneously* We can begin *pulling you from this state of illusion that you are trapped in.*

We pray that you will all do this.

Do not be discouraged. Do not give up. As long as you continue *trying*, that very *trying – whether your conscious mind can appreciate it or not – is manifesting simultaneously* an awareness which at some time will begin to blossom. Then your mind will be aware of it, but it does not mean that your awareness is not growing just because your conscious mind cannot appreciate it. So have faith that your very effort, your trying, your desire, is simultaneously manifesting and you are succeeding as long as you are trying and you have a desire for the light. It is only when you *stop*, it is only when you *give up*, that your advancement slows down so greatly. Try to become *serious*. This is not another form of entertainment on your plane of existence. *It is everything.*

Person Three: Gourasana, after we leave this plane of existence, will some of us be guided to come back and assume a body to teach?

Gourasana: For one in illusion, the desire to come back and teach is just another trap, just another reason to again take birth. Your desire must be focused solely on leaving this plane of existence. Do not think that your help is critical to another. It is not. What may happen in the future of your evolution is another thing. Many leave their bodies at the time of death and with the state of awareness that they have achieved, they wish to come back and teach others, but it is a further bondage. So do not harbor this desire. Your help is not required. Focus all of your energy and your desire on leaving this *plane of existence for good, never to return to this state of illusion again, never to take birth again.*

We will stop.

The Unadulterated Truth is Rare

March 13, 1988, Alpine, CA

(This talk was spoken at a meditation retreat.)

The truth in an unadulterated form is a very rare thing.

You have all witnessed the power of illusion. Sometimes We refer to this as "darkness." The Christians refer to it as "the devil." I intentionally try to avoid rhetoric that is associated with any form of organized religion or processes of the truth, but at this moment I will deviate in this one area, because it is illustrated nicely in the philosophy of the Vedic scriptures. There they refer to this illusion, this darkness, the devil, as Maya. They all mean the same thing in that they are the opposing element to the light. Understand this principle that is captured so nicely in the philosophy of Maya. They consider it – as the Christians do – to have a personification, and the only purpose of this personification is to do something, to do *anything,* to take you away from the light. I do not care what word you use, but for the struggle that is in front of you, it would not be a bad thing, it would not be a wrong way of looking at it to see that this state of illusion, this Maya, is your enemy. It is an opposing element; it is *an active* opposing element that has a particular function. Just as in nature there are so many elements, and they each have a particular function and certain reactions – such as fire. Whatever you may call it, whatever your belief system is, if you put your hand in the fire *you will be burned* – Christian, Hindu, whatever.

Now there is a secret that you may learn so that you can put your hand in the fire and *not be burned.* You can learn to transcend a very powerful law of nature that is binding everyone – it has been demonstrated. In the same way, there is a very powerful element of nature: It is called illusion; it is called Maya. The function of this energy is to oppose the light, to oppose the truth, and it is an active force that is constantly working against you and against everyone. *It is the duty, it is the function of this force to keep you in a state of illusion.*

Now this force has a great intelligence behind it. It is understandable why you can believe it is a personification – and to use that imagery would not be wrong – because *there is a powerful personality that directly wishes to keep you in illusion and is going to try anything and everything to do just that.* This energy, this power, is so great that it rises to the occasion. In other words, there are those that – very easily – are completely in illusion. They are so totally covered over with illusion that *they are not even aware that there is any Spirit.* Try to see the extent of their *illusion.* The only thing that is real, they have not even an inkling of. This is one end of the extreme. But as the living entity evolves and the awareness continues to grow, then the traps of Maya, the traps of illusion, start becoming less obvious.

During this weekend we have discussed a number of cases. The illusion has many tricks. If the illusion cannot get you one way, then it will work on another way. To confuse the issue, even though it is opposed to the light, this opposing element *knows* that it will *not be able to fool* certain people with *total illusion,* so it gives as much light *as it has to – reluctantly – the minimum amount necessary.* Then the illusion uses that minimal amount of light as the binding force and creates as much darkness as possible around that, so that the binding to this material existence is still ensured.

I use the example of Christianity simply because it is known worldwide. We could discuss other philosophies to show this example, but this is one philosophy that everyone is familiar with. It is a very excellent creation of the illusion, because the Christians do experience the incredible power and love that comes from the Lord Jesus, and that experience creates a firm faith. So far, there is no problem. But the illusion has a job; Maya has a duty. If people followed the Lord Jesus as He instructed, they could get free from this plane of illusion, but it is the job of Maya to keep them here. Since the illusion is constantly active, from the very beginning as the words were coming out of the mouth of the Lord Jesus, the illusory energy was beginning to work to change the truth, to do whatever havoc was possible. Who has not heard of the atrocities in the name of the Lord Jesus throughout the centuries? Every atrocity against mankind, against the light, has been done in the name of the Lord Jesus. Even those that are not committing atrocities have accepted a belief *which is a total lie, which is total illusion, and which is binding them to this plane of existence.* They will not be able to transcend this plane of existence, *in spite of their connection,* because their relationship with the Lord Jesus is contaminated.

We discussed at length last night the popularity of "prosperity consciousness." This is also now part of Christianity. This is a new part of Christianity. It has been there for many centuries, but in a small way. Now Christianity has joined the ranks of other groups of prosperity consciousness and is equating material prosperity with spiritual life.

Please understand the intention of My speaking. I am not here to condemn the world. I am not here to condemn these philosophies or these groups or these people. Truly, there is nothing wrong in what they are doing. But there comes a time, there comes a point in your evolution when you will leave this plane of existence, and *in order* to do that, you must give up *all* of the illusions. You must see clearly; you must develop great discretion.

People will say that We are just finding fault. But understand Our intention; understand the purpose. We are not finding fault so that We may put down others. *We are trying to find the illusion,* and if the criticism comes that We are judging, then you can say, "Yes, I am judging, but I am only judging what is truth and what is illusion, because I wish to be free from illusion." And if you are sincere, the illusions will become increasingly obvious to you. That is the nature of illusion. Once you are free, you just see it; it is so obvious.

The Christians say, if you do not accept the Lord Jesus in the prescribed manner that they have set forth, then you will be cast into eternal hell. Now this is a very low level of awareness; there is no one in this group here who is bound by such an obvious ploy. Why? Because your awareness has grown at least to that degree; it is so obvious. God is going to send you to eternal hell and punishment if you do not accept Him in this one instant of eternity? It makes no sense; it is practically insanity.

So in this way all of the illusions will be apparent, because illusion means just that – it covers over the part of you that is aware. So your powers of awareness will not increase unless you exercise them. And you cannot exercise them by having some artificial *blob* of a mentality that anything that goes on is okay. You must develop discrimination, and you must develop judgment.

But understand, *you are not judging people. You have been in illusion for countless lifetimes,* and some of you will be here for many more lifetimes.There is *nothing bad* in the evolutionary process. Nobody is bad because they are in illusion; it is part of the process. What you are judging is what is truth and what is illusion. Now you may judge that in an individual, and that will increase your awareness. When you can see how another is bound by an area of illusion, it will give you a hint: It will help you not fall into the same trap, into the same illusion, and it will aid you in more ways than you can understand.

You already have some idea about what I think of the prosperity consciousness. Now, what I think is one thing, but it is something that you yourself must observe and realize. You see? It will become part of your awareness. You need to become *fully aware,* and you will not be fully aware as long as you are accepting a lie *as the truth!* It is as simple *as that!*

Now you can go to these groups, and you can take the truth and leave the lies. I am not saying that there is nothing out there. But, *I* will not say anything that will be tainted by the trappings of illusion.

My speaking, the very words I use, are flexible and interchangeable. They are not rigid. It is just that I am speaking in certain ways at certain times to make certain points, I say certain things, and if you take just that one thing and make it everything, then it will be a distortion. You must begin to see the overall picture of what I am saying. People may criticize and say that what I am saying appears to be such a negative thing: "Life is bad; it is all suffering; it is all illusion." But trust Me that what I am saying has a purpose, and it is helping an area of your awareness to grow.

The reason that this is so critical and that I have chosen this time to speak on this point at length (and I wish to discuss this to any degree that anyone wishes, and I will stay here until everyone is satisfied with the answer to their question) is because: *Do you see what is happening?! – even as the light is coming, the opposing element, the illusion, is attacking and trying to take you away from the light. I wish – I need you to appreciate and understand this and take it to your heart* SO YOU DO NOT BECOME ONE OF *THE VICTIMS!* You must see it as the tragedy that it is: the tragedy that you will not evolve off this plane of existence. This is Our only interest. If you truly wish to evolve off this plane of existence, you will see the tragedy when someone becomes lost in the illusion again.

You must check yourself. It is not delving into these illusory activities – which is unavoidable for you – that is the problem. It is when you accept these illusory activities as part of the light that they become deadly.

In other words, let us say your goal is to leave this plane of existence. Certain financial arrangements must be made, so you may pursue some prosperity, but you will pursue *just enough* to be certain that your spiritual life will go on nicely. You will not work hard to accumulate unnecessary burdensome things that will bind you for your life. The way you approach it will be different, and that will make all the difference between your getting free or not. Two men can be doing the same exact thing, but the one in the prosperity consciousness is thinking that happiness is coming from the prosperity – that the things he will buy with his money will make him happy – whereas the other man, doing the same activity, is creating a situation conducive for his spiritual advancement. So the same activity in one case is liberating and in the other case is binding.

This is one of many ways that you may test whether what I am saying is not some perverted, fabricated, organized cult or religion desiring to control you. These organizations are all born of illusion. I will be constantly persevering to see that this group will not become contaminated, and if a member of the group is holding on to an illusion, I will expose that illusion. I will not allow an illusion to be perpetrated.

The organizations all have things you can and cannot do. Now, it is a fact that certain things are not conducive to spiritual advancement, but the way I will approach those subjects, you will see, will be far different than the standard moral judgments of society and religion.

I wish for you to have strong faith, I have nothing but the best intentions for you, and I am trying to do everything that I can to free you from this state of illusion. So, if you are unsure of your faith for any reason, then raise the question, raise the issue; but try to hear the reply.

Increased faith will be necessary for where you will be going. You will have to increase your faith in Me and what I am saying. Yesterday I assisted a couple to go to another realm. Their ability to move was directly dependent upon their faith and their trust in Me – and for some of you, this will be very critical. If you cannot have faith and trust in Me, then have faith and trust in what I am saying: faith and trust in this inner realm.

It is natural to be skeptical, *and it is good*. So you should look *very hard* at what has been said and what is being said on a regular basis. I am not afraid to be challenged; indeed, I welcome the challenge. I will not argue with some fanatic who will not change, but for someone who sincerely just does not understand, I will go to great length and time to help them. But I will tell the fanatics to leave, because we do not have time to waste. I will not waste My time and the energy of this group on those that do not really want the truth, that just wish to have some philosophical discussion, some argument. They like to do that. They have organizations and clubs where they come and debate their philosophies, "My philosophy is better than your philosophy." We will not do that.

I have pointed out the obvious lies and darkness in these philosophies – and I used very harsh words to emphasize this – so you also should look at what has transpired. You have all been exposed to some extent; you have all read material that has been spoken; you have all heard Me speak several times. Now, with your most critical judgment begin to look, because there may be something lingering in the back of your mind that is holding you back from moving because you cannot truly believe what I am saying. After all, isn't everyone saying the same thing? Aren't other groups saying that they are the only way; they are the only truth, and you will not be free from this existence unless you believe as they believe? They call this blind faith. It is blind because they cannot see the obvious flaw in what they are saying. We wish you to have faith *with full awareness*.

So you all have an idea of what the ego means, and you may have heard in studying philosophies that one who is truly aware becomes egoless. So you also must become egoless. Your sincerity for the truth must override any disturbances of your ego, because it will get in your way; it will stop you from realizing the truth.

And what I am going to say cannot help but disturb *many egos*. This information will get out, it will become public, and most will not want to hear this. They will become angry and they will attack. So when I discuss a "core," I need to have a core of people *who have unshakable faith, not blind faith, not sentimental faith, not some false belief, false hope! I want you to directly experience the truth so you will know it not only intellectually in your minds, but you will know it in your hearts! You will see the illusion for what it is, so that when you are attacked and someone comes up with the illusion, it will not disturb you because it will be so obvious. It will be just as obvious as if someone comes up to you and says, "If you do not accept Donald Duck and surrender to Disneyland, you will go to hell." You will just look. . . . It will be that obvious in all the areas of illusion. And believe Me, you have not come up against this yet, but their arguments are very persuasive. The arguments of the devil, Maya, illusion, are very persuasive. Why do you think almost everybody has fallen into these illusions,* no matter what level of intelligence they may have?

So when further illustrating and further educating you in the areas of how the illusion is working, offending others will be unavoidable, but I will not restrict Myself. I cannot do that. If I do that, then I will be doing you a disservice.

This body needs to rest for a few minutes. So you can stop the tape. Bring some water.

Person One: Gourasana, on my search for enlightenment, there are times I can feel that feeling of love in my whole body, and I understand that everything around me doesn't really matter. Then there are other times when I go through long periods where I don't have that feeling, but I still feel I'm on the path. The feeling of love, the full awareness of love, doesn't come very often. Does it mean that I am failing, or choosing to not stay there and getting lost in illusion? Or is that the process that we go through: that we get a glimpse, then we fall back, then we want it again and work our way up to it again and again? Is that common? Is that how the path happens?

Gourasana: This is happening with everyone, and this is the proper way to approach it. The philosophies that preach "Stop all illusory activities now," this is insane; it does not work. As I say, it is not that an act in and of itself is taking you from the light. It is true that it is an illusion, but if you are sincerely seeking the light, the illusion will begin to decrease more and more and it will naturally fade.

Some things are not normally conducive to movement toward the light, but you must get in touch with what *you* need to do. What I am about to say is not popularly preached in any philosophy, but there may be a time when the best thing for an individual to do – for a short period such as an evening – is to forget about consciousness and awareness: Take some intoxication; engage in some sex. Do these activities with *some* awareness – not like a meditation, although you can do that also. But just do it with some awareness; begin to pay attention to how you feel. If one has a desire to take some intoxication, then they should observe. See how they feel before taking intoxication. Then again pay attention to how the awareness is changing. Then observe how they feel after taking it. Observe the changes. Do the same thing with sex. Pay attention.

So it is true, these are areas of illusion, but if you do everything that you do with awareness, then you will become free. So even with these areas that appear to be going backwards or going into darkness, if your true desire is to go forward, then even these acts will help you grow. Do you understand the difference?

Person One: Yes, very much, I do. Thank you.

Gourasana: Some people are doing it and *it is darkness*; it is nothing but a source of darkness. But the same *activity* can be there and actually help you evolve. You may touch upon the love, then it may go away and you think that it's gone. But you need to just continue to go back, and that continuing to go back is what will get you there.

Person Two: Gourasana, some of the entities that are talking on the planet right now talk about the illusion, and they talk about knowledge of the illusion. Are a lot of these entities coming from a lot of different platforms? Are some of them in very gross illusion and some of them in just partial illusion? How exactly is that information coming to us?

Gourasana: Yes. It is all different degrees of illusion.

Person Two: Are some of them not in illusion? Some talk about prosperity consciousness or they talk about the science of the illusion, the science of the mind, and how you don't need to look for euphoria somewhere else, that you can find it right here. Am I just misinterpreting what they are saying? Or are some of these entities just in illusion themselves?

Gourasana: Just as I have said, sometimes just total illusion is enough to capture someone. Then sometimes a little light needs to be mixed in to capture someone, so this continues in degrees as the awareness continues. You have some that are preaching – because the illusion knows that it can only hold on so much – they may preach ninety percent truth and ten percent illusion. You understand? Some ten percent light; some ten percent darkness.

Person Two: Are these entities in illusion themselves, or is it just the illusion working through them?

Gourasana: Many of them are in total illusion. "Total illusion" means that they are bound. They have *some* awareness, just as you have *some* awareness, but *basically* you are still bound by illusion. *You* do not yet have the ability to go out and free others from illusion, as you yourself are still bound by illusion. This does not mean that you do not also have awareness. So there are beings that have even more awareness, but they are still bound by illusion. They can teach truth; they can give help; they can give assistance. But they *will not* be able to do *what I am doing: And that is giving* one *hundred* percent truth, no illusion, so that you can become completely free *from* this plane.

Person Two: Thank you, Gourasana. The answer to that question helped me a lot.

Gourasana: But the truth is the truth. That is why we have begun this discussion of discretion. Once you learn discretion, you can go to where there is ninety percent truth and benefit – *because it is the truth.* It is just that you will not be trapped when that *ten* percent is slipped in here and there. You will go, "This is the truth. Oh, there's an illusion. There's a lie."

Person Three: Gourasana, I am going to be leaving here soon, and I would like to extend my gratitude for being here this weekend with you, with us, for offering this vital information. I'll make every effort I possibly can to dispel illusion in my life, to go more to the light – make any sacrifice, at any cost. Thank you.

Person One: Gourasana, I am also leaving and I wanted to say I have grown tremendously this weekend. It seems like most of the things you talked about, I knew. But it was like somebody hitting me over the head with a hammer, and it cleared up so many cobwebs that were getting inside of me. I hope we can do this again soon.

Gourasana: Yes, you see, it is not that you will come and you will hear the same words, and it will be, "Oh, I already know that," because every time I am speaking these words to you it is simultaneously *increasing the awareness behind the words*. So even if I were to say exactly the same words every time, every time *your* awareness would grow, because the knowing is unlimited. It is not that someone will learn it all and then they will not need to come. As we have discussed, the real thing that is going on is a growing awareness in your hearts.

Person One: Gourasana, is there any chance the children can come and listen to you?

Gourasana: We may need a special session with children. They are learning so many things; what we are discussing would create confusion with so many.

Carol: Can we have a special session with the children centered around their questions?

Gourasana: It is possible – if they really care. How many children are sincere? It is just not usual that their attention is turned toward this area at a young age. The parent can usually instruct sufficiently to increase the light. But I am not opposed. You must use your discretion and perhaps just bring a group of children in for a short period, and they may ask questions that are relevant to their existence at that time. It could be very good, but it must be arranged properly and carefully. Definitely do not bring them if they are not interested.

People Leaving: Goodbye, Gourasana.

Gourasana: They say goodbye as if they are leaving Me, but I am going with them. But I understand.

What Sacrifice Will *You* Make?

March 13, 1988, Alpine, CA

(This talk was spoken immediately after the talk called "The Unadulterated Truth is Rare" and was a private session with the Core. The portions of this talk that are of general interest are excerpted in this chapter. The session begins with Carol asking whether the Core should move to a new house that would provide a better facility for people to come and be with Gourasana.)

Carol: Should we consider moving at this time, or should we just try to do our best where we are living now? Change the situation there? It seems like there are several places that we can move to pretty soon, that sound really perfect as far as inspiration for this whole gathering.

Gourasana: Then consider these things.

I wish to begin smaller, more frequent versions of what was experienced during the retreat we just had. People may come earlier and spend many, many hours in a meditative state, and this can be done more frequently rather than waiting so long between times. Up until now the sessions have been nice, but how deep can you go in a two- or three-hour period, especially when the consciousness before and after has been so frivolous? So when you move, consider having facility in your new residence for this. There will not be need for all-night sleeping for everyone. For the handful that cannot travel, it will be very easy to lay out an area for sleeping. And for this, some compensation should be there.

Person One: Can you be specific?

Gourasana: The people that come can contribute. Money is like energy. So when they come and give something, they are giving their energy to help support and continue the growth of this process and this phenomenon. The ones who say they truly appreciate but they will not give: they do not appreciate. You have all given very wonderfully and generously, and *see* your awareness. It is not because you have given, and then I have given you a blessing, that you have more awareness. You do not buy your way into heaven, as they say.

The amount can be modest. Is it necessary to go into the economics? You see what people spend in a month? Some are spending thousands a month, and yet they cannot give ten dollars to read what I have said. Mainly, just enough money has to be there to cover what we would like to do. As I said, it is not that you buy your way or that you get a special benediction from giving money, but it is a reflection of your consciousness. Just like the woman that David and Carol are living with. She has not given *a penny,* and if you asked for a penny – if it were given – it would be given grudgingly. So it is not because she will not give that I say she will not receive the light. Rather, her not receiving the light is a manifestation of the consciousness that she is trapped in. Whereas those of you who have appreciated, and with an open heart have given so generously, have received so much. But your reward was already there before you gave, in your awareness. In this day and age in this country, if someone cannot give some reasonable amount, then they do not care enough, and they will not leave this illusion anyway. They will not do what they need to do, and they will not make the effort that will be necessary to leave this plane of illusion.

Person One: Thank you for clarifying that.

Gourasana: This weekend a minimal amount was given to barely cover expenses so that we could gather and have this time. We would like to increase the amount, and we hope that people will not be offended, but a certain amount is necessary. If they gave as much as when they go to the cinema when they came here, then already there would be sufficient money to purchase some equipment that can be used. Now there is some lack. If they don't think that coming here has more advantages or is worth more than what they get from going to the cinema, what can be done?

(Speaking humorously) Of course, we could sell the light. You tell them: They give Me a thousand dollars, and I will give them the light. The more they give, the more light they get. If they give a million, I'll show them the whole universe. *(Laughter)*

So anyway. Some reasonable, moderate amount.

Person One: Gourasana, on other occasions will you lead us in meditation as you did last night? That was for me the breakthrough that I needed. There is no price to put on that: your personal guidance, your words, even taking us by the hand, if need be, to show us more light until we finally are able to do this on our own. Is this part of your plan to lead us in more meditations? Even in shorter sessions?

Gourasana: Oh yes. Oh yes. This is why I am discussing these practical things. If the facility can be arranged, and more people can come more frequently, then a day can begin early and we may spend the first two, three hours in discussion as we have done, and then the rest of the time in meditation. And we can go very late. So there can be many hours of deep meditation. And, also, I will personally assist.

Person One: That's wonderful.

Gourasana: It is a special power that I am bringing. The power is not separate from Me; *I am the power.* And I can take you. This is why I am spending so much time on these practical matters. *How quickly can we create this situation, so I can use My power to take you to these other realms again? Let us not waste time; let us create the circumstance. Assistance means that it will happen sooner and we can go further.*

It is My sole purpose in coming! David has given his life to Me! Do you understand the significance of that?!! The rest of you are preparing for your death in the future, and he is giving it up now! What sacrifice will others make for the light?!! If they will not give a little money, where is their sincerity? He has given his life. He has told Me whatever it is I desire, I may do it. So if each and every time I come through, it is shortening the life of his body, he is saying that is all right. What sacrifice will you make for the light? If someone will not give the money that it would cost to go to a movie, what can be done?

Now you are understanding even more what "serious" means.

If nobody else cares for the truth and just two or three or four or five of you remain, if nothing else can be accomplished in this lifetime, I will come and spend My entire time with those of you that remain. *HIS*[1] *LIFE FOR YOU AND MY TIME FOR YOU. (Carol and others are crying.)*

We are interested in the death of this illusion, and within a relatively short period of time you can all begin tasting great nectar. But know that you already have touched the gateway to the universe. You have *seen it already* in such a short time. You do not understand clearly what is going on, but *I tell you: you have stood at the gateway to the universe,* and I will take you through that gateway.

I have waited so long for you to come Home. You cannot imagine My desire. I have not forgotten you for a second. And I am only concerned about you. And I am determined. If you can also become determined, then everything is possible.

Come closer to Me – I mean physically. *(People move closer.)*

This is a gathering of love that is rarely witnessed in this way. And as you have seen, it will only increase.

I am Gourasana. I have come to take you Home. Know that it is My love that you feel. Let your hearts burst with joy that you can feel that love. It is a benediction that few have.

Stay with Me here; come here. Come to where I reside and be with Me. My love for you cannot be measured. It is boundless.

It is everything because I am everything.

Do not be distracted from what you know at this moment. When you leave this gathering, do not fall into the pitfalls of illusion. Look for them carefully; use your discretion. Worry not of your relationships with others in

1) Gourasana is referring to David.

this realm of illusion. Concern yourself rather with your relationship with Me. Begin to build your life around the truth and weed out the lies from your life. Begin to weed out the illusions from your life.

I will not ask you to do something beyond your capacity, but can you see at this moment, how one would do anything? What you are experiencing here is so precious. This is what you call unconditional love.

So I must leave for now, but remember, I am always in your heart. At any time you will turn your attention, I am there in My full power. See a glimpse, now, of how glorious it will be when there will never be a separation again, not for a second, not for an instant. And it will be ever-increasing ecstasy and love.

See how your true love for each other increases as it increases for Me.

If we have accomplished nothing else this weekend, I do not think any of you will ever go back into complete illusion again. What a glorious achievement has been made, but see also what a tragedy it would be if one of you again fell back into illusion and no longer cared for the love and the light. Be aware of the illusion. It is not something that will come and overpower you, but if you step into it, it will affect you just as if you stepped into a fire.

Stay in the light. *Come into the light and stay in the light!* Do not listen to those that say it is not possible. And know further *that you have seen the light!*

You Now Exist in an Alien Place

March 18, 1988, Alpine, CA

(This talk is followed by a guided meditation.)

In everyone's heart practically from birth, there is a part, a longing, a desire that is never quite fulfilled. This desire, this longing, is for the light, for the truth. Not understanding this with the conscious mind, you begin seeking from an early age to satisfy this desire in ways that will, of course, not satisfy it. So there is *always* a feeling of dissatisfaction in one's existence, a feeling that something is missing. You see, you now exist in an alien place. It is a place that is foreign to your true self.

It is Our purpose in coming, it is Our intention – if you so desire – to show you what it is that you have been longing for, what it is that has been missing. Some who are here have already begun to experience their true self. They have touched upon the true reality. They have located the place where they truly exist – not this plane of illusion. Just try to understand. These bodies that you now inhabit had a beginning, and they will have an end. All of the paraphernalia, all of the relationships between the bodies, all of these things which have a beginning and an end are in fact an illusion. They are *not* who you truly are.

Now this is very difficult to understand, as you are currently bound by this illusion. What name you call yourself, what your sex is – this is who you think you *are*. You do not know anything else. But yet all of these things – the thoughts, the massive accumulation of information in your minds, not to mention your unconscious minds – have just been accumulated in this lifetime, and they will end with this lifetime.

So you are not that body nor are you that mind, and practically speaking, everything that you know and believe is an illusion. Some of you are a little familiar with this, and for those who are not, this is the beginning point that you must contemplate, because the state of illusion prevents you from knowing who you truly are. So it is like a dream. You have all had this experience. During the night you create an entirely different illusion. It may be similar to your daily existence, or you may change certain aspects; your surroundings, your interactions, may all change.

Now what if you go to sleep and you enter into a dream – you have all had these dreams, these very vivid dreams that seem so real – and you become so lost in this dream that you never again wake? And as the dream perpetually changes, you just become more and more engrossed and bound in this dream. *This is your situation now.* This existence, *as real as it may appear,* is but an illusion. It had a beginning, and it will have an end. It has its characters, it has its interchanges, but it is not real. And who you really are is waiting for you to wake up, come out of this dream, and come back to the true reality.

Now on *this* plane, waking from a dream can be a very difficult thing or have a negative connotation, because the dream that you are in, unfortunately, is frequently a nightmare and you suffer while dreaming. Then when you are waking up, you try to alleviate the suffering, but it is unavoidable. But when you wake from this dream and come to the true reality, what you wake to is a state of ecstasy. It is a state of unlimited love and light. It is a state you come to with full awareness.

Now, practically speaking, you have no idea what is going on. This means you have very little awareness. Of course, this is true to different degrees. Some are totally unaware, some are a little aware. So it is Our purpose in coming to guide you out of this illusion, out of this darkness, back into the light, back to your true self that has no beginning and has no end.

The illusion is very great. It is very intricate, and it is a force that is working against the light. So a great deal of our discussions will be to clarify for you *what is illusion and what is light.* You must begin to discriminate, you must begin to see – this is darkness and this is light. Without this discretion you will not be able to *wake up,* because if what you consider to be the truth is in fact darkness, then you will be bound by the illusion. Just as if you were in a dream, you must understand what is the dreaming. If you believe the dream to be real, then it is not possible to get out. You must come to a state of full awareness of what is the dream state. So We are here to attack the darkness, to attack the illusion, to *expose* the illusion.

The words that are being spoken now in this room are not the true communication that is taking place. The true communication is in your heart; it is within you. The true benefit of these gatherings is not just the words, although the words are helpful. If it were just the words, then you could simply read all the things that are said. But there is a power that is in your heart, and that is moving your awareness. Now your attention has primarily been focused on the illusion, not seeing anything else, not understanding anything else. But as We speak, as you have sat here and listened, your awareness – whether your conscious mind appreciates it or not – has been shifting and beginning to focus on the true reality. *This is how beings become enlightened.* So know that. Try to *feel it* within you. Try to feel the depth of the communication. It is a communication *that is beyond words.* It is like a voice speaking to you, directing you. You can hear it, but it is not with words.

When you begin to touch upon this place, there are many ways that it will manifest that your conscious mind can comprehend, or at least it can appreciate that something is going on. This frequently manifests, for instance, in crying. Because when you touch upon this place, you touch upon your true Home which you have forgotten, and there is naturally an emotion when this connection is made.

For those of you who stay tonight, as We guide everyone to this place, you will see it manifesting in various ways. It may be a sense of peace and just a growing sense of awareness *and understanding.* After you leave tonight, if you will pay attention, you will notice that your awareness *has changed.* You have become *more aware.* And it is important to notice this, because it will give you *the faith* to practice more and achieve more awareness.

You may speak with some who are here, who within *a very short period of time* have realized *a great deal,* whose consciousness has changed *dramatically,* and it is continuing to move at such a rapid rate that sometimes they feel it is a little too fast. This is normally not a problem in the processes of enlightenment, but there is a special circumstance that is being created here; it is a special power that is being brought in to move you very quickly. Because it is the primary intention of Our coming that not only do you achieve some awareness – but that you come to a *full state of awareness,* and *when you leave these bodies, that you never again return to this plane of existence, that you never again take birth in this world.*

So as you sit here tonight, try to feel the power that is within. It is like listening. Something is going on, and it is going on *now.* Do not be frustrated if you cannot comprehend or feel or hear at this moment. Simply try to put yourself in a receptive, open state and continue to listen. And what will happen – what *has happened* with many that are here – is that you do begin to hear; you do once again come in touch with the true realm, and it is a *realm of overwhelming love and ecstasy.*

But there are *so many* misconceptions holding you back from beginning this process. The majority of the processes of truth are riddled with lies. And as this is the case, everyone is filled with misconceptions of what they must do *before* they can have the truth. So We will be attacking the lies in the processes. Now understand, these processes *are* giving light. They *are* giving illumination. They *are* giving some awareness. You can see people that practice certain processes *do change; they do become more aware in many areas.* So We are not condemning the processes. We will only condemn, point out, and fight against the *darkness* – the *illusion that has become mixed in with the light.* For while you may follow a process that has light and you may grow in awareness, as long as you are holding on to illusion or darkness, you *will not get free from this plane of existence.* So We will only help. We are not saying that you must stop a process that you may be involved in, but We *will* point out what aspects of the process are *darkness, are illusion,* and if you will remove the darkness from the process that you are practicing, you will move so much faster.

So at times it may appear that We are just criticizing *everybody*, but if you will *please* pay attention, you will see it is only the illusion and the darkness that We are attacking, that We are exposing. To clarify for some of you, I will give an example from the Christian faith. The Lord Jesus *truly* only taught the love and the light. But through years of perversion of His teachings, they have now come to a conclusion and propagate, as *His teaching,* that if you do not do certain things that *they* have formulated, if you do not follow Him *exclusively*, then you will be cast into an eternal hell, and there you will reside and be punished mercilessly for eternity. Now this is a lie. It is not true. We wish *that you would follow* the teachings of the Lord Jesus *properly*, if you are going to do that. But understand, as long as the followers of Lord Jesus hold on to *this tremendous lie,* they will *not* get free from this illusion. They will *not* go back to what they call heaven because they are still bound; there is an area of their awareness that is in total darkness. So We are not attacking the Christian faith; We are attacking the darkness and the perversions of the truth that have taken place.

In addition to this, We may at times point out darkness and illusion that is going on in an individual. We, of course, *are not against anybody.* We are only against the illusion and the darkness *that is binding you to this plane of existence and is perpetuating a state of suffering.* There is also some happiness on this plane, but it is so little that you are settling for.

We do not want to be misunderstood in this area, so I have spent considerable time and I will repeat these things in the future. We are not against any organization. We are not against any individual. We are only against the darkness. We wish that you would become free from this state of illusion and darkness and come into the light. It is your true Home – and it is *waiting* for you to return.

So if you would be interested in getting free from this illusion, then perhaps there is a question that you wish to ask that will assist you in achieving this state. Know that anything that is separating you from this state is just an illusion; it is a trap; it is filled with misconceptions. The illusion would like you to think that to achieve the light will be harder, more impossible to achieve than it is, so you will not truly even attempt it, as you will be afraid that you will have to give up something in order to achieve the light. This is the nature of illusion. It convinces you to stay in illusion. It is a force; it is a power. Try to understand.

What are your questions?

Do not think that your questions, in any way, may be unimportant or trivial. Any obstacle between you and the light is not trivial. What may seem to be a small thing in your mind and not worth mentioning, upon discussion can be opened up, and a whole area of darkness can be exposed. So do not be intimidated in any way. There is only one mood that exists here, and that *is to do everything to help you from the state of illusion into the light. It is unconditional love.* It is hard to trust that, as you have not had that experience before. But whatever you are doing, whatever you want to do, we will only help you move forward.

Person One: Gourasana, I am not sure I understood you when a few minutes ago you were explaining the power that the illusion has on us in this life, in this material world. Were you saying that the illusion has such a power that it makes us think that we have to give up what we have here in order to advance our consciousness? Are you saying that it is illusion that you think you have to give up everything? Because I feel like I've just given up. It's just incredible where I'm at; I don't really know what to do with myself. I don't know what is next. I desire a lot of silence. It's very hard for me to relate to so much of this world that we are in.

Gourasana: But I was not speaking to you. When I speak, as time goes on, people will say, "He is contradicting; He says one thing, then He says another thing." But all of you are on a path, *and it is a highly individualized path.* That is why these general processes are not such a good thing if you truly want to make great advancement. The blanket processes have set rules, "You do this. You do this. You do this. You don't do this. You don't do this. And then you get the light." There are some people that happen to benefit nicely because their path is parallel to some of these teachings. But in general, most are missing out because they are trying to do or not do something.

This is why I am saying these words are not the true communication. They are just giving some direction. The true communication is within your heart, and you must learn to listen, ultimately, with it. I can guide you with the words, but there will come a point where you will be within, and then you will begin to move quickly. So you must learn to have some patience.

It is generally taught in all of the large organized philosophies that you must not do certain things, and if you do those things then you will not get the light. There are a great many such teachings: "If you smoke, you will not get the light. If you take any intoxication, you will not get the light. If you engage in sex, you will not get the light." There is nothing preventing you from getting the light. As an example of what I mean by "highly individualized," there are some of you that should try to become freer, let go of guilt and fear that is binding you. In other words, for someone who is bound by a religious belief – that it is bad to drink some alcohol, and that if you drink that alcohol it will be a sin and then God will punish you – *for this individual it may be good to drink some alcohol to break that guilt and that lie.* Now I am not recommending that you drink alcohol, I am just trying to give an illustration of how it cannot be just one blanket process. It has to be *highly individualized* according to where *you* are at and what *you* need to do. Now on the other hand, there are those that are drinking alcohol and smoking cigarettes, and it would be best if they stopped it entirely – as soon as they can – not with a sense of repression and guilt and fear, but through an awareness.

This one common lie that is perpetrated, that God is going to punish you if you behave in a certain way – *this* is one of the darkest lies. It is born from illusion and darkness, and it binds you in and of itself, because rather than experiencing a loving relationship with the Supreme, you have a part of you that is constantly afraid. So you are *paralyzed* and cannot move. That is why I say that for some people it would be good to break this *paralysis by rebelling against this lie.* Not that I am saying they should go out and drink day and night or engage in sex day and night. I am just saying some rebellion would be good *for them* in their *particular state of awareness* because *they have been frozen by guilt and fear of the Lord!* And they should *do these things just to break free from that fear!* And know in their hearts that the Lord does not punish. Just begin to see the illusion in this concept – *that He will punish you for eternity!* Just begin to see how the darkness works and prevents you from getting free from this state of illusion, and see the magnitude of the illusion. Without guidance, how would it be possible to get free?

Person Two: Gourasana, if you hurt someone else, are you punished for that?

Gourasana: The punishment is already there at the time of the hurt. To have a consciousness that you would intentionally hurt, that consciousness is the punishment. It is not that you hurt someone, then a punishment comes. *Your hell, your punishments* are coming from your awareness, from your consciousness. So those that hurt others have created their own hell. But even the most evil of these beings – evil of course, I mean, by their behavior – if they would come to a state of awareness, then there would be no more hell; there would be no more punishment. This is where the concept of this hell has been derived – one of the areas. Whatever consciousness you create, whatever universe you create, that is what you exist in. The consciousness of one who goes out and harms another intentionally, maliciously, the consciousness they have created is not good, and they are suffering from that consciousness. So you can see how some have accepted the philosophy that they are being punished because they are suffering, but they are suffering because of the consciousness they have created. Not that there is an outside force coming in and punishing. As soon as they change that consciousness, then the hell stops.

Person Three: I am considering relocating. I am feeling that for my inner development, if I am in a natural setting where there is clean water and air, that this will support my inner development as well as my total being. Can you please comment on whether the relocation would be good for me?

Gourasana: There are only two things that I consider. If what you do is taking you toward the light, then it is good. If it will put you in a situation where your true awareness will grow, then it is good. If it is a move that will put you in another area of illusion or darkness, then it is bad. *YOU must develop the awareness to perceive the difference between the illusion and the light. This is the only way you will attain a state of full awareness.* You must begin examining each and every thing that is in your existence and ask, "Is this taking me toward the light or is this taking me toward the darkness? Am I getting distracted from the light, or am I truly creating a situation where I can go within and find my true self?" You must begin to observe. You must understand.

I will not become a crutch, because the crutch will also keep you in this world. I will help and guide and direct, but you must develop *your own spiritual strength and awareness.* It is not that I can make you aware. *You must achieve your own awareness.* I can guide you, and there is a power to help pull you toward the light, but except for a few things I will not be giving such specific advice. This type of thing, to be honest, is not so helpful because it is a crutch, and it dulls your own awareness.

This is what has happened with philosophies and different paths of awareness. They say, "You do this. You don't do that. And then you achieve this." So they have set up so many rules. Indeed, there are scriptures that have all the rules of existence – how to bathe, how to eat, how to sleep, how to dress – that mindlessly so many people are following this, and it is just mechanical because it has all been spelled out for them. So they mindlessly and mechanically are going through this process, and they are not making very good advancement spiritually, because they are not going within and getting in touch with their true self for the answers. Rather they are depending upon an outside structure.

This does not mean that guidance and help is not there and will not continue to be there. But I am not here to cast some light on this plane of illusion so you may have a happier dream, a happier state of illusion. That advice you can get at other places. This is not what We are doing here. "Should I marry someone, should I not marry someone" – like that. Indirectly, sometimes suggestions will be there. But you must begin to go within and get in touch with your true self, where the true communication is going on, and be guided from that place. As you practice this more and more, it will become clearer and clearer what it is you should do and what it is you should not do.

Person Three: Thank you.

Person Two: Does karma exist?

Gourasana: Not as it is commonly taught. It only exists in that everything you do has an effect upon your consciousness. So your state of awareness, the consciousness that it creates, will force you to behave in certain ways. And behaving in some ways will create suffering and pain, so it may appear that it is caused by an outside force, but it is truly only your consciousness. This is why teachers of karma say that once you attain a state of full awareness, karma stops, the cycle of birth and death stops, no matter what you have done. But, of course, the activities that you do can put you into a state of illusion that will bind you for some time so it will not be possible to get the light. You see? Just as everyone who has come here tonight has created a consciousness that now has opened a door, through which they may – if they pursue it – come to a state of full awareness. But if they begin behaving, doing certain activities, there can be *another* consciousness created, which rejects the light. So the light will no longer be available, as they will not be able to take it – you see. It *is* that simple. It is just here to take. Nothing is stopping you except yourself. So if you want the light, if you desire the light, take some assistance and *you will get the light.* But again, the karma that is commonly preached – that if you do a wrongful activity, then the Lord will punish you – is one way to communicate to a mass of people, but it is not the truth.

Person Four: Gourasana, I value ownership and financial status, but I see it impeding my consciousness and slowing me down from entering into the light. How can I open my heart to achieve consciousness and light and let go of my desire for financial status?

Gourasana: This is a good question, because again there is a concept that first *you must give up* the desire for something or *you must stop* the activity. *It is illusion,* but it is not necessary to stop it before you get the light. As you gradually achieve more awareness and more light, the illusion that you are speaking of will simply disappear. Understand, it is an illusion; this means that, in fact, it truly does not exist. You can see that certain people in the group have different illusions than yours. Just as you are not bound by *their illusions* (it is not binding you at all) so it will be with *your illusion.* As your awareness grows, your illusion will become like the others' illusions that are not an illusion *for you.* You see?

In regard to the area of finances – as I said, I do not give specific advice, and remember that this is not something I am saying *to everyone* – my general recommendation in the area of finances is that on the one hand, you do not have as your work something which is so disturbing to your mind that it consumes so much of your time that you cannot adequately devote time to the light. This will vary from one individual to another, and this is why I am emphasizing it is just a suggestion.

But on the other hand, try to live *simply*. This does not mean that you need to live in deprivation or in a bad environment. It means to try to see where excess spending can be reduced so financial burden will not be there. You will see one man and his family, and they will make a certain amount of money, and they will live a certain way, which is fine. But given twice as much money, they will spend twice as much money. And given three times as much money, they will spend three times as much money. And on and on, until the man is making millions, and he is spending millions. So try to live a simple existence. It can be very nice, but the things that people are normally buying to bring happiness to themselves are excessive and are distracting them. Plus the financial burden puts them in a bind. They are bound financially to a situation, and this can hurt them in their progress.

Person Four: Thank you.

Person Five: Do you think that you can be balanced, working in the light, have sufficient finances, have everything in this material world, and be doing it for the highest of yourself and for other people?

Gourasana: Yes. But it is a question of where is your focus? If your focus, if your attention is that you have all of these things, and then in your spare time you want the light, then you will be bound by illusion. The same exact existence with a different consciousness will enable you to achieve a state of full enlightenment. In other words, if your goal is for the light, for the truth, for achieving a full state of awareness, then *these things* will only support you. But *it is* a question of your focus and your desire. And your desire must come ultimately to a point where you want nothing else but the light, the love, and the truth. Around that desire so many things may or may not manifest. It is not so critical. But with this perception, these things will not bind you to the material existence. In other words, if you are in a profession that produces large sums of money, and in this profession your mind is not too disturbed or distracted so that you cannot begin to go within and achieve awareness, then the money that you produce from this profession will not bind you and you may still have a nice house, a nice car, nice clothing. Try to understand the difference. On one hand, all of these things will bind you and trap you in this illusion, but with another awareness or perception, they will not. Generally speaking, they do.

Person Four: I have seen the light. I have danced in the light. I want the ability to do this more frequently and stop the patterns and impediments. And I am wondering if the light I have danced in is the true light or does it expand and go further than that?

Gourasana: It is *unlimited*. You have had a glimpse. Even if someone thinks they have come here out of idle curiosity, it is truly because they have had a glimpse, and that glimpse moved them enough to take time out from their illusion to come here. But yes, it is unlimited; it is *beyond* your comprehension.

You can move in a very short time. What we are doing here is not promising something in the future. We are not asking you to behave in this way or that way, and then sometime in the future you will begin to get something. What We are doing here is We are taking you to the light *now. Just try to see. Just make the effort and try to perceive that as We speak there is a change in your awareness that is taking place.* The mind does not understand; the mind frequently does not even have knowledge of what is happening. It is a feeling, it is a sense of awareness that is changing. And *it is changing for every single person in this room and it is changing now!* We are not giving a teaching that you will leave, you will go out and you will practice, and later you will get something. We are giving some advice, but know *that the real phenomenon is happening now.* There is nothing that is stopping you from going within and moving faster, becoming *more* aware. And if you can come to these gatherings and pay attention to your awareness before you come, pay close attention, and then after you leave again examine your awareness, you will see that there is a difference. As you become more in tune, as you become more sensitive, then *this* will become more and more apparent until all *doubt will be removed* about what is happening here.

But desire is everything; let your desire for the truth grow. Let your desire grow to be free from this state of illusion. You can see; you can look around and see how people are bound by it, and by that binding they are suffering, and practically they are mindlessly going through life not understanding *anything* that is going on. Let this frighten you a little bit for incentive. Let it frighten you that people are so hopelessly lost in illusion that *they have no idea that they are even in illusion.* They are so bound by illusion, they are not even aware of the *possibility* of Spirit. They truly do not believe that there even is another realm of existence. *And it is the only true realm! This is an illusion!* Just try to understand the significance of the circumstance that is going on. What everyone is taking to be reality is total illusion. And what most, at best, are getting a glimpse of is the only true reality. And you are all simply walking around as in a dream, not knowing, not understanding. Just going from one scene to another, to another, to another. Just like in a very long movie. Not understanding the purpose behind it. Not understanding anything. Simply acting out one scene after another.

Try to understand. It is your desire that will take you there. There is no qualification that you must have. Listen. . . . Your true self is beckoning. It wishes you to wake from this illusion, but you have not been listening. Try to listen. Try to hear.

Person Four: Is achieving true cornucopia a vehicle to be more in the light?

Gourasana: This word, cornucopia, has so many definitions.

Person Four: What is the true definition?

Gourasana: There is the cornucopia of material abundance; you could use it in that way: that you will have everything that you desire materially. But if I were to use this word, it would mean spiritual abundance – it would mean unlimited abundance. I do not wish to mix the two. There is a misconception that one necessarily comes with the other. But I can tell you that there are many that have full spiritual cornucopia and materially they have nothing. It is the spiritual cornucopia that We are after. You should know that when you have achieved this, all of your desires will be satisfied – and then *much more* beyond your comprehension. In this existence you are settling for so little.

There is a tendency to think that by giving up something in this material realm there will be a lack, that you will be missing something, but you should know that it is what you are holding on to that is causing you to miss something. There are many that are sitting with no material possessions to speak of – eating almost nothing, having no pleasures of this material world – and they are sitting in a state of ecstasy and love that is beyond your comprehension, and they desire nothing, nor do they need anything.

So We are encouraging that the focus of your life and the focus of your attention be on becoming fully aware and achieving the light. That is where the focus should rest – ultimately. This does not mean that you need to cease to engage in these other activities. Certain activities, as you progress, you will naturally lose interest in. It will not have to be such a struggle, or a repression of desire. Just as when you were a child you desired to do certain things, to have certain things, and if they were taken away from you, there would be much disturbance and crying due to your attachment. But as you have grown, your attachment for these things has gone. It is no longer binding you. So in the same way you do not need to endeavor separately so much. The things that are illusion will gradually simply diminish, and you will lose interest *as you experience something better.* Not that first you stop *everything* that gives you pleasure and then somewhere down the line you will get some spiritual pleasure.

But it is important to begin to focus your attention on the light. There is no activity that will stop that desire; only *you* will stop that desire. You can be engaging in the act of sex and desiring the light. Generally, the common philosophies preach that this is something that is *preventing* you from the light, and that you must stop or restrict this activity or you will not get the light. But it will not stop you. It is true that this is a strong attachment, but I do not want to worry you, because as you become fully aware the attachment will diminish, and simply the desire for that type of reciprocation will be gone, because it will have been replaced by a reciprocation that is more ecstatic than anything you have ever *experienced* in the act of sex, *and it will be continuous.* So you will have no desire, of course, to have *less pleasure.* So you do not need to separately endeavor as much as is being propagated by the common philosophies. It is a question of your desire and your focus.

Person Four: But still, when you put the focus and desire in there, you are dealing with the conditions of the real world. You need to survive.

Gourasana: Focus in where?

Person Four: Focus on making money to survive, even though the will and desire to achieve the light is there. How do you avoid that conflict?

Gourasana: First you must become patient, because it will gradually change. Now if you are doing something (as I have stated several times tonight) that is creating such a distraction, such a disturbance in the mind that you find it is not possible to focus or shift your awareness, then it may be *necessary* for you to do something *differently.* For instance, a businessman may be a very big man in a corporation and be making large sums of money, but his job is taking his entire life. So it may be – and I am not recommending that you quickly abandon what you are doing, give it time first – it may be that after some endeavor for some period of time when he sees that this is too much, that he will not achieve what he desires in this position, then he will have to leave this position and take another position, perhaps one that is more conducive, that will be more peaceful, that will give him more time, more freedom.

And create an atmosphere; wherever possible, whatever you do, if there is a little something you can do in your workplace to remind you of the light – it will help. There are some who are fortunate enough that they could have a little music playing, music as we will play tonight which induces a meditative state. So while they are working, they can be going within. You do not need to sit down and do nothing else to be within and to be evolving. So those that are fortunate in this area could do something like that. For others, it may be a phrase that strongly strikes their heart and they can write this nicely on a plaque or a paper and place it where, throughout the day, they frequently will see it and it will remind them.

Or when there is time to take food, during that time period you can create a meditative state. You see, it is just a question of focus. It is waiting here for you, but you have just lost focus. So now We will lead you through the maze of illusion and help you to begin to focus. So before you go to work, while you are preparing your body, you can create a meditative state. You can play some music; some people like incense. So many things – you must think of what it is that sparks it in *you* so that you are centered and within when you arrive at work. Now, due to the insanity that you have experienced in the workplace, you may lose focus: You are out in the illusion, you have become distracted, and you are out of touch. But you can take a little break, and in just a *few minutes* you can totally calm yourself, focus within again, and be *just* as centered as you were. And as you practice, this will become easier and easier to do until you achieve a point *that no matter what is going on,* you will be centered. But as I have said, in order to get to that state, some may need to change their position.

So many opportunities to go within: when you rise, when there is a little break of time that they allow you, you can take that time to go within. When it is time to take food, *that is a very long time;* if you just spent that time every day going within, being receptive in a meditative state, you would make so much progress. After the job is finished, at night before you go to sleep, if you have had *no other time* – your existence is so chaotic, so many problems with the children, the family, the work, and the problems of this world, if somehow that day you didn't even have a minute to sit down – when you go to sleep, if you can just at that point enter into a meditative state *while you are sleeping,* you will be moving and *you will be advancing.* Just see. There is *no one* who cannot make advancement. It is simply your desire. If you want it, then there are many ways that you will get it. And as you progress, the ways will unfold more and it will become clear what you should and should not do, and you will move faster and faster and faster.

Person Four: When you're doing that and you let your impatience get in the way, is your impatience your impediment? Most of your advice you just gave me, I follow. I've been centered all week, through very major business decisions, but I just can't see the light as I remember the light.

Gourasana: Yes. You must not do this with expectations. People have an experience one time. . . . There are some in this room who have had experiences that are very great – yet if the next time they sit down, they expect at least as much or more, then the expectation can hamper them, because it changes, it is different every time. There may be *some* similarities, but it is an unlimited realm, and the way it will *come to you,* the way your awareness will grow, will vary from individual to individual and from time to time. So you must not have expectations. You simply must *do it.* You simply must go within and just be receptive. The impatience, and the frustration, and the fear, and the doubt, they will come and you must just try, gently, to not give them much energy. And with practice it will come. In other words, when the impatience comes, there will be a point when, due to your evolution and your *separateness* from the illusion, you will see it as something separate, and you will say, "Oh, here comes the impatience again." Now see what happens when the impatience is there. "I want it. I want it right now. I do not have it now. I want this so. . . ." And you will be able to observe, and as you continue to observe, the separation from the illusion will continue, and the illusion will gradually lose its power until the impatience will disappear – simply because it no longer will have any binding power. So try *not* to give it energy.

But in all endeavors, while there is a *great desire* that you want to let grow, you must approach the obstacles with a gentleness, a loving gentleness. Just gently push them out of the way. Do not be too hard on yourself; at the same time let your desire grow. You may have one period in the day when you will meditate, and you will come home and there will be a woman there, and she will desire sex and there will be a conflict in you – but do not be overly concerned. Do not give this too much energy – that here the one time you have in the day, the desire for sex has taken you over and now your entire period for meditation will be taken up. Go ahead and engage in sex, but you can do it with awareness, and simply observe.

And as I have said, no matter what the day brings, no matter how chaotic and distracting the day is, when you lie down to sleep at night – *and you should all practice this* – possibly if you could put on some music it would be nice, something soothing. But even if that is not possible (perhaps you do not have that facility), you can just go within and feel the peace or whatever it is that you feel. And in that state when you go to sleep, while you are sleeping your awareness will be moving and your awareness will be shifting. So there is no reason, there is nothing that is stopping *anybody* from going toward the light *except their desire.*

The woman who does sex for a living, she may rise in the morning, and throughout the entire day she may do nothing but engage in these acts – which are very distracting to her – but at the time of taking rest she can do this, and her consciousness will evolve. And even though she is in an occupation that is generally perceived to be against the light, she can be going faster toward the light than many that are sitting in church praying.

Try to understand, *it is your desire that is creating your universe.* If you desire just to have things in this world, then your energy will be focused there, and you may or may not get them. But even if you get them – you see so many who have so many things, so many vehicles and homes and servants and clothing – and of course they are not happy. And believe Me, even in the highest states of happiness that are achieved through these things, it is *nothing* compared to the true happiness, the bliss that is waiting in the spiritual realm – which is the only true realm.

So do not think, "Oh, I will have to give up this; I will have to stop this because this is an illusion." No. You can enjoy to the full degree of your capacity areas of the illusion that you wish to. It is just that by increasing your desire for the light and beginning some practice, you will evolve and you will grow toward the light.

Person Four: Thank you.

Gourasana: The only reason that you will not succeed is that you will give up, that you will stop. There is nothing else that will happen that will prevent you from achieving this goal – especially with the assistance that is now being offered. Practically, it is guaranteed.

Are there more questions?

We will be meeting frequently, and you all are welcome to come and ask. As you come into difficulty, then We can help you through the difficulty. By your very coming here, you have become – rather I should say, you have entered into a phenomenon that will fulfill all of your desires. Your faith will increase as this proves to be true; you do not have to go away with any firm faith. Simply have enough desire to continue, and it will be *proven* by your own experience, not by some words or influence from someone else. It will come from a direct experience. Now this is what We are going to do.

Guided Meditation

(Often when Gourasana spoke to a group, He would lead a guided meditation after His talk. All of Gourasana's speaking, if you are focused within, will take you deeper, but the guided meditations are specifically designed for this purpose.)

We are going to begin the true purpose of the gathering. This will be going within and finding this true realm that is there waiting for you. This is a practice of the utmost seriousness. Do not be *impatient* if you are going to stay and practice. Just go within, and if you feel nothing else than a relaxed state, perhaps a little peace of mind, then be satisfied and just try to go deeper and experience *more*. Give up your conceptions of how it will be when you have gone within. Do not be distracted by what others are going through; as you will see, it will be different for every single person. Do not be inhibited or concerned about others around you. If you have a feeling or a desire to cry, then let that desire take you over and do more. Whatever it is that *you feel* you should enter into, allow yourself to enter into that. There will be certain commotion, but do not let it concern you if you have not seen it before.

We will start the music. Get into a comfortable position. If there is something that is extremely annoying about your body, then try to take care of it now. If you need to go to the bathroom, or whatever it is that you need – some thirst – take care of it now; create a comfortable situation *now*, so that once we begin, you can concentrate on what is going to happen for as long as possible without being disturbed by your body.

Is there any question on this?

(Meditation music starts playing in the background: "The Fairy Ring.")

So now, focus only on yourself. Try to exclude from your thoughts those around you. Do not let anything distract you. Do not be inhibited from whatever you feel. Do not be afraid of failure. There can be no failure. It is just a question of focus. When you go within you may not be able to appreciate with your conscious mind where you are, but you will be within.

Let yourself go deeper within. Let go of all the illusions of your life: who you think you are, what you think you must do. Let go of the illusion and go within in a receptive state, desiring to know the truth. Look within. Pray that it may be revealed to you, that you may begin waking from this dreaming state that you have been in for so long.

Do not be concerned if you become distracted. Simply go within again.

To give you a hint (if you do not understand this going within) as you go within, the reality of this room that your body is in will begin to lessen. It is similar to a state of sleep for some, although it is with an awareness.

Now feel yourself being freed from the bondage of time. Let your mind go. Let go of this illusion of time: that you have a certain time period in which to go within and then that time period will be over. This is an illusion.

Try now to let go. Understand that there is no time, and you have forever to go within and search for this place that is within all of you.

It is everything that you truly desire. Let it draw you like a magnet. Let it pull you in. Let it pull you into this realm. It is a realm of unlimited love and light. It is everything you have been seeking, and it is here now waiting for you.

There is nothing more you must do. There is nothing more that your mind must understand. There is *nothing* that is preventing you from going within now and experiencing this realm – tasting the nectar of this eternal spiritual realm, which is your true Home.

You have no other concern at this time. Let all your concerns leave you. There is nothing else to do.

Even My words, if they are not important to you, if what I am saying does not concern you, if you have already located a place, do not be concerned with the words. Remember, My true communication to you is in your heart. Go within and hear. Listen to the truth that will free you from this state of bondage that you are in.

Pray for help. Pray for guidance. Pray that you will achieve what you so desperately want. It is something that you have not found in this realm of illusion. It is something different, but it is what you have been searching for.

Be at peace.

You have just begun the journey inward. Already you are moving closer.

Now some of you are beginning to feel the Presence that is within you. It is like a gentle whisper. You are not sure if even you are hearing it. Have faith that you *are* hearing it.

Let go. Too much you are hanging onto this realm. Let go and you will fall to your depths. Go deeper. Want nothing else. It is everything.

You have just begun. Do not let frustration stand in your way. Do not let expectations stand in your way. The only thing that will stop you from achieving this connection is if you stop going within.

It is not something your mind needs to understand. There is a part of you, your true self, which understands fully. Let this part of you take over, and let go of this illusion, who you think you are.

You are doing well. Be satisfied. No matter what level you have reached, do not think you have achieved nothing. It is not possible to achieve nothing in this process. As you endeavor, there is simultaneously a manifestation of awareness that is taking place. Every second that you are desiring, every second that you are going within, every second that you are praying for the light, your awareness is growing and you are coming closer. Try to feel the Presence. Just try to *feel* the Presence.

You want to be attentive to what you are doing, but the attention is coming from within. Do not let what you have experienced in the past stop you. Do not expect to have the same experience now. Go within and receive what is waiting for you now.

You see, you have just begun, yet you have come closer. Try to appreciate the movement in your awareness.

If you are thinking, "But I feel a resistance, a holding back," do not hold yourself back. Let go. Let go of it. Come here.

If I could just show you what is waiting for you, you would not cease your endeavor until you had achieved it. But you must come here, inward, to see it. *You* must make the effort. The assistance is there, the help is there. Take it.

Illusion Means Just That

April 8, 1988, Alpine, CA

The truth cannot be known, cannot be found, with words. The words can assist you, they can give some guidance, some direction, but that is all. You must all go deeply inside.

Some of you are situated nicely inside, but now go even deeper. You see, it is *only* within that you will find the truth. This is where you *must* focus your attention. If you come and you only listen to the words, you will practically have missed the point in coming here. How many different ways have the masters throughout the centuries tried to communicate the truth in words? How many thousands of volumes of words are there? But you can read every one and still not know the truth.

I have come here to assist you, to guide you – if you are willing – to the true realm of existence. But this realm can only be discovered by going within. And as you endeavor to go deeper, to go within, you will find obstacles. It is these obstacles that We wish to remove.

We are not gathering for a philosophical conversation. This is not an intellectual discussion of some ideas where you will listen and then go away and think about it. It is Our hope that you will make the endeavor *now*, that you will go within *now*, that you will not wait for some philosophical conclusion and then proceed at some later date with some meditation. This is one trick of the illusion. Not living at this moment is one way that you are bound by the illusion; your awareness is not situated *now* – which is all that there is.

So try to see your awareness change. It is important that you appreciate the difference in your awareness. From the time you come until the time you leave, it is possible for your awareness to grow a great deal. So go deeper within and find the truth.

So ask questions: How do you find this place? What do you need to do? What are your obstacles? This is Our concern. Time must be spent in discussion until you have reached a certain point; then we can sit together in silence and the true communication can go on.

When you listen to the answer, be in a receptive state. Try to be open, and try to listen with your heart. Have your attention focused *within* when you are listening. Your mind will hear some words and understand, but the *real* awareness will come from within. If you have any questions, ask. Do not be afraid. Many will not ask, but it is so important. What else is there? What you have known is nothing but illusion. Can you see that? You can only remember your existence in this body, and you have had countless bodies. See how your awareness is limited by this illusion.

You see, for those that are situated within, there is no need at a certain point to even speak. Every moment that passes, awareness is growing. Go within in a receptive state. It is like a listening.

Gayle: Gourasana, can you speak to us more about the illusion? Sometimes it is just so obvious to me, and then other times it's hard for me to tell the difference. People say so many different things and I don't know what to believe.

Gourasana: Yes, the illusion means that you are being deceived. What you consider as reality is not reality. And then you change your consciousness – and there can be unlimited dramatic changes in your consciousness – and these changes can simply be, and almost always are, just another state of illusion. In this way, everyone is bound by illusion and is simply going from one illusion to another illusion, never truly knowing the truth.

The beginning point is that you must begin to see the duality; you must begin to see what is light and what is darkness, what is truth and what is illusion. You must begin this practice. When you perform an activity, is that taking you to the light or away from the light?

You may say, "But I have so many things that I must do; I have so many responsibilities." But most of your responsibilities that you have taken on are unnecessary illusion. Too many are wasting their time creating so much money so that they can live in this illusion so nicely. But it is such a short period of time before you will leave this body. If you spend that time trying to enjoy this illusion, then you will have wasted your life. To the degree that you can spend your time not enjoying the illusion but trying to *see the illusion,* to that degree your awareness will grow.

It is possible to become fully aware, but *first* you must ask yourself, *what is it that you desire? What is it that you truly want?* The reason that most do not grow very quickly in their awareness is because of their lack of focus. I am not saying that there should be deprivation. There needs to be sufficient clothing, food, and shelter, but the unnecessary aspects of these things are a waste of your valuable time. You will be sorry at the time of death, because you will not know what is going on, because you will not be aware, because you will have spent your time devoted *to illusion. And now you're leaving the illusion and you have known nothing else! Now what will you do?! You are going to be forced to give up this illusion that is all that you have known. Do you understand? You will be forced, and at that time you will be sorry that you have no idea where you are going, what it will be like.* How will you be prepared at the time of death? Even if you cannot bring yourself to a stage of full awareness, which is very difficult, at least pursue this enough so at the time of death you do not die in a *bewildered* state, not understanding at all what is going on or having any real faith.

But it is a very powerful illusion. It has you convinced that you must do so many things that you must not do. How will you break free, *and do you wish to?* Do you wish to just have a little light so that you feel a little happier in this illusion – or do you truly want to find the true realm of existence, the ultimate reality, *the only reality?* What is your desire? You must focus, and you must make this your only desire if you wish to succeed. Now when people hear that, "the only desire," they think that I am saying, "Stop everything and just sit down and meditate," or something like that, but that is not the case. You see, it is just: Where is your attention focused? Where is your energy going to be primarily focused?

And I tell you, the existence you have now will only become better. If you have a wife and family, and you as a family are trying to enjoy this material existence, if you will change this consciousness and try to find the light and the truth, then you will see that the family as a unit will become much happier and freer, because the children also only want the light and the love.

If you do not have this desire, then consider yourself unfortunate, because what you are settling for, this miserable state of illusion – where no matter how happy you think you are or how happy you think you will be or no matter how happy you can get in this realm of illusion – it is nothing. *It is nothing.* And by holding on to this illusion *you are missing everything.* The little pleasure you get out of this, practically speaking is pathetic; when there is so much waiting; everything is waiting.

Try to let your awareness grow and encompass the magnitude of what We are discussing here. You entered into this realm of existence countless lifetimes ago, and have been taking birth after birth after birth. Now it is possible for you, *if you wish,* to finally graduate, to finally leave this plane of illusion. Everyone should try to appreciate this point. You are *only aware of this lifetime.* That is all you can even remember. *Yet there was never a time that you did not exist.* Try to understand this point. *How limited your consciousness has become.*

It is only due to this great illusion that is covering you, this darkness that is covering you, that it is possible that the only thing that you are aware of is this current state of illusion that you have created. This body, the bodies around you, and the exchange between these bodies is all you are aware of. (You *may* know a little something else.) So how to get from that state to where you can see that this is *all illusion* – and you can exist in the light with awareness? Then at the time of death there will be no fear, there will be no attachment. If you are fully aware, there will be no desire to return, because you will be free from the illusion. You will see through the illusion. Illusion means just that – it is just an illusion.

When you were a baby, when you were in a very small body, you took pleasure in certain activities, due to the illusion of that moment, of that time, which now in an adult body it would not be possible for you to enjoy. Why? Because *that* illusion is gone. It has been traded in for *another* illusion and then *another* and then *another* and then *another*. This is how you are existing from day to day. You are just gradually changing your illusions. The illusions that were binding you ten years ago may not be binding you today. Some may be, but there are certain illusions that are no longer binding you.

The secret is to continue to change, but instead of changing into another illusion, *start changing into the light. Start changing into the truth.* Instead of stepping into another role of illusion, *try stepping into the light with awareness and understanding* as you step out of the illusion. It is not that you can totally stop the illusion and then suddenly be totally in the light. It is an evolution, but *it is* an evolution that can move very, very quickly *according to your desire.* If you have little desire, then you will move just a little. If you have a great desire, then what cannot be achieved? And if you can make it *your only* desire to find the truth, then how can you fail? Because it is all based upon your desire. What is it that you truly want? What is it that you are looking for but not finding in the activities that you perform in illusion: that love that is not quite fulfilled, that longing that never quite goes away? No matter how many people you are with, you are dissatisfied and longing for something more.

You get a new automobile and your happiness increases, so you have been fooled by the illusion. You have come to the conclusion that the new automobile produces happiness, so you become addicted to a new automobile and this becomes important for your happiness. You acquire a new house and this produces some happiness, so you have been fooled by the illusion. You think that the house is producing some happiness – and on and on.

Of course, simultaneously, if you will pay attention, with every single thing, you will see there is always the other side of the coin – the suffering that goes along, the price that you must pay for these things, the dissatisfaction that comes. "The house did not quite fulfill, it did not quite live up to my expectations, so I'll sell that house and get another and then I will be happy." The happiness is always waiting in the future, "Once I have done this. . . ." It is never now. "Once I make more money," "once my health is good," "once we have acquired a new house," "once the children are born," "once the children leave" – or maybe "when I die, then I'll be happy."

See how the illusion is deceiving you? You are convinced that you must do and have certain things in order to be happy, and it is not true. In your heart you know it is not true. The people who are trying to produce their happiness in this way can look at those who have much more than they will *ever* have, and they can see that they are not happy, that they are not aware, that they are bewildered and have no understanding of what is going on. The rich people, they do not have to work. They have a house such as you will never have. They can have new automobiles every day. They have so much that is completely beyond you, and *they* are not happy. And you think you will be happy when you get a car, a house? These things are binding you to the illusion.

Now that does not mean *necessarily* that these things need to be given up, but there are *many* cases where it would be good to give them up because you have created too much excess in your existence. You have unnecessary things that you must work so hard to support, which are not producing happiness. Once your happiness comes from within, more and more, these things will become unnecessary and you will quit striving to make money for these things, and you will use that same energy and striving to go within.

The only way that you will be able to break free from this *powerful* illusion, which has you *totally bound,* is by your desire. All you have to do is begin to change your desire. Begin to see the illusion. Begin to see the duality. Begin to see what is light, begin to see what is dark, and reject the darkness and take the light more and more. As you do this, your awareness will grow more and more rapidly. This is how you can evolve *very quickly.* There is so much special assistance that is coming in. Do not be so unfortunate that you will not take advantage – that you will just remain in illusion.

Change your desire now. Look at what your desires have been. Look at what they are now. What is it that you want? Look at all of your desires. In the whole spectrum of your desires, which of the desires are for truth and light and which of the desires are just continuing your illusion? See what percentage of your spectrum of desires is for the truth. If you see that your desire is just a small part, then is it any wonder that your awareness has not grown much? You see, you can desire nothing else but the truth and other things in the spectrum will still be satisfied. It is a question of your desire. If you are looking for happiness in a house, then your energy is focused on that, and you will be bound. But if you only want the light and you want a nice facility so that you, or you and your family, can have a nice facility to find the light and the truth, then in one case the house is binding you and is darkness, and in the other case it is a sanctuary, a church, or a temple of light. It is a place that will increase your awareness – the same place. You see, it is just a matter of your consciousness. In one case it is binding you, and you will never be satisfied. And in the other case, your happiness will only increase as you go within and find more and more of the love and the light that is awaiting you. The proper car that you need for practical existence will not bind you, if your existence is to find the truth. You need to go to work; you need to buy food; you need to do so many things. It is a necessity. So the very same things, the car, the house, the family – depending upon your desire – will either bind you, keep you in darkness, and perpetuate the illusion, or the very same things can increase the light, the love, and the awareness, and produce *true* happiness. So try to make this your only desire. You will not be missing anything on this plane of illusion, and you will be experiencing a realm where there is an ecstasy *that is beyond anything that you can remember.*

So how far have you traveled since you have come? How deeply within have you been able to situate yourself?

Carol: Gourasana, I have a hard time getting very deep. I get to a point where I don't have any thoughts and I get peaceful. But as far as getting really deep, I get stuck and can't go deeper. It seems maybe nothing's happening.

Gourasana: It is important to appreciate what you have achieved spiritually. It is important to appreciate the changes in your awareness. More and more you must do this. This is another thing. This is another problem. This is another common obstacle. People meditate, they practice, and they think that they are not getting anything; but it is not possible. As long as there is *an endeavor*, as long as the very act of *trying* is going on, even if you have no understanding of what going within means – your higher self does.

So *you*, your mind, what you are aware of, this being of illusion that you have created may not understand what is going on, *but there is something going on* – and your awareness is growing and you are becoming freer from the bonds of illusion *while* you are making the endeavor. It is not possible to stand still. Everyone's consciousness is evolving in this plane of illusion no matter what activity they are involved in. It is just a question of speed. How quickly are they evolving? Will you leave in this lifetime, or will it be millions of lifetimes more? This is *very* important to know.

You must begin to appreciate and see what you have achieved. You all have areas in which you are aware, and you can see areas in which others are not aware. As your awareness increases, this will just become more and more true until you will begin to see how some are practically in *total illusion*. They have *no idea* what is going on. And you will begin to perceive the different degrees of light and awareness that people have. But you must begin observing, and you must begin to observe with discretion. You must see: is this truly the light or is it darkness?

And then the additional difficulty is that frequently the two are mixed, so this creates confusion. The best example of this is the organized philosophies. People can go and feel the light and the love to certain degrees, so they accept the whole thing that is being handed to them. But with the light they are accepting so much darkness, which prohibits them from moving very quickly, so they are bound in another illusion and their growth is stunted.

Still, they are better off than someone who is doing nothing, because there is light, there is love, and that is increasing, which is why they have so much faith that they continue to practice – whatever process it may be: Yoga, Christianity. But because along with that light they have accepted darkness – things that are not true, things that are lies, things that are illusions that are manufactured over a period of time – they are again bound by another illusion because their discretion is not good. If you can go to these processes and just take the light and leave the darkness, then you will move *so much faster, so much quicker.*

You must have discretion. See how subtle the illusion is. See how at every turn you take, the illusion is waiting to snare you again. One desires to know the truth, so he begins to search. He goes out and he comes to an organization, and they are preaching the light. So he can see in his heart that he desired some light, and he found some light; here he can experience in his heart that this is light. So he accepts *everything*, but he accepts so much darkness with the light that although he is better off, still he is bound by illusion. So when you look at the processes of truth, you must develop discretion to weed out the darkness that has been interwoven in the philosophies, and reject the darkness.

The very powerful, incredible light and love of the Lord Jesus – and all He preached was light and love, that is *all* He represented. *All* He wanted *is that everyone would come and take the light and the love of the Lord,* but over a period of time things have been added, and now, generally, they preach that if you do not accept the Lord Jesus exclusively, then you will be cast into an eternal hell, eternal darkness, where you will be punished for your rebellion. This is not the teaching of the Lord Jesus, and it is a lie. It is a lie that they have manufactured. They may have manufactured it out of sincerity as motivation for people to accept the Lord Jesus, because they thought they knew better. But the end result is that most who are accepting the Lord Jesus – and they *are* experiencing love and light in that process – they are also accepting this *terrible darkness,* this *illusion* that is interwoven in it. *The Lord Jesus is nothing but love and light. Do you know what that means? Do you think that He is some cruel personality that if you do not accept Him within this one tiny period, this one tiny life, that He will cast you into a hell of punishment eternally?! If you think this, how can you really know the Lord Jesus?!* So again, bound by another illusion. But you can go to this process and just take the light, just take the love, and with discretion reject all that is darkness. Then you can move so much faster, so quickly, because you are not bound by further illusion.

So this is going on – you have so many processes, so many paths of truth, but they have become quickly contaminated. So quickly they become contaminated that the truth becomes less and less and less and less and less, and the darkness increases until the truth is the small part and the darkness is dominant.

Person One: Gourasana, whenever fear creeps into a philosophy that is being taught, should we use our discretion to think that if there is fear, then there is darkness in the philosophy?

Gourasana: Yes. If it produces fear, then it is still contaminated. But understand that there is also a need. That's *why* these processes exist and are very popular. What

We are doing here is simply weeding out the darkness so that you may evolve quicker. But it is a fact that in some cases the lie, the fear of eternal darkness, motivates one to desire the light. But it is not sufficient. It will not get you out of this plane of existence in this lifetime because it is too contaminated. But still, it has its purpose.

Understand, there is a reason for this existence and there is even a reason for all of the darkness. But if you wish to finally evolve off this plane of illusion, you must become free from the darkness. It no longer has a purpose for you. The illusion no longer serves a purpose. So you want to give it up. You need to get out of the darkness and illusion, so you must begin seeing. But for the masses, yes, the processes all have these terrible fears they are motivating the people with. "Here is your choice. You can come with the Lord Jesus and experience the love, the light, and the ecstasy of His association eternally, or you can go to hell and *suffer horribly,* beyond your imagination, eternal darkness and damnation and punishment. What is your choice?" "Oh, I'll take hell."[1] So it serves a purpose, because people are so densely bound in illusion. What will motivate them to do something to get free from this illusion? So the fear becomes a necessary tool at times. But whenever the fear is being taught, then you should be careful.

Person One: Gourasana, I understand you to say that some people have bad discretion and that to see the illusion you need good discretion. How do I build better discretion between darkness and the light as I'm exposed to the illusion and seeing it in its duality?

Gourasana: By practice, by beginning to see, by not just going and experiencing, but by seeing what is illusion

1) Gourasana is speaking ironically.

and what is darkness. When someone is speaking to you, is it illusion, is it darkness, or is it light? When you are experiencing something or you wish to do something, is that desire something that will take you toward the light or is it a distraction, is it illusion? When you look at teachings, when you read the books of teachings of truth, see how much is darkness – and they vary greatly. Some are mainly darkness. This is how you become aware, by practicing and becoming aware. You must make the effort. You must want to become free from illusion, and that desire will help you. You will start to see the illusion because you need to see the illusion in order to become free from it. You will know it; it will become obvious to you. It will not trap you again because you will know it for what it is.

For example, let us assume that everyone in this room is free from the illusion of heroin addiction. So if I come up to you and I say, "Here, this is some heroin; would you like to take this? It is being offered," because you are at least that aware, you will say, "No. It is just suffering. It is just suffering. It is just illusion. Why would I want that?" And you will have *no interest,* and there will be some repulsion. This is how it will become, as your awareness grows, with all areas of illusion. When the illusion comes, you will say, "No, I don't want that illusion. Thank you." It is very difficult to see your own illusion, but you can begin by seeing the illusions that others are bound by. It will help you to understand your own illusions, ultimately.

You can see a man who is totally unhappy and dissatisfied with life, and all of his effort, all of his existence is put into producing money, because he thinks that once he achieves that goal, *then* he will find happiness. Even sometimes when he thinks that the money will be used for finding the truth, it is still just another trap, because his attention is focused on one thing primarily, and that is to make money. And he thinks after the money has been achieved, *then* everything will be fine; then everything will manifest and grow. In this way he is *bound* because he is simply going day after day into the illusion, and the happiness is ever eluding, not quite able to be achieved, never quite able to be grasped. So many examples: see how others around you are striving after something they think will produce happiness. You can *see* with the awareness you have already achieved that it definitely will *not* produce happiness. See how they are bound by that illusion.

So begin to see, begin to practice. Then you will start to get a hint of your own illusion. That is harder to see. You know from experience. You can go up to someone who is heading for disaster, who has made a decision to enter voluntarily into darkness, and you know that they will only suffer; you try to help, but they are so completely covered over with this illusion that no illumination can get through and they are not able to hear. In this way they suffer, because they cannot receive any light. How many do you know like this? How many instances do you see where people are searching after happiness in an area that *you* know, and so many others around them *know*, are aware, that it is only going to produce unhappiness and they will *never* be fulfilled. Yet they are bound by that illusion – you see. They are thinking, "Oh no, I will be happy." So this is everyone's predicament. Everyone is thinking they will be happy in these pursuits. But it is just illusion, and satisfaction will never come. The longing will never be satisfied.

Person Two: Gourasana, an obstacle that I am becoming more aware of is I find it easier to go deeper when I am here, when I am listening to you or meditating in your presence or listening to your tapes. I can't seem to make the leap of locating my depth without being close to you. I think it is an illusion for me to be dependent upon you. How do I go from this experience of finding the light with you into taking it with me when I leave here?

Gourasana: It is not an illusion. When you are here there is special assistance. There is nothing wrong with taking assistance. Indeed, take as much as you can. Find as much as you can. If you find that you cannot meditate alone well, if at all, and that you can only do so in a group, then be with a group. It is true that ultimately you will not need this. This is true when you reach a certain stage.

We are not saying to reject help or assistance; do not misunderstand. Assistance *must* be there. You will *never* get out of this plane of existence without assistance. You can go to church and pray to the Lord Jesus that He please show you the light and the truth, and you will move; you will create more awareness. There is nothing wrong in that; assistance must be there. The association of others who are seeking the light is important, because the influence of others is such an important factor in your evolution. You want to disassociate yourself, as much as possible, from those that are totally bound in illusion, because they will tend to pull you into the illusion with them. But in the same way, association with someone who is seeking only the light will tend to pull you into the light. So there is nothing wrong in taking assistance. Taking assistance is not an illusion.

But there comes a point when through assistance – and there are so many types of assistance that you need – you will get in touch so securely with the true realm of existence that there will come a time when you will no longer *need* assistance such as this. Although you will still like these types of things, because as you go deeper, you begin to appreciate more and more what is going on when we gather together.

But the assistance is also there when you are by yourself. So when that is happening, when you are by yourself, you just must try harder. And you simply must practice. Some will say, "I do not have time to sit down and meditate." But this may not be necessary. You could continue just a day-to-day existence simply observing the illusion *in whatever you do* and your awareness will be growing simultaneously. Even while you are involved in activities that you know are illusion, that knowing will increase as you begin to observe. You will begin to see more and more clearly how it is illusion and how others around you are in illusion, how the illusion is working by leading persons from one thing to another and from one trap into another, how even so many offerings of the light are truly just another trap of illusion. So there is no excuse; there is no reason you cannot grow in your awareness. No matter what you are doing, no matter what it is, you can grow at a faster rate if you will simply make an effort while you are performing that activity.

If you wish to get intoxicated, when you do it, do it with awareness. *Pay attention.* If you are drinking, pay attention. You are going to begin – you taste. Pay attention to the taste. Then observe as the alcohol goes into your body; pay attention to the changes that go on. Look at your thoughts and see how they change as the consumption of alcohol increases. Do it with awareness and observe, and you will actually advance while you are performing the act. Those that are bound by these things will only become free from them from awareness. If you do it, it is not good to suppress it so much if it is something you always desire – it is better *to understand it;* then the danger in the future will no longer be there. As you observe the effects of intoxication – if you do it every time and this is your only meditation, and you get intoxicated one hundred more times – at the end of those one hundred times do you know how aware you will be? And then it will come to a point where you will see so clearly; you will have become so aware that you will no longer desire to become intoxicated, because you will have observed that, yes, there was a point where there was relief. But then after some time an anxiety came in, the body started to feel bad, terrible, unusual; a depressed thought came into the mind, "Have I behaved in a way that was repulsive?" The next day there was so much pain and bad feeling and how long was there actually pleasure? In this way, you will see that overall it is not something you wish to do anymore.[2]

So you see. I say these words "Give up and let go," and people are afraid and repulsed, because they are afraid of giving up things that they are convinced are bringing them happiness. But I am not saying to give up artificially. I am saying to see the illusion and give up with awareness; it is the only way that you can truly give up. The only way the illusion will not again trap you is when you see through it. You see it so clearly that it is nothing that will bind you again. There is nothing there that will distract you again. Just as I gave the example of heroin, so all of the illusions will become like that. And there will come a point where you will become free from the illusion, and at the time of death you will be leaving this place, and there will be *no* illusion that you wish to come back for; there will be no illusion that you wish to be in again. And that is how you

2) If you are addicted to alcohol or any other substance, we recommend you seek professional help.

will evolve off this plane of existence in this lifetime – with awareness, not artificially giving up everything and then sitting there constantly desiring the things that you have given up because your mind has become convinced that there is happiness there, until after years of repression you finally break down and go back to those things.

But sometimes breaking the bond of illusion is a little painful. I am not saying that it is easy to give up. Even once you have understood that there is no pleasure in intoxication or other illusion, that it is only suffering, there is still an effort of *will* that must be exerted. There is still some pain and discomfort and difficulty that will be there in overcoming it. It is just that you need to come to the point of performing the act of giving it up with awareness. You cannot mindlessly just give up. You must do it with awareness; then it will not trap you again.

Person Two: Is this how we must rid ourselves of all the illusions, by being conscious of their effect on us? We must simply see our illusions, our addictions to relationships or to commitments or to work or to certain pleasures or self-indulgences? We must simply see it, experience it and be conscious of it, and see it for what it is?

Gourasana: Yes. But there is another thing: once you become more aware in *one* area, as you become free from illusion in *one* area, simultaneously the illusion *in other areas* also becomes less dense, less binding. So if there is an area that you do not even want *to think* about giving up, then don't be concerned. Work on an area of illusion that you can give up, and as you become freer from illusion in other areas, the one illusion that you could not even consider giving up will become less binding. Then you can turn your attention there, and that also will be broken. So it is not that you have so many illusions and you must individually work through each and every illusion. As your awareness grows from practicing, (I gave the example of drinking alcohol), doing an act with as much awareness as you can, after one hundred times your awareness will grow in many ways besides just on the issue of drinking alcohol. You will have become aware of many other things, because that very act, which is generally considered to be one of total illusion, will have helped you to increase your awareness – if you practice it as I have stated. Do you understand?

So even an act that is generally binding you, if performed with awareness, will not only free you from that one thing, but your overall awareness and consciousness will be evolving. You will have grown so much in so many other areas. No matter what your situation is now, no matter what you're bound to, *there is a way to become free. No matter what it is.*

And it is the practical difficulties of the individual cases where more discussion is needed. And I know that in a group like this, it is sometimes too embarrassing or difficult to openly discuss, so, also, I will be more and more available so that you can come privately to discuss your individual problem. What is your illusion? What is binding you? What do you need to do now, practically? Do you understand?

First you make the decision to want the truth and have the desire. Then you must begin to act. It cannot just be something in your mind, just intellectual. You must take the things that you know you should do and begin to act, begin to do them. *If you do not act, your awareness will not grow.* Practice observation, looking and seeing – is something illusion or is it light? That is acting. You must act, and the more you act, the quicker your awareness will grow.

And you can move *very, very quickly,* because every second of the day your awareness can be moving. No matter *what* activity you are involved in, you can be evolving very, very quickly. And it is happening now; it is happening. There are some that have moved so quickly in the evolution of their consciousness; it is astonishing. So take whatever *help* is there. When you see that something is producing light, then take the opportunity and increase your light, increase your awareness.

But reject the darkness; always be looking for the illusion. I can say one thing, and everyone in this room will take it and they will tend to want to fit it into their illusion. You can ask different people who have heard so many of these teachings, and if you are aware, you will see how they have taken the teachings, and they have changed them a little bit and fit them into their illusion.

So you must begin. Discretion is important. Without it, you will just be trapped in another illusion. If it is an illusion around the Lord Jesus, if it is an illusion around any process, it will just be another trap if you do not pay attention and observe.

So hopefully, up until this point you have not wasted your time. No matter what you think, if you go within you will find the truth, and if you have been using this time to go within, then you have been finding the truth; you have been getting closer to the truth whether your conscious mind is aware of it or not. The very effort is producing a result. So we will have a period now where you can redouble your efforts and go within. But before we begin we can take a break – whatever is necessary to get comfortable.

True Reality Appears to You as a Dream

April 15, 1988, Alpine, CA

It is not an easy thing to find the truth. There are so many thousands of books that have been written about the truth, trying to give those who read them some idea of the truth. But if it were possible to communicate the truth with words, then you would simply need to read so many books and then you would know the truth. But it is not possible to know the truth with words. The words will give you guidance, will give you an idea, a hint, in which direction you should go and in which direction you should not go, but that is the best that can be hoped for. This does not mean that there is not a power behind the words – because there is. You can read something that will inspire you or give you further insight, but ultimately you must go beyond the words and find the truth.

The communication that is going on here, the true communication, is at a level that is beyond your mind and these words. If you wish to hear *this* communication, then you must be situated within. If you *only* hear the words, it may give *some* help, it may give *some* assistance, but the true communication that is going on here is *beyond* the words. Your conscious mind may not understand or appreciate what is going on. It is an increase in your awareness that *will* take place if you will focus your attention within.

Mainly, everyone gathered here is only sure of this plane of existence – what you can see, what you can touch. But this plane of existence is an illusion; it is nothing *but* an illusion. The only reality given to this plane is because of time – which is also an illusion. You have all existed for so many lifetimes, and yet you are not aware of more than this one lifetime. Rarely, someone may *glimpse* a past life, but that is all, briefly a glimpse. I am saying this so you will appreciate how limited your consciousness is right now, because you are not aware of anything more than this plane of illusion and this one lifetime. I am speaking practically. Of course, many of you have glimpsed the true realm of existence. But so many, even after exceptional experiences in the true realm of existence, come back to this plane of illusion and doubt that it ever happened, as if it were a dream. So see how much work needs to be done, because *this is the dream,* and the *only true reality* appears to you as a dream.

We are not trying to discourage questions, but We desire, as much as possible, that they be pertinent to the condition at hand. You know nothing else but this plane of existence. Even though there is no beginning to your existence, you can remember nothing else but this limited infinitesimal period of time. And the true reality, the spiritual reality – most of you are not even sure if it exists. So how to change this? How to change the awareness, how to change the focus? What are the obstacles in your way? You have so many misconceptions of how it will be, of what spirituality should be like, about how one should behave when they are in a spiritual consciousness. Practically speaking, you have nothing *but* misconceptions, and if fortunate, perhaps understand a couple of things clearly.

One of the important elements in moving your awareness, in changing your consciousness, is to first focus your attention here and now – not what will happen later, not what will happen tomorrow, not what happened today, not what happened yesterday. This type of thinking is one way that you are being bound in this illusion. And it is through guidance that We hope some of you will attempt to become free from this state of illusion.

Ultimately, you will all leave. This plane was never meant to be permanent or eternal. It is just a question of *when* you will leave. And while We will help many in their evolution, We wish that those people will come who wish to finally leave this plane of illusion and enter into a state of full awareness, and never again take birth in this plane.

So if you have any question, if there is anything that you need to know that might be of some help. . . . Sometimes it can be the smallest misconception, or what appears to you to be the smallest misconception, that is holding you back from true awareness. I have said this so many times; still, there is a difference between hearing the words and truly hearing. But you all have formulated concepts of what it will be like – or what you would *like it* to be like – as you evolve in your spiritual awareness, and you must let go of these conceptions because they are primarily misconceptions.

So if there are any questions, please ask.

Person One: What is the correlation between your head and your heart and intuition, and acting on the proper one in the proper situation? Or is there a proper situation? Or is there a proper one to act on? Or is this where cornucopia comes into play?

Gourasana: The use of the words is all right. It is good to be able to distinguish. Obviously, you have to be able to distinguish when your awareness is focused on this plane and when your awareness is focused within – or as you say, between your heart and your head. Your heart – this is when you are focused within. When your attention is focused within, to the degree, to the depth that you are within, to the clarity in which you have focused – to this degree, you are in touch with the true realm of existence. It is the plane of true love that you feel, but that true love comes from within.

It is a place of focus. If you are only aware of this plane of existence and you are not focused within at all, then any real love is not possible. But at those times that you do feel real love – sometimes it is said that happens when you are *touched* by something – actually *you* have touched on something that is within you, and that gives you love for others. So you need to distinguish where your attention is focused.

If your attention is in your head, as you say, then it is as if you have come out of yourself and are fully in the plane of illusion. And therefore you are very disturbed by whatever is going on, on this plane of illusion, because you are not *aware* of anything else. But when you go within – that peace within that is spoken of – and you look out from that place within, then even when there is so much disturbance, still you can feel that peace and that love.

And as this connection with the true realm becomes stronger and more concrete, then you will come to a point of full awareness where you will be unshakable, where you *will see* this plane as nothing *but* illusion, nothing *but* a dream.

So no matter *what* takes place on this plane, ultimately it will not affect *you* because *you* are not this illusion. Also, you should realize that the truth cannot be figured out. You cannot take the words and the facts that are presented and through a process of thinking come to an end result of truth. Your hearing, your awareness, will only grow from being focused within.

Knowing comes from within. It is not something that you are separate from in your true state. It is only the illusion that separates you from knowing full awareness.

Person One: How do you alleviate the illusion?

Gourasana: First, you must begin by seeing the duality. You must begin seeing what is illusion and what is light. If you do not do this, if you do not distinguish, if you do not discriminate, then you will go from one illusion into another illusion. You must be able to perceive what is illusion and what is light, what is truth and what are lies, what is light and what is darkness. You must simply begin to observe, see how the illusion is working, and see it as an illusion. This is how to begin. This *everybody* must do. You cannot accept the darkness and the light together. You must distinguish. If you do not distinguish, then you will move from one illusion into another, *even on your path of searching.* Yet if you *can* distinguish and only take the light, then you will move very quickly and will not be bound. So this is a very important exercise that everybody must perform. If you cannot see the difference, if you cannot distinguish, there is no question of awareness. Not being able to distinguish means that to *that* degree you are *not* aware.

Person Two: Gourasana, since you have kindly disillusioned me about the importance of some of the physical changes, the astral experiences, and the psychic experiences that we talked about last week, I find that I'm left with a very simple meditation: only a prayer, simply asking for the light. Is this sufficient, or can you teach me a better meditation?

Gourasana: Yes, a constant prayer will get you to the light. You do not need to read so many books, do so many things. Sometimes these things help and assist, so you take assistance where you need it, but there comes a point when it becomes simple. And this is good, because *desire is everything. It is everything* – if you desire to know the truth, if you desire to see the light, if you desire to know what is going on: Why am I here? Why is there so much disturbance? No matter how hard we try, we cannot make this a place of peace. No matter how hard. They say once the people are fed and clothed, the diseases are cured, on and on, then this will be a place of peace. But it will *never* be a place of peace, *because this is not where you belong. You do not belong here. You are spirit, eternal. You have no beginning and you have no end. And yet you are caught in an illusion, which is preventing you from knowing your true self, the true existence.*

So see, what is your desire? What is it that you truly want? Do you just want to make this existence better in this plane of illusion, or do you truly want to know the truth? And where in all your endless desires is your desire to know the truth; where have you placed it? Is it somewhere between a new car and a new house, and the truth, and where will I eat tonight? Then how much truth will you receive? *If it becomes everything, if it becomes your only desire, then you will have it. It is as simple as that.* But who will listen? Who will hear? And once they have heard, who will act? Who will take the steps necessary to become free from this plane of illusion? And this will answer whether you will be free in this lifetime or even the degree that your awareness will grow.

If you make a list of things that are important to you, and knowing the truth, knowing what is going on here is buried far down the list, then you can understand why you do not *experience* much, why you do not *understand* much, why your *awareness* isn't growing so much. Somehow or other, even if it is further down the list, you must move it. You must make it your *only* desire, because it is the *only thing that will satisfy you.* The other things you are doing are just perpetuating this state of illusion. To just desire the light and nothing else – *just the desire* – that will give you the thing that you desire.

Know this: All of your desires are being fulfilled. *Desire is everything.* Even if somehow or other, you do not feel this desire strongly, a meditation of prayer would be very beneficial (as it is for everyone). Prayer, the state of prayer, is an asking with sincerity: "*Please show me the truth. I wish to know.*"

It is very powerful and it will change your desire. Even if it is not your number one desire, it can become your number one desire through this prayer, this expression.

Prayer has so many aspects. There is a trusting, there is a faith that when you pray there is a receptor of what you are praying – a benevolent energy that can satisfy that desire. And your true self knows this, so it inspires you to pray more. Even the people that profess not to believe in another realm, when death is close, or great danger, even if they have given thought to nothing else but this plane of illusion, they will cry out, "Oh God, help me!" Because for that moment of seriousness they may focus within, and of course in their hearts they know what the truth is.

Person Two: That helps me. I've been feeling that this was too simple or childlike to be of any real value, but what you've told me is very useful. Thank you.

Carol: Gourasana, how do you get through hard days? Today was such a hard day for me. So many things were going wrong. How do you stay equipoised and within when so many things are bad and not working out? How do you keep from becoming agitated or bothered by that?

Gourasana: First, there are two things. You must see if the activities that you are performing are what you should be doing. Are you performing unnecessary activities that are distracting you? And you need to alleviate, wherever possible, the distracting influences. You must try to make your existence as peaceful as possible. Or at the least, have a period of time that can be peaceful. For some, this may only be during sleep, although almost everyone can find time. But even during the sleeping period – I'm talking now of someone who is very bound up with so many responsibilities that from the second they wake until the second they go to sleep, they are engaged; they have no time to pay attention to anything else – they can focus their attention within while they fall asleep, and during their period of sleep (this is true of everyone) they will evolve and they will become more aware.

So, as with someone like this, also *you* must focus within, and when you are greatly disturbed, then you can know that your attention is *not* focused within. The difficulty is that you accept this disturbed condition for so long; you do nothing to interfere. As soon as you see that your attention is not focused within, then you should rectify this. If you are greatly disturbed and agitated from something that is going on in this plane of existence, that means that your attention, your focus within, has been lost, temporarily at least. And you need to rectify that. This can be done in an instant, or it may take a minute, or it may take a few minutes – whatever. But the difficulty is people *accept* these disturbed states of mind and then the problem becomes worse. It becomes compounded until it seems endless because your focus is lost. The insanity of this plane of existence takes over, and you become lost in what is going on here, lost in all the conflicts of this plane, which are unavoidable because of the duality. You cannot avoid it; it is impossible to avoid difficulties in this plane.

But if you are centered within, if you are focused within, then you will have peace. Because no matter what goes on here, if you are centered where you truly belong, you know that it doesn't really matter so much, and you have your peace – no matter what. It is difficult to get to this state where you are *never* disturbed, but if you allow disturbance to go on hour after hour, then it is *only your fault*. It is *not* this world, and if you blame this plane of illusion, then it is *another trap. It is your fault; it is your responsibility. You create your own reality.*

This does not mean that this plane of illusion will function according to your desire. It means that you will get in touch with your true reality. So that no matter what transpires on this plane, you will be properly situated and will have no real difficulty. So you must check as soon as it starts; as soon as the great disturbance comes, *you must stop* and say, "Why am *I* disturbed? Why am *I* so upset? This is just the duality of this plane of illusion, the constant suffering and conflict that is going on here, and yet *I* am disturbed?" It is your being of illusion that you have created interacting with the other beings of illusion, which means endless conflict and suffering and turmoil.

But when you bypass this being of illusion you have created and go within, then *your relationship* with everything will change and it will create a peacefulness even in those around you who are *not* centered within. Because *your* awareness will influence them. But if you get lost in illusion and you think that you are this body and this mind, and on and on, all the circumstances surrounding this body – if you think this is your existence, then you are lost in illusion again. So you should not tolerate this state for any length of time. This is a main mistake that everyone is making. You should immediately stop it; you should immediately do something – arrangements can be made, somehow, or at the soonest possible opportunity. Do not let this illusion go on unchecked. You have *found* the true realm. You *know* what it means to be situated there. Now there is no excuse. Others are simply trying to find that place, but for *you* there is no excuse because you know where it is. And if you do not take the trouble to go there, then who can you blame for the insanity that is created around you?

Carol: Sometimes when interacting with so many different people, so many different situations, and with people who have so many problems in their lives, it becomes hard for me to keep their problems from becoming my problem, because of the great disturbance that's going on in their lives. Sometimes I just lose it. It all becomes too much, especially when it's all in one day.

Gourasana: So you must *begin* the day centered. And as soon as the first disturbance comes, immediately correct the situation. Do whatever is necessary to correct the situation.

And then when other things come, you will be properly situated so they will not disturb you. You see, if you are centered within, you will see the things that are happening for the illusion that *they are*.

When somebody is angry at you or you are angry at someone – on and on. On this plane there is incredible conflict between people, so much misunderstanding, and so little true communication. You can see, and you should begin to see the illusion, how it is just the illusion. How could such a condition exist without the illusion? This is why, one of many reasons, that it is Our desire that you finally leave this plane, because in so many ways, it is distracting. Even if you just did not have these bodies, how much easier it would be. So much trouble and time you must spend just for the body. Practically your whole existence is centered around this body – feeding, clothing, bathing, making money to do these things. Then taking care of the bodies around you, and then the bodies in the world. It is an endless task.

But if you let a disturbance in and you accept it, accepting it means you have played into the hands of illusion. You are letting it disturb you, you are letting it take you over – then you have made a mistake. You say you have had so many disturbances in one day – with the first disturbance you were captured by illusion. The first disturbance that came, you *allowed* yourself to be captured by illusion, and then in that disturbed state, when another thing happens, then more disturbed and more disturbed. This is how people are almost constantly living in a bewildered state, not understanding anything that is going on – simply, madly trying to do something or other to satisfy the immediate cravings of the body and the mind. This becomes the whole focus of existence. This is all they know for sure. And madly they are running around trying to do something, but of course, happiness is never found. It is not possible.

Gayle: Gourasana, when I'm really in the midst of confusion like I was today, that's when I just scream out to know the truth; and what happens is, when I begin to look at the duality, it gets harder and harder to see what is the truth. One person says, "Oh, this is the way," and another person says, "This is the way." You have to read this scripture, and follow this teaching, and everybody seems to have their own truth, and then I begin to question what I think I know is true. I get very confused. I mean, I know what I want and that seems to be my only clear desire. I know I want to know the truth and I know I want God in my heart. That's the only thing I want, but what confuses me is when I start to talk to other people and they say, "No, no this is the way." "No, no this is the way." "This is wrong." "You're doing it wrong." And people question your existence and your motivation – who you are. Anyway, sometimes in the midst of all this confusion, it seems like then I *really know what I want.* And that is I just want this illusion to be ripped away so that I can really see clearly. And it really hurts sometimes to begin to see. *(Crying)*

Gourasana: Yes. Yes. It is not pleasant. Breaking the illusion is very difficult. That is one reason I have said you must give up your conceptions of how it will be. There will be periods where it will appear to create *more* separateness rather than the oneness with everyone that you seek.

Gayle: That's what's so hard, because you can see the separateness so clearly.

Gourasana: But you can see: The separateness is created by the illusion, by the belief. It is not possible to be separate.

Spirit is one. The incredible power of the illusion creates the separateness. And in this way, a mother is turned against son, the son is turned against father, brother against sister, friend against friend.

It is not where you belong. No matter how hard you try, it will never be a nice place to exist. It can be tolerable; it can be better, but it will never be very nice on this plane. *Never.* It is not possible. The separateness is illusion. A rigid belief in the truth creates a separateness. The truth is ever changing; it is unlimited, and it is beyond the comprehension of these minds that you have. But taking the words and applying them literally, with no flexibility, look at the chaos that it has created. Look at the separateness that it has created on just this one small planet – how the *belief* is separating one from another. But you must see: Does the belief have the darkness in it?

Gayle: Yes, it definitely does.

Gourasana: It almost always does. But when one is bound in illusion and you can see that illusion, still, it is all right because that is what they desire – to be in that illusion. So what can you do? You can do nothing. But you must see the illusion and not be confused, and think it is somehow your problem or your illusion.

The great religions of the world have one goal, purportedly, and that is to come to the light. Yet between the religions there is so much hate and condemning. So this is what I am saying: You must see the duality; you must see the darkness. Someone seeking the light may take up a religious process. Now, there may be light in that religious process, but if they also accept the darkness, the lies of the religious process, then they are bound in another illusion. They may still evolve spiritually to some degree because of the light, but simultaneously they are being bound by the illusion they have accepted.

If you can discriminate between the darkness and the light, then you can go out and just take the light and reject the darkness and move very quickly. And some have had the intuition or the sense to do just that – to reject many of the rules and regulations of organized religion and just take the truth and the light. Just one example that everyone knows is in the Christian faith: the love and the light of the Lord Jesus. It is undeniable. What could be greater, what greater light could there be? Yet somehow they have perverted the philosophy to a point where they say that the Lord Jesus, who is nothing *but* love and light, is teaching that there is an eternal hell of darkness that you will be cast into if you do not accept Him. This is not symptomatic of an all-merciful Father. This is symptomatic of a demented being.

So in this way, there are so many more areas of darkness, and some are more and more subtle. So guidance is necessary. But you cannot pretend that the darkness is not there. You must see it separate from the beings that are in the illusion. It is not like here is a man who is killing, and so *he* is bad, or is condemned in *any* way, eternally. No. It is an eternal being who is in an illusion. So you can hate the illusion; you can hate the darkness, but you can still love the being – although, it is not desirable to have this being around you who is in the illusion of killing. You do not need to have certain people around you in order to love them. Because of your limited vision all you can see is illusion, so when they come into your existence, all you begin to see is the darkness of their illusion, and the love dissipates. So until you come to a stage of true awareness where you do not discriminate, you need to be careful with whom you associate.

Person Three: Gourasana, there is this feeling in me that is telling me that what I am feeling is just an illusion, and I'm sure that it probably is, but I just need help to get free of it – this whole responsibility trip. When something occurs that theoretically in this illusive world we would be responsible for, how do we not let it affect us? It's like I almost feel like I'm obligated to feel this feeling of guilt or responsibility. I feel like if I didn't feel these things, this feeling of guilt, which I know is an illusion, then I would be putting out vibes of complete rudeness, insensitivity and not caring. All I pray for every single day is to just have every illusion that is known to me dispelled. All I want is the light and I'm doing everything I possibly can. When things happen like what today brought, it's like I don't even know what else to do. What am I not doing?

Gourasana: Yes, you may care for the light, but caring for the light will reflect in your daily existence in that you will be *care–full* in what you do so that it does not create so much distraction and disturbance that it takes you away from the light. Your *whole being* must be careful. Not that you just meditate with great care and desire, and then you come out and you mindlessly inhabit the world. You must be *careful* in everything that you do. *Take care!* The path of truth is not one of mindlessness; it is one of great care. As soon as the body becomes diseased, you immediately take steps to correct the situation. You do not carelessly let the condition go on until it becomes critical. You must use care in arranging your existence. Simplifying is very important. You should simplify as much as possible so there are not unnecessary responsibilities; but in those responsibilities you cannot escape, that are necessary, you must be careful. And when you are not careful, then unnecessary disturbance comes. You must be aware of what you are doing, and this awareness must increase. Awareness means just that, *that you are aware*. If daily you are eating something which is poisonous and which is creating disease within the body, then where is your awareness?

Person Three: It just overwhelms me how one minute our awareness can be so crystal clear, and the next minute we can just be sound asleep. It's very frustrating.

Gourasana: Yes, but if you will trace the point of clarity to the point of bewilderment, you will see that you did something to get to that point of bewilderment. *You* did something. This is what people do not like. This is why the organized philosophies are so popular, because they say all you need to do is you follow this set of rules; you do these things and you do not do these things, and then automatically the end result will be there – but it is not like that. You are fully responsible every step of the way. Help is there, assistance is there, but as powerful as that assistance can be, ultimately *you* must take the responsibility. You are not like a puppet on a string. It is not like that. So when there is great disturbance in anyone's life, they need simply to begin to look and see where it is coming from and what can be done to solve the problem.

The existence here must be created; it must be conducive. And it will not be conducive as long as you mindlessly perform the activities that are necessary. If you eat mindlessly, and therefore you eat poison, you will become diseased and it will create disturbance. If you drive mindlessly and you have an accident, who will you blame? Becoming aware means in all areas. Take great pains and time and trouble to see to the details of your existence. It is a very complicated plane that you exist on. So you need to first simplify it as much as possible. And then you must become very aware of each and every detail of interaction that is going on on this plane and become adept at dealing with these things so they do not become a distraction, so that everything goes smoothly. In this way you will minimize, greatly, the disturbance.

Person Three: And therefore the simpler our lives become, the more light will then manifest in our lives and there will be less suffering?

Gourasana: No, these things do not follow what I am saying. You are drawing a conclusion.

At the same time that you want to simplify and prevent unnecessary disturbance (it is a plane of disturbance), you must become detached from excessive happiness as well as excessive distress. You must *become* equipoised. If you become elated on one hand when something goes very well in this plane of illusion, there will be an opposite effect of depression and disturbance when it does *not* go well. You must become balanced in your view of this plane of illusion. If you are watching a movie and someone in the movie has great wealth, do you become very happy for them, and when they have a disease, do you become very sad for them? Maybe a little. This plane of illusion is like that. You may have some financial boon, some success, but do not be overly happy. What is it after all? At the same time, when there is suffering, equally, be detached. See yourself separate from this plane. Do not be attached; *do not try to create happiness on this plane,* because when it is not happy, when it is not what you are trying to create, you will be unhappy. In this way you will be in illusion as everyone else, bouncing back and forth between happy and unhappy. You must become equipoised. You must, or you will suffer. From Our point of view, your excessive happiness and your suffering are the same, because they are both symptomatic that you are focused in the illusion too much. So avoid the extremes.

Person Three: Thank you very much.

Lynn: Gourasana, can we experience being centered and living in the light now, and having a sense of peacefulness, calm, a unity and harmony?

Gourasana: Yes. But your steps bring different results as you come to the light, and you must not be attached to *this state* until you come to a state of full awareness; because there are things you must do and you must let go of in order to become free of this illusion. And you will come to something you are holding on to very tightly – an attachment, a concept, whatever – and when it comes time to let go, you will not be very peaceful. At the same time, there will be an ultimate peacefulness, a knowingness that you are on the right path, that you are doing well; so it is not a disturbance (like a disturbance on this plane) although it may appear to be so to others.

But yes, initially, when people, through reminder or effort, go within, the initial experiences are usually positive, what you think is positive: feeling love, some beauty, some peace. But as you begin to shift out of the illusion, other things come up that have a negative connotation, and you must not be fooled thinking that you are not going toward the light. Because letting go can produce, for instance, fear – everyone has some fear that they must overcome. Assistance is there and it can be accomplished. But backing away from fear is one main area that is stifling growth, spiritual growth. So if you can feel that peace within, that calm within, that love within – this is good. Hold on to that and let it increase your faith that you are properly situated. But as you go deeper, you may come upon fear. Just know that there are many things that you must go through to come to a state of full awareness. Just see what has to be done to break this illusion.

Person Four: Gourasana, I'm having trouble breaking my attachment to helping other people change their lives, and I want to surrender that. I know it's illusion that they have to change their lives. I'd like some help with that.

Gourasana: Yes. This is another obstacle. It is an obstacle when you are ready to leave this plane of existence, truly, because you cannot change another; you cannot give light where it is not welcome. You can offer something, but if they will not receive it, then what can be done? The only way that you will see this in the true perspective is when your awareness shifts out of this illusion and understands truly what is happening. You see, let us say one thousand lifetimes ago you were not prepared to make any serious steps to leave this plane, and that of course was no problem, because that was part of the purpose of your evolution in this plane. In the same way, there are others now – most – that are simply not ready to leave. And while there is nothing wrong with that, still you can see you're wasting energy trying to help – that it is futile. They do not desire to leave, or maybe they do not even desire illumination in certain areas. You see, when I say it is your desire that is everything – *this is* what is creating all of the situations. No matter how much you talk, no matter how much you try to convince, no matter what you try to do to get another to the light, if they do not have the desire they simply will not do it.

It is another trap, because the help that is needed on this plane is unlimited, whatever area you wish to help in.

If you wish to help in the basic things such as feeding and clothing – it is an endless task.

If you are doing the right thing or not in helping others, can be judged by whether it is increasing the light and your awareness, or whether it is something that is a burden or distraction. *You need to help each other,* but when you try to give help where it is not welcome, then it is a waste and a burden. You must wait for someone who is receptive to the help, and *there* give the help. Then it will produce more energy rather than less. So giving also must be done with consciousness. But giving must be there; caring must be there; helping each other must be there. Help means just that, not that you carry another's burden for them. You assist them, perhaps guide them in how they may better carry their own. Too many fall into this trap of humanitarianism, and take the weight of the world on their shoulders, as you say. They are constantly burdened in helping others and they achieve no light. So for leaving this plane of existence, it isn't good.

If there are no more questions, then we can concentrate on the true communication solely. Sometimes the speaking distracts from going within. So now prepare yourself for going within. Whatever is a comfortable position, whatever you need to do.

You Will Not Break Free Without Assistance

May 6, 1988, Alpine, CA

Today, one who is very serious about coming to the light chose darkness. You see, you *choose* to be in illusion, you *choose* to be in darkness, and you are *choosing* to remain there. It is of your own free will. But I would not let him stay in darkness, *even though it was his desire, because he has asked Me to help him.* Without the assistance he received today, he would have stayed hiding in darkness. He would have continued to avoid the light. See how critical this consciousness is. He asked Me, "What should I do in what I am about to undertake? Could you please give me guidance?" So I gave him some guidance. But he chose to ignore that guidance and went into darkness. But The Lady and Carol went to where he was hiding to assist him. By no accident they had the words with them that I spoke to him, and still he resisted to some extent.

Now, instead of being in darkness he is in the light. You do not know what that means; *if you knew, you would not stay in this darkness. You would not cling to this illusion. You would move heaven and hell to get to the light, and yet,*

I come to you and you sit there and you resist. This is the power of the illusion.

So when you ask for assistance – even if somehow or other you make the wrong decision and you choose the darkness – if you truly want the light, it will not be allowed. Of course if you persist, if you will no longer listen – just as today he would not listen even when confronted with the truth, so long it took to change his heart – but if you come to a point where you will no longer listen to the truth, stubbornly you wish to stay in darkness, then you will stay in darkness. Then your desire will be fulfilled. A little free will may be surrendered, but if you insist, then you can go back into darkness; you can stay in illusion. But even though in the light, will he stay in the light, or will he again choose darkness?

This is going on constantly. I have spoken of this so many times. You have seen it so many times in such a short period, and here again today – what an example. Here is one who was determined, who had dedicated his life to finding the truth, but instead of trusting, instead of having faith, when he touched upon some fear he chose to hide in illusion. There he would remain were it not for outside assistance. So while it is very difficult to overcome this state of illusion, if you will take the assistance, if you will receive it, then it will be possible. But if you again deny the truth and hide in darkness, what can be done?

So you saw this today: The darkness – and the light.

So you can try to help each other, and if you are sincere, and to the degree that your help is pure, to that degree you will be able to help each other. Because her [Carol's] desire was pure, now he is in the light. Had it not been so. . . .

So how will you break free from this illusion? It is not possible without assistance. Even one sitting alone, meditating, is receiving assistance. You simply cannot see the assistance, but just as certainly as *you* receive it, so does he. But the illusion is very distracting; it is very strong – so many disturbances. So *special* assistance is being provided. The one meditating alone knows that he wants nothing else. His desire is so great that he has given up everything that you consider to be pleasurable, to find the truth. So for him, special assistance is not required, for his illusion is not so dense. But this is a rare exception. Most are totally lost in illusion and have no idea what the truth is.

Hearing means, not just that you hear the words. True hearing means that your true self has received the message, that you have heard with your heart. The symptom that you have truly heard will be that you will act upon what you have heard. Not just, "Oh yes, I have heard these words before, I already know this." If you already knew and understood what I was saying, you would not be in illusion. The only way you will know is if you will focus your attention within and in that state, listen. If you are situated within your heart and you hear from your heart, it is far different than just listening to some words. This is not a philosophical discussion. The words help; they do help. They give direction where to go, some hint. But the knowing, the awareness, will only come if you will go within and find the truth.

This *is* a meditation: Your listening should be a meditation. It means that you listen from another place. It is a hearing that is not with the ears, and it is a seeing that is not with these eyes. It is an awareness of something else, something other than what you know on this plane of illusion. It is something else, something *different,* far *different.* It feels entirely different, and those that have experienced this, know. Their attention is focused on this plane of illusion and their consciousness is a certain way, and then they go within and focus their attention on the true realm of existence *and everything changes.* They have not moved; they are still in the same place. The only thing that has changed is their focus of attention. And they find themselves in another place, or at least they are touching upon, experiencing, another place.

While it is the nature of things to come back from this place (this true realm of existence) to your plane of illusion and *doubt,* while one is within and experiencing the true realm of existence, there is no doubt. There has been at least some period of time when several in this room have been totally absorbed in another plane of existence other than *this* realm of existence; even if for a short time, purely, without doubt, they know what they experienced. So they are striving to connect permanently with that place. Why do they wish to do this? Why does one dedicate oneself so completely to this? Because once you have touched upon the true realm of existence and you come back to this plane, you again want to go back as soon as possible, because this plane of existence is not very nice, and it is not your Home. It is not your true realm of existence.

Yet one who is in total illusion will hear this and say, "I do not understand," or they'll be in total doubt or cynicism because it is not within their experience – and it is something you must experience.

There is a part of you that is buried, that you have forgotten. It is your true self, your true identity, and your true self knows where Home is. So there is a desire within everyone that goes unfulfilled. Nothing satisfies this desire. Whatever you do on this plane of illusion, you will never satisfy this desire – this desire to go back to where you belong, to leave this plane of illusion and go back to your true realm of existence. It is like a pain and it never truly goes away. When you wake in the morning, it is there. When you go to sleep, it is there. Even while you are dreaming, it is there – this nagging, this urging, this desire for something, but you do not know what.

Whatever you do on this plane – and most people are trying desperately to satisfy it – nothing will satisfy this desire. However much money you have, however much sex you have, whatever intoxication you take, *whatever you can do on this plane of illusion, you may do that and still you will not be satisfied.* That is why those that seemingly have *everything* on this plane are not satisfied any more than you are. Though they live in a palace, have many servants and can have practically any desire fulfilled on this plane at their whim, they are no more satisfied than you.

This is the nature of illusion. Illusion means just that. It is like a dream that you need to wake up from, and until you do, you will not be satisfied. For whatever happens in your dream, you will just be dreaming. This is a very deep dream and to wake up requires an effort. But it is possible; it can be done. It is not that you practice some meditation, that you do something for so many years and then you will get it. If you will begin the endeavor *now,* you will start receiving *now.* You can start experiencing *now,* no matter what state of consciousness you are in. If you have some desire to know the truth, then you will begin to experience it. But it is very subtle in the beginning. And when it becomes obvious that one is touching upon the true realm of existence – by obvious, I mean because of their outward manifestations – there is still doubt. The illusion is so strong that they come back from experiencing ecstasy and wonder, "Was it real?" Yet they know in their heart it was, so they endeavor.

You might think, "But if I do this, then I will not be satisfied. I want to do so many things." So try, with your intelligence, to look at the many things you wish to do, then look around you and see others who have done all of the things that you desire and *see* how they are not happy or satisfied. If you would practice this exercise just for a few minutes, you will see who isn't satisfied. Temporarily, they may appear to be satisfied, which is confusing, but you will see they will lose that happiness.

Just as one may desire to become a great musician, one of the greatest, be famous, have so many thousands of people come to hear them – there are many like that, that are succeeding in this endeavor – but even while they are succeeding they are not happy, they are not satisfied. You can examine anything that is written or spoken about their lives. You will see, even while every night they stand on a stage and have thousands of people come just to hear them and give them so much money that they have anything they want, still they are unhappy. And they must take intoxication to continue on, because they do not have the strength, they do not have the will to keep up this facade, this illusion. So they must take support from intoxicants.

Take a hint. Others who have gotten much more than everything you desire are not satisfied. *Take a hint.* Save yourselves time and find out *what it is that you are truly looking for.* And if you can somehow or other summon up this much intelligence – and even without experiencing the true realm of existence, somewhere know it to be true

– if you can summon up just enough desire to make the endeavor to find the truth, then you can succeed. Because to succeed, you first need to begin. Once you truly begin, then you can succeed. Then you can know the truth. Then you can be self-satisfied. This is why the man that is sitting alone in the cave for decades, some for centuries (you do not know about this), can sit there with nothing you consider to be pleasurable. Yet they are fully satisfied and do not need to go anywhere other than where they just sit, because *they have found everything.*

It is like you are living in a coal mine, deeply buried underground, mainly with suffering and darkness, but in this dark hole, occasionally you get some relief. While sitting there and suffering, someone brings some intoxication to you, some diversion comes, but when the diversion is over, then again you are faced with the reality of your situation, where you are.

But one who has climbed out of this hole, out of this dark place, and has come outside and sees the whole world is there, realizes: "I have been hiding in this dark place. I was attached to what I thought was pleasurable: when they brought me something to drink, something to eat, so I did not wish to leave this place. Others spoke of another realm, but I did not believe it enough even to go and look for myself. Even though they told me it was so much greater than anything I could ever have in this dark hole, I would not even go and look for a moment. 'No. Do not bother me, I am happy here. There is nothing else. I do not believe you.'" But one, where somehow or other the words strike their heart, and they take the necessary effort to climb out of this deep hole, even enough to get a glimpse of the light, *they will never forget that light. Never!* Even though they will climb back down and stay in that hole, *it will never* go from their consciousness again – the impression on the consciousness *is that strong*. They may sit in the hole and suffer and try to forget about it, but once they have seen that light, it will *never* leave their consciousness.

One who is fortunate enough to again go and look and go further and further and further and experience more and more, then there comes a point where there is no turning back, because they will *never* be happy with anything down in this dark hole of illusion again; because they have been outside, free in the light, and have seen a place that is unlimited incredible beauty – *inconceivable*. It is inconceivable to you, because you have such a *limited* perception of what beauty is. The most beautiful thing that you can think of on this plane is nothing. It is like a well-shaped piece of coal – at best.

So this is what We are asking you to do. If you have not yet taken the time and the trouble, if you have not yet made the effort to crawl out of this dark hole of illusion, *even once*, to get *a glimpse* of the truth, of the light, *then I urge you to do this tonight*. And if you do not feel you have succeeded by the end of tonight, then try it again, and again. It will not be so long before you do begin to experience. There are so many opportunities waiting for you. It is an unlimited wealth that you just need to tap into. *You just need to take it*.

Do not be satisfied. Do not be satisfied with this existence. *Do not let your goals in life be limited to goals of illusion that everyone has been pursuing since time immemorial and has never been satisfied with, and at the time of death cry out, "Help me, because I am lost and I am afraid, and I do not know where I am going. I have no understanding of where I have been, of what is going on, because I did not take any time to understand what my life was about, what my existence was about, what the truth was. Now it is my death and I am afraid, because I am about to leave everything that I know, including my body. What will be left?"*

Do not allow this to happen. You do not have to give up anything now. That is not what is required. Yes, you will ultimately give up this plane of existence, but it will happen gradually and you will control the pace. But if you do not do it voluntarily, at the time of death you will be forced to give up everything you now know to be reality. It will cease to exist for you. Even who you think you are, which is all situated around this body – you are a man, you are a woman; you are of this race; you do this for a living, you have this personality; you live in this state; you live in this country; you live in this world – it is all an illusion, and when you die, the illusion will all be taken away.

But because you still desire to be in illusion, then again you will come back and take birth, and you will have another lifetime of illusion. You will be somebody else entirely, and who you were will be totally forgotten. Just as now you cannot remember who you were in your last life – what you did; what were your desires? You can barely remember parts of this lifetime. Can you remember when you were three months old? Can you remember when you were six months old? Rarely, maybe a little bit. But just look back and see how this period of time, the beginning of this lifetime is already faded so much that it is almost lost to you, because since you were five years old you have become another person entirely. And in this way, you are going from lifetime to lifetime to lifetime to lifetime through countless lifetimes assuming different identities of illusion.

So the question is: When will you tire of this? Will you just stay in illusion, die, again take birth, again illusion, die . . . ? Or do you want to *finally* find something else? Do you finally wish to connect with the true realm of existence? This is what We are doing here. We are taking people from this illusion, from this dark hole, and We are bringing them out into the true realm of existence, into the light. And ideally, at the time of death, in a full state of awareness, they will never again take birth on this plane of illusion. This *is* possible for everyone. You only have to desire it. *If you want it, then you can have it.* There is assistance now *that is very rare;* there has never quite been this assistance. It is a special time. So this you must ask yourself: Do you want to know the truth? Do you want to have a glimpse of the truth, and will you make an effort to have that glimpse? Will you, until you have the experience, function on intelligence and intuition, knowing that there is the truth, that there is spirit, knowing that this realm obviously is temporary? Even this planet may last for so many, many, many years, but it is doomed. It will come to an end, just as it had a beginning.

For a few minutes you can put on some music, and for a few minutes you can go within, summon up some sincerity, and try to focus your attention within. Then from this place of seriousness and desire to know the truth, if there is any question, we will at that time discuss whatever it is you need to know to find the truth. What is pertinent now? What is it that you need to know to continue, or to even begin your path? So go within in a meditative state and see: Is there even a desire? If you are not sure, then see if you can find *that* in these few minutes. Is there even a desire within you, even the tiniest desire to have a glimpse of this light that I am speaking of? See if that is there.

Person One: Gourasana, is it predetermined when we will make that final decision to let go?

Gourasana: Things are not so concrete as some would believe them to be about the future. There is always flexibility. There is a certain destiny that you may take birth with, but you can change that destiny by changing your desire. Just as you have experienced, sometimes you change your mind; you desire to do one thing and then for whatever reason, even without some outside influence, you desire to do something else. So destiny is that you have decided to do something in this lifetime, but you can change your desire at any moment. And you can change it back again. Just as we saw earlier tonight, one who has experienced the true realm of existence – and he has experienced it, it is very rare in this world to have experienced it so well – yet even this one changed his desire, to some extent, to stay in darkness. In this way, at any time you can change your desire. So do not be afraid to try to find the truth, because at any point you can go back into illusion. If that is your desire, your desire will be fulfilled no matter how great your state of awareness. If you change your desire, that desire will be fulfilled. It is not like: "Oh, I am not ready yet to become aware. It is not my destiny. It is not my karma." These are all traps of illusion, and the traps are practically endless. That is why some guidance, some assistance, is necessary for almost everyone.

Everyone in this room can leave this plane of existence in this lifetime, and within a very short time everyone in this room can have an experience of the true realm of existence that *will be so strong,* which will leave such an impression on them that they will begin to pursue this until it becomes the only thing. They may do something else temporarily; that does not matter. It will not stop them from becoming aware. But their main focus will change to becoming aware.

In other words, you can still have marriage and family, so many things that you may desire; they do not necessarily have to stop you. It is just where your main attention is focused. What is your goal in life? If your goal is to make a million dollars and you achieve that goal and then you die, what will have been accomplished? But if your goal is to become aware and you achieve that, then you have everything. That does not mean that on the way you cannot make a million dollars. You see. It is just, where is your attention focused? It is not that along the way you cannot engage in sex or you cannot pursue so many careers; it will just be a change of your *primary* focus. You will see that your life is executed in such a way that your environment is conducive for spiritual growth. It will not stop you. You do not need to stop the endeavors necessarily; you just need to change your focus and see that that is taken care of properly.

Person Two: Gourasana, if it is fears that keep us attached to this plane, will you give us a clue as to how to identify these fears and to live with them, deal with them or how to dispose of them? I know that I am stuck in those fears even though I don't know what they are yet.

Gourasana: The way you get stuck is when you avoid the fear, when you refuse to look at whatever it is that is making you afraid. That is when you are not moving. If you are not moving, if you are not experiencing, if you sit there and feel that nothing is going on, then you are refusing to do something. You are resisting. You are afraid to face certain

1) Gourasana is referring to a transformational seminar.

things. You have had this experience. There is this structure[1], this format, this seminar that you have gone to, and in this structure you look at these things. Don't you?

Person Two: Yes.

Gourasana: That is the power of this structure. Even one, like this man today, who did not want to face something – he was too afraid to face something, so he was hiding literally in another place, an entirely different area of this county – but once he faced the fear, he came back into the light. But without persuasion, the outside assistance he received, he would not have done it.

This will be the next thing for those that are stuck. We will have another format, another structure, that we will work within until you do face what it is that you do not want to face. Because as you have seen in this seminar you have gone to, when you *do* face your fears, when you *do* face the things that are at first unpleasant – you have seen so many cases where one was terrified, totally afraid – and yet the end result was ecstasy, an ecstasy rarely achieved on this plane of existence.

So in this seminar . . . just see what takes place within just a few days! How quickly your awareness can grow if the endeavor is there. The structure is just one that leaves you no alternative. Of course it is voluntary. Just as now, you can either do it or you can not do it. But you make a commitment, and you desire to know the truth so much that you will see it through. Even in a few days of your life, those that see it through achieve a level of awareness *that is astonishing!* People grow more in their awareness in these few days than most do in a lifetime. It is so powerful! Once you make that decision to find the truth and then act – and you make the endeavor – how much you can receive.

So if you are stuck, then somewhere there is a problem with endeavor. Something is not being done. You are not doing something properly. So this is a problem. We will create a process to assist, but do not wait for the future, which may not come for you. There are many steps along the way, but there is basically just one problem, and that is that you do not wish to let go of this illusion. There may be many reasons why you do not trust the true realm of existence – you doubt it. Whatever the reason you will not let go of the illusion, you will stay here, just as the man in the hole. He knows if he stays there, that someone will feed him and clothe him, and he will have some relief. So he hangs on to this, as pitiful as that existence is, because he will not trust. Even though *so many* have come back and have said how wonderful it is, he will not trust enough to let go.

Person One: Gourasana, it takes so much bravery and courage to face our fears. Sometimes we know we can't do it by ourselves. We place ourselves in situations where we're almost telling someone to push us because we don't think we can do it by ourselves. This is the situation that I find myself in a lot of times. A fear will come up and it is so difficult for me to face it by myself. I feel like putting myself in a situation like the seminar where you are almost forced to face it. Then you know you can shift beyond the fear. There's that one place where you need to find the courage and bravery in yourself. How can I find that? How can I help build that in myself?

Gourasana: One thing is commitment. This is what you make when you go into the seminar. You make a commitment that no matter what, you will see it through. You know you will not leave, and you do not wish to leave until you have achieved what it is you have come for. So your commitment is one thing you need to analyze. Did you come here tonight with a commitment, and how strong was this commitment? How far did you set your goal tonight, and will you stay until you achieve that goal? Yes, assistance is there.

Person One: That is an excellent question of focus, and it will help greatly when arriving here to focus in on that question of commitment. That's something I wasn't asking of myself. It will help me in the future and at this moment.

Gourasana: Yes, at this moment, *now,* this is all that there is, so you need to ask yourself, what is your commitment *now?* What will you do *now?* What do you wish to achieve *now? You know,* more than most, that this plane is just an illusion. You have seen through the facade so much. Yet, why will you not leave it behind? Because you do not trust? Because you are afraid? Because you do not have the faith? What are the reasons that you will not allow yourself to go tonight? *And you can go tonight.* You see, you know. You have seen it in the seminar. Those that just make the decision, "*I will do it today,*" *by the end of that day they do it. Why? An impossible feat, seemingly, but they decided to. They wanted it and they made the commitment, and they did it.*

So what is it that you would like to achieve *tonight?* What area are you dissatisfied with? Most do not even understand that it is an illusion; they have not even given much thought to this. It is important to come to this platform that you have come to, but once you understand you are in the dark hole – that this is not what you want – what is it that is preventing you from letting go of it and moving to another place? Words do not need to be there. It is not something you need to think about. But you need to go within, and you need to make a commitment. Will you let go *tonight?* Will you let yourself, *tonight,* see more light than you have ever seen before? Summon up that determination, that effort, that desire, and make the commitment. And in that state of mind you can achieve it. Even if the commitment is that you will just do *as much as you possibly can;* you will just let go as much *as you possibly can;* you will tolerate any fear that comes *as much as you can.* You will let go *as much as you can.* You will come to a point where letting go will become easier and you will experience a new problem, and that will be hanging on.

So there comes a point when you need to go beyond the words. You need to leave them behind. If you have heard what has transpired tonight, truly heard it, then you can begin to act. There is a part of you that knows what to do if you will just let go, if you will just desire to know the truth, and if you will just look earnestly.

Anyway, it is a great task, and ultimately it is a task that must be performed because it is not the design that you stay on this plane of illusion eternally. There will come a point when everyone will leave this plane of existence. The question is: *When* will you leave?

We hope you at least will give it a chance. We hope that in this lifetime you will at least make enough endeavor to get a glimpse of the light, that you will not be satisfied to sit in total illusion, not knowing what is going on. We hope that you will take a little time out of your life until you at least get a glimpse. Give yourself that much of a chance. Do enough *so that you can at least get a glimpse of the truth.* And if you do not see any way to do this, then I would recommend that you try this seminar that has been arranged, because you will *at least* get a glimpse of the truth in that period of time. It is a short period of time. It is a small investment of your life to get that one glimpse. Those that will not even get this glimpse are certainly very unfortunate.

Is there any other question?

If you wish to stay for the meditation, then you can begin preparing yourself. Whatever you need to do to get comfortable, for however long you are going to stay. If you do not wish to stay, of course, this is the time to leave. But the meditation is what we have been talking about. Actually, several here have been in the meditation from the beginning; that is the true benefit of this session. Meditation is available even while I am speaking; some are sitting and they are within, and they are mostly not even listening to the words and they are going so far. But now in earnest we will begin a meditation.

Desire Will Save You

May 27, 1988, Alpine, CA

(This discourse was given at the start of a weekend retreat. Meditation music ["Angel Love"] is playing softly in the background while Gourasana is speaking. A guided meditation follows the discourse.)

Your consciousness is evolving. There is no time that passes that your consciousness is not moving. The issue that we are dealing with here is how quickly your consciousness is evolving, how fast your awareness can move. What our gathering for this period of time has been designed for is to move your awareness as far and as fast as possible. And though it may seem to be a short period of time, you can move very quickly and you can move very far in this period. What we are attempting to do, and what we are succeeding in doing, is to move out of the normal evolutionary time to another speed.

Those that have been around for a little time, they can tell you that awareness can move very, very quickly. Some who have come have achieved states of awareness, stages of realization, and have been taken over by such overwhelming love that the state they enter into can be called nothing but ecstasy – and this in such a *very* short time. Normally this rate is not seen, this accomplishment is not seen for many lifetimes – what some here have accomplished in weeks.

Now, most here are a little familiar with what has been going on, and I know you have all heard something, but for those who have never come before, you may wish to ask or discuss a little. This time is setting the stage for this period of growth we are about to undertake. You must give up your concepts, your misconceptions, in so many areas; one area is how quickly you can evolve, how quickly your awareness can change, how quickly you can experience the true realm of existence, how much illusion you can break through in such a short time.

This is not a situation to come and just feel a little relief from the struggle in the state of illusion, like a vacation where you come and feel a little peaceful and relieved before you go back into a state of suffering. This is a period where according to your desire, you can move your consciousness a great degree from where it is now, where you can accomplish a much greater degree of awareness than you now have.

This plane that you have lived on for as long as you can remember is just a plane of illusion, and who you think you are is just an illusion. Practically speaking, you know nothing *but* illusion. The exception is that you may know a little truth, you may have a little understanding, a little awareness about what is *really* going on in the universe, but the reality is mainly you are covered in illusion so densely that you are not even aware of the true realm of existence. It is like a figment of someone's imagination, whereas in the true reality the opposite is the case. This plane that you consider reality is just an illusion. This is just a dream. This is just a figment of your imagination, more or less. And your true Home, the true realm of existence, is where you belong.

So try to understand your situation a little bit. Try to understand how completely you are in illusion, thoroughly covered in illusion, you and those around you: in the city, the state, the country, the world. Everyone is deeply covered in illusion. Because once you remove all of the things that you are not, then what is it that is left? You are not the body – that is apparent. It had a beginning and it will have an end – that is certain. The personality that has been built around this body will have an end. Your mind, which is made up of so much endless information, is also just an illusion, because what is in your mind, after all, but information you have received from this plane of illusion?

So what We are doing here is directing you to the true realm of existence, to your true Home – something other than the illusion that you have only been aware of. We want to take you from this plane of illusion and move you into another plane, the true realm of existence. This is done simply by a change in your consciousness, in your awareness, because the true realm is right here.

This is not an easy thing to understand, and it is not an easy thing to accomplish. Yet I can tell you, there is a special power that is present here that will make it possible where normally it would not be possible. And no matter how dense the state of illusion that you are in, you can move. The only issue is your desire: your desire to know the truth, your desire to find out what is really happening, what is really going on. You know that you take birth; you exist for some time either as man or woman. You do so many things, so many activities, then you grow old and then you die – then again birth, and then again the same pattern over and over and over for countless lifetimes.

How you will move your awareness is by an act of will, of desire. But you are not alone. It is not solely up to you. You must make the effort, that is true, but the assistance that is available to you is very great. And you can move very, very far if you will but desire it, if you will just will it. But you need to understand the extent of your illusion; you need to be convinced as much as possible what this means, this illusion. Most can barely remember even this lifetime. In the early ages, the first few years, maybe a baby can remember a little, some more than others, some practically nothing.

In the same way, you had a life before this – and who here can remember that life? Rarely someone can sometimes remember one instance, like a dream. Just like your early, early childhood is like a dream, you may rarely remember something from a past life like a dream. Yet you had a whole other existence in the life before this: You were born either man or woman, you grew up under different circumstances, then you died, and then you took this birth. And before that, another life; and before that, another life; and in each and every lifetime it is just as it is now in this lifetime: you cannot remember anything else but this lifetime.

So although your awareness and your consciousness are so great (your *true* self, your awareness is so expanded, so great), now, because of the illusion, your consciousness is so covered over that you cannot even remember who you are, or the point of your existence. Your awareness, your consciousness is so dulled you cannot even remember your last life, and you have taken *countless* births on this plane of illusion. But even if that is hard for you to grasp, just understand that *in this lifetime alone* what do you know? What is the extent of your awareness? You have beliefs; you have things that you think are true, concepts about the way things are – spiritual things – but what are you truly aware of? What do you truly know?

So of course, especially during this time, the mood *is serious,* because We want you to try to *wake up.* Now you are in a dreaming condition, *not knowing* who you are, *not knowing* why you exist, *not knowing* what is going on. You are just in a dream. You are going from one activity, to another activity, to another activity seeking some elusive happiness that never comes. A little temporary satisfaction and then that is gone, then suffering. It's like a dream and sometimes like a nightmare.

So whatever level you are at, begin to wake up. At least, begin to wake up. Do not think that you are *so* caught in illusion that you cannot become free, because it does not matter what level of illusion you are in or what level of advancement you have achieved. What is going on here – there is so much power that if you will make the effort, if you will put in some time and perseverance, you can grow so quickly that you will surpass many yogis and many seekers who have been seeking for lifetimes.

While this may sound fantastic or doubtful, what is going on here is not something that you may refer to as a "belief system." It is not a belief system where you *believe* in something, therefore you practice something for so many, many years and hope that sometime in the future God will save you or something like that. It is something where you will be *practically* getting the experiences. And the experiences that several here have already had in such a short time – you can only find similar experiences chronicled in books: yogis and masters who have gone through similar experiences.

Try to understand. This is not just words. This is not just some belief system where We are saying to you, follow some moral code, follow some rules, follow some regulations, and then God will bless you in the future. What We are doing here is We are asking you to make the effort, but you will have practical, direct experience. Of course, according to your desire, your effort, your will, and your determination, those experiences will increase. And as I said, We have seen tremendous experiences that have happened in such a short time: Where one is sitting in this room – like some of you now, you are just in this room, in this plane of illusion, and your awareness has not moved beyond this plane so much – and then suddenly it begins to move. The room is the same and the circumstance is the same. Nothing has changed around you. Yet you, sitting in the same place, are moving somewhere else. Several have experienced this to great degrees: moving through dimensions, moving through unknown territory while sitting in the same place, going to other realms and other experiences and finding so many wonderful things. Some have *come to the light and been in the light and the overwhelming love that is there.* They stay in states of ecstasy for hours, crying from joy from the overwhelming love and light that they have come to – moving, you understand, from this plane to a whole other realm of existence. Not some belief, but direct experience – practically unheard of.

There are cases of masters on this planet, great yogis, who with certain powers can also take individuals and move them like this, but it is very rare to find in America. I do not think you will find any. There are some in India who have this power.

But it is not easy to understand this other realm when you are caught on the plane of illusion. "Illusion" means just that. The true realm is cut off from you. You cannot *feel* it. You see? You do not feel the unlimited love and light and ecstasy that is there, because you are covered in illusion. And the illusion is so dense, of course, how many even believe that there is any other existence? Some *believe* that there is another existence, but it is just a belief. There is not much direct experience. They *believe there must be more than this*, yet they have not experienced it directly.

Now the ones who have been through this structure, this training[1], have had some experience of what it means to move your awareness from this plane to another plane or to somewhere else. Many felt that love; if even a glimpse, they felt it for some time. Whatever you experience here, even if you are only able to obtain a glimpse, I hope that this will give you enough faith to continue and to find more and more. Because as you grow in awareness, this plane of illusion becomes less of an illusion, and you become situated more and more in the true realm of existence and what is going on becomes clearer. You do less stumbling around blindly with no clear direction to go in, other than some artificial goal that you set in your state of illusion.

But each person is unique, and the problems for each person are highly individualized. This is why these blanket organizations, these blanket philosophies, these blanket religions are not so effective. They try to set some rule, some standard for everybody, when everybody is *so widely different*. In an organization where there are millions, maybe

1) Gourasana is referring to a transformational seminar.

a handful are getting the real truth. Generally speaking, their awareness, their freedom from this illusion is not very great. Yet you can find those whose awareness is very great. They have achieved a good state of awareness, but they are the exception. They are very rare. Because the illusion is so complex and there are so many traps along the way, without personal, individualized guidance, it is, to be frank, *impossible* to break free from this illusion.

That does not mean you cannot become more aware; that does not mean that doing other things will not increase your awareness. I am not saying that. What We are trying to do here is – for those who desire it – *to completely, completely, break free from the illusion and enter into a state of full awareness.* Now this is something that is practically unheard of. And although there have been similar promises made, you can look at the organizations that make these claims and see the individuals just are not achieving that awareness. Yet here, with just a handful, so much awareness has been achieved in such a short period of time.

So during this time I have come to help, if you will take the assistance, you can move very quickly. So if you wish to talk to Me, discuss semi-privately – if it is something so intimate that you wish to speak in front of no one else, it is so embarrassing – then that can be arranged. Otherwise, we like to have semi-private, not the whole group, but mainly you and I can discuss things and maybe a couple of others can listen, because all of you have *similar* problems, and advice that will help one will also help the others. So if it is not something too intimate or embarrassing, then perhaps you can allow some others to be present. I am here to help you *individually* to *understand* your existence, to *understand* what you need to do, to *understand* what is going on. I *can* give guidance if you will accept it. But some things are very embarrassing, I understand, and if you wish, we can be totally alone and discuss.

Take advantage; take advantage of this opportunity. Because of your state of illusion, *you do not understand the opportunity that is here for you.* Try to hear that. *You do not appreciate or know what is available to you right now, and all you need do is to take it. There is so much waiting for you.* Try to understand. If you have ever felt that love in your life, try to imagine the realm where the love *is unlimited,* and practically where it is more than you can contain – it is *so great.* And who of you can say that you do not want this love? Who of you can say that this love would not satisfy practically everything? Because it is a love *that does satisfy everything.* It is love and light beyond your comprehension, and it is waiting for you *now.* It is waiting for you *here.*

This love is right here. This light is right here, and the only thing separating you from it is your illusion. Try to understand this. It is an unlimited realm, and your experiences in this realm are not with these bodies and with these minds, although when one enters into a stage of ecstasy, these bodies may manifest outward symptoms. The experience is your true self in your Home. You are going Home to where you belong.

You all have heard some stories. How is it that these yogis, these saints and sages, these masters, throughout the centuries, can sit alone in a place where there is nothing materially to comfort them? The heat comes – there is nothing to cool them. The cold comes – there is nothing to warm them. They have practically no food or clothing. Bugs crawl on their bodies. They sit on a very hard place, yet they sit there year after year after year in stages of ecstasy.

How is that? *Where is that ecstasy coming from? What is so satisfying that they can sit there alone for decades in stages of ecstasy? What have they found? What they have found is what you can find! Know that! Believe that it is possible* because it *is possible! Do not believe those that say that it is not!* If you will make the effort, you can begin to have the experiences, and in a relatively short period of time you can also begin to taste the sweetness of the true realm of existence, until quickly you will come to a point where even though it may not always be love and ecstasy, *you will be aware of the true realm of existence* – where you are not so much aware of it right now – *twenty-four hours a day.*

You can ask several who have just been coming a short time, and they are becoming more and more aware that all night long while they sleep they are doing something else, that something else is going on. They are not lying there in a state of unconsciousness at all. Indeed, they wake up, so-called "wake up," and feel that they have been working *the hardest* while they have been sleeping. *And this is the reality,* because as you live during your day in a dreamy state of illusion, when you go to sleep in that same state, then your sleep is like that: more illusion, more dream, just as your waking existence is a dream – practically, it is one continuous dream. As you begin to turn this around and your daily existence becomes aware and conscious, this carries over into your so-called sleeping state so that your *sleeping state* is a state of awareness and consciousness, even though you may not be able to remember particular things.

If your desire is not so strong, if it does not have so much meaning for you, then try to find that desire. Try to let that desire increase. Try to pray for that desire to know the truth. Of course, *any* that have come this weekend have some desire; there is enough faith, enough trust that you are giving up two days of your life to see if you can *find* something, see if you can *experience* something. *And you can. You can succeed at this no matter where your awareness is now, no matter how deep your illusion is, no matter how dense your illusion is, no matter how far gone you think that you are.*

The standards that have been set up by the organized religions are so harmful to true paths of awareness. They lead you to believe that if you drink some alcohol, you are so much further lost than one who does not; this is not necessarily the case at all. So no matter what your habits, no matter what your illusions, no matter where you are in your life, you can achieve a full state of awareness. You all just have different illusions that are covering you, and when you are guided through these, as your awareness grows, as they disappear, you will achieve the same state as everyone else no matter where you began. But it is *not easy.* It is *not easy,* but it is *so rewarding – so rewarding.* And it is not like so many belief systems where the reward is years and years in the future: "Do this practice for so many years and then sometime way in the future you will get something." If you will *pay attention* this weekend, if you will begin to pay attention right now, pay close attention to your consciousness, you will see that it is moving.

As you begin to perceive *any* change *at all, do not judge your changes, do not judge what you are getting, do not judge how you think it should come to you.* Simply notice – *change.* Then this change will gradually give a hint how you can change more and more, so that even though we are going to be here for just a matter of hours, in these hours so much awareness can be achieved.

Indeed, you can achieve more awareness in this short time than most will achieve in a lifetime if you will *but desire it, if you just want it, if you will just make the effort.* And you can come to Me practically *at any time* and discuss, and other help can be given.

We ask while you are here that you remain in total silence, not speaking a word. Do not try to understand with discussion. If the truth could be understood with discussion, so many philosophers who have read so much and have discussed so much would be aware. But generally, they are not very aware. They just know so much philosophy.

Discussion will be allowed in the group or personally with Me. If, of course, for some practical matter you need to speak, then you can speak to those of the household here. But try not to break the silence because there is a power in not speaking. Some of you may have heard of the principle of not speaking. The Buddhists practice not speaking, silence. Silence creates an internal power; it creates an opening *within,* and when you speak, *especially unnecessarily,* that opening is shut off.

So we are desiring to just go within here, within to the true realm of existence. Not speaking will help to open up more and more the path within. Try to understand the importance of this request and, of course as with anything, it is a request. To the degree that you make the effort, to that degree you will achieve. There may also be some other instances where special circumstances for help are there, because when you go within, as you start to truly look at things, there are issues, things that frequently need to be dealt with. They are like dirt that needs to be cleared away, for some more than others. So in the beginning of this process – you all have had this to some degree – you know you come to places where there is fear or great sorrow. This is part of the process and you may need to spend time on these areas. This will help your awareness grow. There are two in this house who are very expert at helping you to work through great fears and great problems if the need arises – and I think it will arise this weekend. One is Carol and the other one is called Gayle. They are very expert at helping, because they have an awareness and an understanding of how to guide you through so many difficulties.

Everything has been arranged for you. Everything is here to help you. The ones who already know, because of what they have received, wish to help and share it. Yet they could go with Me somewhere in the woods and live a very simple existence and do so much, but instead all of this facility has been arranged for you. They have put in so much effort and time. So much care has been made to see that everything will be nice for you while you are here, that all your needs will be fulfilled – physical, mental, and spiritual; all will be met while you are here. You can have so much while you are here. We hope that you will *just take* – become greedy this weekend and receive help in your life so that you may leave with so much more awareness than you arrived with. See *how far you can move in your awareness. See how much you can change your life in such a short time. Put all of the effort that you can, all your desire and all your will into this period and move. Take advantage of something.*

I do not know where else you can go and receive help in so many areas. There is not a strict structure that you need to follow. If you feel the need to be alone, then there is so much facility here. (*Speaking to assistant:* You know, there are some outside lights that can be turned on so if people wish to go and walk, they can walk.) You can walk outside. The property is fairly large and beautiful. Of course, during the daytime there are many places you can go and be completely alone and reflect if you wish to do that.

If you wish to meditate in the group, there will be constant meditation going on, if you wish to do that. If you wish to consult or associate with Me, that is going on. If you have come across some pain, some suffering in your heart that is too much to bear and you need help and assistance, and you need to just cry or scream, or whatever you need, to release and work through these things – these are all illusions – then assistance is there. In other words, feel free to do whatever you need to do; just always, of course, do not take away from others. This does not mean that if you are in the group and you are feeling something, and you wish to cry that you should stop that – no. If it becomes so intense, *then* we have arrangements for other rooms that you can go in and release as much as you need to.

So again, take advantage, and feel peaceful and free here. Even the eating has been made in such a way that when it is convenient *for you,* you can go and have so many wonderful foods – very healthy foods have been prepared here, a nice variety – so you can go at any time. Sleep when you wish. Rise when you wish. If you wish to swim there is a lake. Whatever. The *main thing is to stay* in a meditative state. Do not waste your time here. Do not treat it as a resort.

The only other thing is, I know that a couple of you have the habit of smoking cigarettes. If you cannot help but do this, then if you please, when you do this, go away from the house and always outside, so the air passes over you. So while you smoke, your clothes do not collect the smell so much. Do not smoke inside any enclosure. Then if you could be even more polite, stay outside for a few minutes after smoking, so that the odor of the smoke can dissipate. We do not want to make you feel uncomfortable and, of course, not unwelcome for any reason, but just in this area be considerate. Also, of course, for this period of time there should be no need for any form of intoxication.

Know this, no one here is judging you. This is not the perspective We have. We just see there are true beings, your true self, and there are different forms of illusions that cover you over. That is all. We do not see your true self and your illusions as one thing, "Oh, here is a person that does this." No, "Here is a true living entity who has this certain illusion," and We are only concerned with how to help you free yourself from this illusion.

No one here is condemning anyone for their illusion, but the reality is that you are condemning yourself by your illusion. You are condemning yourself to this plane of illusion, and if you will allow assistance and help and become *free* from this illusion, then you no longer need be condemned. So open your hearts and speak freely. You can speak freely to Me. My concern for you is unconditional. Whatever you may think of Me, do not think you can offend Me by your doubt or criticism or by whatever else you may say. Try to take as much advantage as possible. Do any of you have anything that you would like to discuss about this period?

Cindy: Gourasana, I feel so much joy in my life right now, and the more joy I feel, the more connected I feel. I want to break through this wall of illusion. I can't seem to get that, but I feel very connected. Do I have to die to leave this plane? What can I do?

Gourasana: No, you do not have to die physically, but I can tell you that as you begin to lose the illusion, it feels like dying. That someone needs to die physically is of course not true. This is not a common problem among people who meditate or find awareness – that they die. It is just that as you become free from the illusion, it feels like dying at certain points. It feels tremendously like dying. And although you do not know this and it may be hard to understand, the "death" experience that you may go through, the different stages of dying that you may go through, can be even *worse* than normal death, because at normal death, you are not giving up the illusion. You see? You are just leaving one body and again you will take *another* body and continue in illusion. So you are holding on to your false self, the illusory self, although the circumstances are always changing. But as you *break free* from the illusion, as you begin *to achieve a full state of awareness, that dying* is *much more profound because it means that once you leave this plane of existence you will not return.* At the end of *this* lifetime in illusion, you may be leaving one husband or one wife and some children, and mother, father, family, friends, society, and you feel that pain of separation, but when you give up the *whole illusion,* then it can feel like dying. But you do not need to worry about this. You can deal with this problem if it comes.

Cindy: I just want to go Home. I want to break through this, and I can't seem to break through it. I feel so strongly and long for it so much. I do not feel any fear. I feel a lot of joy in my life right now. Everything is very beautiful, yet I'm ready to leave it all behind. I feel that there is something that is stopping me. I don't know how to get through this.

Gourasana: Well, it is good that you have the desire, because desire is everything. Desire will save you. Desire is how you will go through to the other side. But the illusion is so dense, and although tremendous strides can be made, practically it's not possible to just, in a few minutes, go to a full state of awareness. *It is possible;* I am not saying it is impossible, and *incredible* strides can be made. But there are steps that you need to take to move through this illusion. You see there are so many complexities to the illusion. The illusion is so dense. You are so bound by it. There are so many traps to it that you need to be guided through. In this period you can go so far and see so much light. While it is wonderful that you have the desire, let the desire grow, and begin to move through the illusion.

If you want personal help, not just talking – talking is one thing, talking is trying to get you to understand – there is something going on that is much greater than the talking. If you need personal help from Me and you would like personal help from Me while we are meditating, then at any time you can just come to Me and ask that now you would really like to move through this illusion as much as possible, and I will take My time and work with you. You will see that you can move tremendously.

Cindy: Yes, I would like that. Thank you.

Person One: If I have a desire to move my awareness but at the same time I am feeling a blockage, is that a mixed desire that is fighting my own desire to want to be free, because I also have a desire to stay in the illusion? Or is it that the desire to be free is the main desire, and then there are other things that I just cannot understand?

Gourasana: No. You do not need to make it so confusing. You can just see it this simply: There is the desire to become free; there is desire to find the love and the light and the truth; and then there is the illusion that is stopping you. Whatever form the illusion comes in, it is just an illusion. *Whatever form it is, it is just an illusion,* and the illusion *can be dispelled.*

There are so many forms of illusion. This is why I say it is highly individualized, and it will require individual work with different stages and different problems. You are all so different. You all need to do different things, and will experience different things. I don't know if the members that have been around for some time would like to discuss – if there is an opportunity this weekend or at some other time – how different and variegated their experiences have been? There is one man that I have taken into the light several times. There have been those sitting there in illusion, and with just a touch, they have moved into the light, seen the light, and felt the love.

But the experiences are all very different. What one needs to go through to get there is also highly unique and individual. Your main illusions, your main problems are all very different. Misconceptions: You may have a misconception that is your main obstacle. For instance, you may not feel worthy, which is a misconception. So even though you desire the light, there is a part of you that does not feel worthy. Now that feeling of unworthiness is illusion. Until that particular problem is overcome, *you will be bound by that illusion,* the illusion that you are not worthy: "Well, who are we? Here we are in this room; who are we to achieve a full state of awareness? Don't we have to do something first, become so pure or something like that? We have been told so many things." Generally, this is how it is preached.

You see? Try to understand all the misconceptions and things that hold you back. There are so many, but they vary greatly from one person to another. In another case, it may be ego, just pure ego. So many different problems. Another may be fear, just fear. You know it is there, but you do not trust it, you do not have enough faith to let go of your illusion, so you are just simply afraid and that fear has you paralyzed, unable to move – so many different problems. Or you are just "stuck," which means that you sit there and nothing happens. You hear them say, "I am stuck. I am not moving in any direction," but that's not such a big problem. Getting you to move is not such a big problem. No one is stuck, truly.

I will point out again: In the time since you have come into this room or since you have arrived today, see if you can notice any change in your awareness. Can you feel something different? Are you quite the same as you were? It is important to appreciate the changes because, I tell you frankly, the changes go on hourly. Actually, they are going on minute by minute, but because your awareness is not so keen you don't notice. So in the short time even that we have discussed, if you can stop now and look and see: Is there *any* difference?

Do not think that wherever your consciousness is at, that it is bad, because there are many points of frustration that you must come to, to move on. You come to a point where you are bored; you are just tired. Suddenly you do not care so much about consciousness; you are tired and do not really care to hear any more or think any more about it. Perhaps you would like to do something else – watch some TV or something – whatever it is that you come to, it is just an obstacle. Know that. Any thought that prevents you, prevents that desire that was expressed by this lady *(Cindy)*, it is just the illusion keeping you trapped.

When you no longer care is when you are in the greatest danger. To have the desire she expressed, this is *so* fortunate. I cannot emphasize it enough. *It is so fortunate that you want to find the truth.* That you *know* that you are in illusion, that you *know* there is a barrier preventing you from experiencing the unlimited love and light that is waiting for you. *It is so fortunate to have that desire to try to break through that illusion. The worst thing is when you do not care.* But everyone who has come, obviously, *they care* to some extent. Otherwise, why would they come here when they could go to the beach or a nightclub to have fun?

If you have this desire, be appreciative of what you have, *because this desire is an indication of your awareness. Appreciate* what awareness you do have. *Appreciate* whatever you do have, because in this plane of illusion these things *are so precious.* You find hardly any in this world who really care at all or who even believe there is anything else. And even if someone believes, they hardly ever really care enough to make an effort to break through this illusion. So even if you have the desire and you are not able to execute as you would like to – you cannot give up bad habits that you know are holding you back too much – just be grateful that you have the desire and try not to let this desire die.

Conversely, try to let it grow. *Pray* for more desire. *Let it become everything, because it is everything.* This plane of illusion is nothing. *It is just suffering, endless suffering.* You have no idea what is waiting for you in the future, but one thing you can be certain of is that there will be suffering. If I told each and every one of you right now how you would die, how would you feel? Yet, you *will* die, and in a certain way: one of cancer, one of heart failure, one violently. You see? It is not a nice place to be. Just as you have suffered in the past, you will suffer in the future. This is not your Home. This is not where you belong. And I have come here to show you how to become free from this plane of illusion. *It can be done. It can be. Do not listen to those who say it cannot,* because *they do not have the faith, they do not have the desire. So they have just given up:* "Oh, it cannot be done, so I will not make the effort. I will *just stay* in illusion, and try to make a happy situation in this illusion." *But like a fish out of water, whatever you do, you will not be happy, because this is not where you belong.*

It is so obvious; if you can just begin seeing the illusion, it is so obvious. It is not where you belong! You see the people with so much money, practically unlimited money, but *they are not happy.* The ones with so much fame, they are practically being worshipped, *they are not happy.* Whatever you are hoping for in this lifetime, whatever goal you are trying to achieve, thinking it will bring you happiness, someone else has achieved it and excelled in it, and *they are not happy. So take a hint and know it isn't on this plane that you will find it.* If you are seeking fame, if you are seeking money, if you are seeking an ideal love relationship with another, if you are seeking it in your children, if you are seeking it in your society, if you are seeking it in your country, if you are seeking it by creating peace on earth, in whatever way you are trying to accomplish happiness on this plane of illusion, *you will not succeed. No one has succeeded. No one ever will succeed, because this is not where you belong! The only ones that succeed are the ones that have gone within, have gone beyond this illusion, have found the true realm of existence, have felt that love, have seen that light, have had that experience with their Lord.* These are the ones that have some happiness. In no other endeavor will you find any peace or happiness. You are just chasing something that you will never capture.

Also during our talks, during our meditations, if you find that you are too tired and you are growing sleepy and cannot pay attention, then quietly go outside and revive yourself. Take a shower; walk outside. The air is very cool at night here. You can sit outside, be refreshed, and continue to meditate. Do not allow yourself to fall into a dreaming state. Or if you are just too tired to continue, period, then take rest so that when you rise, you can again give maximum effort.

I'll tell you that even while you sleep in *this house* this weekend, you will not be sitting still. We will not leave you alone, even while you sleep. And if you will pay attention, you will notice something is going on even in this state you call "sleep." So do not think you will be missing out if you are sleeping, because even in your sleep something will be going on.

Any more discussion? Anything? Is everyone situated comfortably? Does everyone have what they need? A proper place to sleep? Bedding?

Lynn: Gourasana, I notice people have fear when I invite them to come here.

Gourasana: It does become a little frightening. This is a mistake that many make in their search. They come upon a fear and think, "Well, this cannot be 'spiritual' because 'spiritual' is all love and light, so, if I am feeling fear, this must be darkness." Yet there are so many fears that one can come across in their journey to the light. Misconception again.

You must not let *anything* stop you. Know that *anything* that stops you is just an illusion. There is no outside force, per se, that is trying to *get* you. It is just that you're *allowing* the illusion to control you – that is the problem. Yes, there *is* a force of illusion going on, but it is because *you allow it to go on,* and you will not let go. It is not so much that the illusion is holding on *to you;* it is that *you* are holding on to the illusion.

So as I speak to you collectively or individually, when I tell you to let go, to give up, I am saying to let go of this illusion, the whole thing: who you think you are, what you think is going on. It is just a letting go. Do not try to figure it out, just try *to feel it more.* It is just a letting go. You know that none of this is real; part of you knows that none of this is real. So as you move faster, you need to *let go.* So you will hear Me say this, and there will come a point where you will grasp it more and more. You need *to let go* of this illusion. You need to *give up* this illusion, and you need to move into another realm.

Cindy: Gourasana, what is this fear? I do not see or feel this intense fear. What is it?

Gourasana: Ultimately, the fear is finally letting go of this illusion. You might call it the core fear. You have other fears that may come up. Perhaps someone was hurt – let's say a woman was hurt by a man in her life, so she is afraid. She has a fear, and that can hold her back. Or she has been hurt or abused by men, so she has anger and hate, and that needs to be worked through.

Cindy: But the most intense fear is that of giving up the world of illusion?

Gourasana: Yes.

Cindy: And that is just at the point that you break through?

Gourasana: Yes. You do not have to *worry* about it. Things come in different ways and at different times. It is never the same. I can just tell you, practically, even though I have just been here a few months, in that time every single individual who has worked with Me has been filled with misconceptions that have held them back. They are seeing one person experiencing ecstatic symptoms, and they are thinking that they want to do that. So when they meditate they are trying to become like that. That is not what they should do. That is not what they need to do. So they are creating a block, because rather than accepting what it is they *need* to accept, work on what they *need* to work on, they are trying to do something else; so they are creating a resistance.

You must open your heart and be receptive to whatever comes, and it varies *so much*. It may just come gently and just be love – sweet, gentle love. Or there may be an intense fear. There *may* be. There may be a great struggle through darkness, and then coming out into the light. Or there may just be a continual growing of awareness, understanding, more and more and more aware. Each individual, so highly individualized, each person – how things happen, how you will grow in your evolution. I am discussing all of these things mainly so that you do not get caught up in these misconceptions, caught up in thinking that it should be a certain way, or you want it in a certain way. Give up what you want. Surrender; there is a higher Source that knows what you need. Give up how *you* want it. "Oh, I want to sit down and I just want to feel the love." So you sit there. "I do not feel any love, *but that is what I want.*" Well, that may not be what *you need* to experience. You have to be *open* to what it is you need. Be receptive, be submissive. Surrender to what it is you need. Then it will come.

Do not go into your meditations with expectations. Expectations will stop what should come. In the same way, when you go inside, do not *expect* the fear as if you are waiting for it: "When is the fear going to come?" I am saying these things so that if someone comes to a point where they *feel fear,* they will not mistakenly back away from it and say, "Oh, I do not want this. This is not awareness. This is not consciousness. This is fear. This is bad, so I want to hide from this fear." You understand?

Cindy: Yes.

Gourasana: Again, I am speaking so many words, but try to hear the communication in your heart more than your head. Try to understand with your heart what I am saying. I am speaking of so many cases, so many instances, giving hints here and there – some guidance. The true communication is going on at a deeper level.

The main thing is that you must throw out as much as possible all of your conceptions of spiritual life, all your conceptions of God, all your conceptions of the universe, all your belief systems, how you think it is, how you think it should be. Because you are in illusion, and whatever concepts you have formed, whatever beliefs you have formed, they are contaminated with illusion and it will not be like that at all.

So you need to *give up.* You need to *let go* of all of *these things* that you are holding on to, and be receptive. Be receptive. Be open to the truth, so when the truth comes you can take it and move and not be blocked by a belief. You see? Just as there are belief systems that more obviously stop people, so also each one of you has your own private belief systems, your own private concepts that hinder you. That is why I say we will work with your individual beliefs. These artificial ideas that you have, about how it should be or what it will be like or how it will come, will start to become apparent to you as you go further and further.

Person Two: Gourasana, is it true that at some point in the journey, even desire itself has to be given up?

Gourasana: For practical reasons, I will say no. That is not true, because that concept is completely misunderstood from this plane of illusion. What has happened is that those who wish to achieve a stage of desirelessness have misunderstood what desirelessness means, so they have made it something bad. They think you should feel no love. There *is* a state you achieve in full awareness where you are *fully satisfied,* therefore you have no more desires. It's not that you artificially try to be free from desire, which is not possible, but there is a stage when you reach full awareness where you are fully satisfied. So in that sense, there is no more desire. You become desireless. But that will be an automatic by-product of full awareness. It is not something that you need to achieve separately or work on separately.

This is a large obstacle for many millions of people on this planet. They have misunderstood this so much. Their concept of desirelessness is so distorted that they have created another illusion. That is why I say: Without guidance, practically speaking you will not get out, because even those who are searching so sincerely are just becoming trapped in one illusion after another. There are so many paths, but the paths themselves are so riddled with illusions that they are trapped in other illusions. They may receive more light, that is true. They may receive more awareness, that is true, but simultaneously they are receiving more illusion. So they are just stepping from one illusion into another.

This issue of desirelessness – which is very dominant particularly in the East, like the Buddhists – they are just not understanding properly. Desirelessness comes when you have achieved a full state of awareness; you are without desire because you are *fully* satisfied. You no longer desire love because you have *become* love. You are fully immersed in love. You no longer desire the light because you have become immersed in the light. There is nothing that is not satisfied any longer. In that sense, there is no more desire, and you have become desireless. But that is not something you need to worry about. *Now,* you need to build your desire. Now, you need to *increase* your desire as much as possible, *because it is your desire that will save you.*

Person Three: Gourasana, how do you distinguish illusion from truth?

Gourasana: You must begin observing. You must see the duality. The only way that you can *see* the difference is by beginning to see the difference. You must see what is illusion, darkness, and you must see what is truth and light. After a time, even a short time, what is illusion, at least certain aspects of the illusion, start to become very obvious. It is a practice that you need to begin. Just see: what is illusion and what is darkness.

We have had so many that have come and they moved very far in their awareness. It was obvious that they were going toward the light. The light has certain symptoms: They were becoming more aware; they could see what the illusion was so much more clearly. Then they came across some fear – usually, of course, the fear of letting go of their illusion – because the illusion was really starting to go. You see?

Now some of you are just talking about it, but there will come a point when it *will start going,* and you will be losing something – you will be losing the illusion, and you are very attached to this illusion. You have had it for countless millions of years. It's not such an easy thing.

So at any rate, they came to a point of fear because they were moving at such a great rate, so they did something to again cover themselves with illusion. They acted in a way where they would be separate from the light, where they would no longer be around a situation that would take them toward the light. Rather, they created an environment that was conducive for illusion, for darkness. Quickly they created more illusion so they could hide from the light. This has happened to several: they have hidden from the light and they have allowed the illusion to cover them again.

Observing the duality is a beginning exercise. We have discussed this at length many times before. Again, not only may you discuss this with Me, but The Lady and Carol have become expert in many areas of this, and they can also help. But you need to begin. This is the beginning stage. Everyone needs to see this. You *must* see what is illusion and what is light, and the only way to do that is to begin to see it, begin to practice seeing it.

For instance, let us say you go into a church and someone is speaking. When they are speaking about the love of Jesus, you can see, you can *see* the light – their face, their countenance will look different. The mood, the awareness in the air, will be different when they are talking about the love and the light because that is the truth, that is the light. But when the same man starts talking about hell, the eternal damnation, "If you do not do what I am telling you, then you will go to hell for eternity," you will see his countenance will change, the mood will change, and depending upon your awareness, you can actually *perceive* darkness come. This is just an example: The same man speaking at the same place, but on one hand he is speaking the truth: the eternal love and light of the Lord Jesus, and on the other hand he is speaking a lie, an illusion: that the Lord Jesus – who has nothing but love and light – is going to cast you for eternity into hell where you will suffer without any hope of ever leaving. What a huge lie they are preaching! So again – duality.

So you need to begin to see, because this is what is happening: People are going to the organized philosophies, and they are accepting the whole thing without discretion. You must develop discretion. You must see what is light and what is darkness, because they are interwoven. And the confusing aspect is that they are most interwoven on the paths of light. You see, it is the common pattern of this world of illusion: the fanatic Muslim, the fanatic Christian, the fanatic Hindu. Why? Because they have had some light, they have had some experience with God, but they have also accepted *darkness* with it, and they have become so interwoven that they have accepted *the darkness as light,* so they are bound in illusion. You see? They do not have discretion, and because they cannot distinguish between the light and the darkness, they have accepted darkness as light. Therefore they are bound by illusion, and at the time of death they will take birth again because they are not fully aware, because they have allowed this darkness to bind them continually.

On the paths of awareness, this is so obvious. This is why you have the Muslims – they also are worshipping God; you do not think they feel some love? Of course they feel some love when they worship. Again, like the minister, they're worshipping purely, just love. They feel that love, but then they believe that if they kill a Christian they will go to heaven, so they have accepted a lie. And the Christians believe that if you do not believe exactly as they believe you will go to eternal hell. It is a lie. It is illusion.

So in this way everything is riddled with darkness and illusion. So you must begin to use your discretion. You must begin to see the duality. You must begin to distinguish between what is light and what is darkness. You *must* do this. If you do not do this, what will happen is the darkness will get you. It will be interwoven with your light and while you may be *very aware*, the darkness that works its way in will still bind you, and you will *not* get out of this plane of existence. And that is what We are doing here; We are breaking all of the illusion and darkness so there is nothing but light.

Cindy: Is it true that light or awareness does attract the darkness?

Gourasana: No, it doesn't attract, but you could say this: Just as there are laws of nature – like you put your hand in the fire and it burns you, no matter what your belief system, it will burn you – so there is a law of nature, and that law of nature is the illusion. It is a force that is real. You can say it is an active force that is trying at every step to keep you in darkness, to keep you from full awareness, to keep you from the light. No matter what stage of awareness you are at, it is always a real possibility that the darkness will come and capture you; the darkness will come and distract you and take you away. At any stage of awareness this is a danger. So the light does not attract the darkness, but it is always a real danger that you must look out for. Never feel that you are beyond the power of illusion.

But if you are sincere, then the help is there and you can break it. You can break the illusion, but assistance is necessary. No one leaves this plane of existence without assistance. It is not possible; it is not possible! There are so many traps.

Great yogis – they become so advanced but they are caught in another trap. They become trapped in their power. They think they are so great. They can leave the body at will. They can go to other planets. They can do so many mystical feats. But even though it is a higher power, it is just a higher material power; it is not spiritual. These powers of clairvoyance, leaving the body, astral projection, auras, these things – it is all just material. It is *all* just illusion. It is *higher* illusion. So you see how again people are getting trapped? They are doing this astral projection and they think it is something spiritual. But it is not spiritual. It is just another material power. They are not necessarily nearer to the light and love than one who cannot do this.

Cindy: Has any soul ever broken through this wall of illusion?

Gourasana: *Oh, yes!* Everyone will eventually break through. Everyone will evolve. This plane of existence was never meant to be eternal. Although the length of time is so great, it can seem eternal. Everyone eventually will evolve off this plane of existence, but it is not happening very frequently. It is the natural order of things. It is just one stage of your evolution, this plane of existence.

What We are doing is unusual in the speed of evolution that is possible and the rarity of it. Even if in all of Our endeavors, only a few achieve a state of full awareness, that in and of itself will be *very rare*. That even *a few* leave this plane of existence for good is so rare, but it is always going on. It is not eternal – this illusion. It is just a question of when are you ready to leave? Do you wish to stay or not? If you wish to leave, then you can leave. If you wish to stay, then you will stay. This is for those who wish to leave.

You can go to sleep very soon, but for now if you would *wake up*. Those of you who are a little sleepy, you should *wake up*. Whatever you need to do: Stand up, adjust yourself, but wake up just for a little bit. The state that you go to sleep in will determine how much you will move while you are sleeping. So even if you only remain alert for the next half an hour, it can make all of the difference. It can double, triple, quadruple the degree that you move while you sleep tonight. I know that some of you are tired, but try to put in as much effort as you can. Even if it is just a short period, thirty minutes, then all facility is there, and you can go to sleep. But if you will move your awareness now during this period of time, when you go to sleep the work will go much faster; much more will happen while you are sleeping. This is very important.

We have discussed so much tonight to try to lay groundwork, especially since there are several that are new. Even while you are sleeping you can be growing. Throughout the weekend, you do not need to be in here meditating in order to be moving. You may wish to walk on the grounds or talk privately – so many things. But for now, at this point we will all meditate together.

Guided Meditation

(Often when Gourasana spoke to a group, He would lead a guided meditation after His talk. All of Gourasana's speaking will take you deeper inside, but the guided meditations are specifically designed for this purpose.)

Your true self, your higher self, whatever you wish to call it, *knows* what to do. There is a part of you that knows what to do. Even though you may be in illusion and not understand clearly what "going within" means, if you can just let yourself go . . . it is like a feeling, another part of you taking over.

Also, there is a presence in the room that is assisting you, and of course the association of others in the room will help you.

So we are going to begin a meditation. If you need special assistance, I will be coming around to some extent and helping. Or, if you need personal assistance, you can come up here and sit next to Me, and I will help you. Or, again, I will be going around, personally.

So now be alert.

(Music starts playing in the background: "The Fairy Ring.")

So begin to go within now. Make yourself comfortable. If you find that you are not comfortable, change your position. Do not be distracted by those around you. Someone may be crying, making some noise, whatever. This is an internal process. You find the true realm of existence by going within. This is where your focus is – not on what is going on around you, but what is within.

Everything is inside. Everything is within. This is where your focus should go.

As you go within, just let go *of everything* that you know, because everything that you know is just an illusion.

This is not time for discussion or trying to understand. Try to hear the communication in your heart. Do not try to understand the words so much. There is a part of you that understands. Go within. You have all felt this love in your life. You have all felt this pull. You have all felt this calling in your life, but you have been distracted by the illusion. You have been covered by the illusion. It has prevented you from experiencing the true realm of existence. So now let go of the illusion and let yourself go within. And whatever experience comes to you, *let it come*. Do not deny any experience that comes to you.

Try to understand. Everything that you are looking for *is here,* and *it is now.* You can find it now. There is nothing else but now. Tomorrow does not exist; the future does not exist. People go through life and they are looking for love from their mother, their father, their husband, their wives, their children, their brothers, their sisters, while all the time *that love that they have been searching for is within.* The completion that they have been looking for is within. The peace that they have been looking for is within.

What all saints and sages, what *all* masters and yogis, what *all* teachers throughout the ages have been trying to communicate is *this place within.* So many different ways to get there, but the end result is what *they are trying to communicate.* And it is *so great.* It is *so powerful.* It is *so wonderful. It is everything.*

So make some effort. Be patient with yourself. Let yourself go – and there is like a *flow* that will *carry you* from this plane of illusion and begin to carry you into the light. But along the way you may run into your obstacles, your fears, your pains; so you must deal with them as they come. Do not hide from them any longer. Whatever comes, accept it.

And if the emotion of going within moves you, let it move you to the fullest. Do not hold back. This is a time to move. Before, we discussed, and there was a certain movement in awareness. Now is the time for experience, more experience. Do not hold back. Do not be concerned about others. Let yourself *go*. Let yourself become free from this illusion. And if you find yourself frustrated and just sitting there, unable to understand or move or know how to move or to go within, then you can pray.

> Please, even though I do not have much desire and I am so lost in illusion I do not even know where to go, *please help me. Please guide me.*

Always do something. Never sit idly. If you do not feel anything happening, if you do not perceive any movement, then you can pray. The prayer does not even have to be in words. It can just be the desire. The desire is a prayer.

> Please show me the truth. Please let me feel that love. Please let me be free from this suffering.

There is a presence in this room. See if you can notice. Since you have come tonight you have been *in this presence,* and it has changed you. See if you can notice the difference. See if even a little, you can perceive the presence that is here, that is calling you. It is like imagination, yet it is the only reality.

You may be having an experience, and your mind will say to you something like "You are making it up." But it is a reality; it is something that is happening. Trust and let go. Know that there is nothing here that is not benevolent. There is no force here that does not have your full interest at heart. There is nothing here but love and light.

We care so much. We are praying that somehow or other you will move your awareness closer to the light. And at the least, you will pray to have the desire, so your desire will increase. No matter where you are in your awareness, you can pray to have the desire to find the truth and the light and the love. Once you have the desire, then you will be saved, because the desire is everything; desire will save you, just the desire.

Try to understand. If you just have the desire for that love and you will not settle for anything less than the unlimited love of the Lord that is waiting for you, then you will succeed – *if you just have the desire.* And if you do not have it, then *pray for it.*

Feel yourself move. Feel yourself move from this realm. There is personal assistance going on with each and every one of you at this moment. Try *to feel* that presence. Try *to feel* that assistance. Try *to feel* that help. You are not wandering blindly; you are being guided. If you will just trust and let go of your concepts and your illusions – and just let come whatever comes, then you can have everything.

We have just begun this journey. We have just begun.

You hear of "love" on this plane of illusion and you have become cynical and you have not trusted, because love here has always been so contaminated. But here, the true realm of existence, it is unconditional love that is waiting for you, *no matter what your behavior, no matter what you have done, no matter how unworthy* you think you are. These things are all just obstacles of illusion.

Try to take some of this unconditional love now. *Try to feel it. Whatever you do you will be loved – unconditionally – whatever you do.* You have heard so many lies and distortions about the Lord – as if He condemns you for your behavior, as if He does not like you because of your behavior. These things are lies – as if He would punish you for your behavior. These things are all lies. The reality is you create your own suffering; you create your own hell.

Hear not My words so much as My desire. That is the communication. I am calling you. Come here to this realm of existence. It is a love that you want so badly. It is a love that is so fulfilling that once you have it you need nothing else.

So many different words to try to get you to understand in what direction to move. But the underlying communication is My desire to have you leave your plane of illusion and come here to the true realm of existence, for here it is only love and light.

Hard to see? Yes, because of the illusion. Let go of the illusion and come here. *Now*. Why not now? Why wait another day? Even if you can only glimpse it tonight, let your desire grow. And if *only* for an instant, *feel the love that is waiting for you – if only for an instant. It is so powerful you will never forget.*

Do not let one more day of your life pass without *feeling* some of this love, some of this light, some of this truth that is waiting for you. It is everything.

I am Gourasana, and I can take you Home, because I know where Home is. And I can lead you through your illusion because I can see your illusion. *What an opportunity you have.* It is a gift being offered. Please take it.

Try to capture the mood that is here. Try to capture the presence that is here. Try to capture the seriousness that is here. And if you can do this as you fall asleep, while you sleep tonight your awareness will move so much.

Just continue. Any effort that you make is simultaneously producing a result. Even if your conscious mind is not aware of it, if you are making an effort, you *are* moving and you *are* increasing your awareness, even if your conscious mind is not aware of it.

So just continue to try. Just continue to make an effort. Just continue to care and have a desire for the light. It is only when you give up that you stop moving. That is why if you carry your desire to your sleep, you will move even while you sleep. The desire is so strong, it is so powerful.

On the Other Side of the Greatest Fear is the Greatest Love

June 3, 1988, Alpine, CA

We use the word "meditation." You could use many definitions of the word "meditation," but one thing that defines it is that it is something other than sitting and thinking about things – or thinking, analyzing with the mind what is going on. Because as has been proven, no matter how much thinking you do, you will not find the truth by this mechanism alone. Meditation suggests an experience that goes deeper, that is beyond thinking. There may also be thoughts and words in the mind, but if there are just thoughts and words in the mind and nothing else, then everything We are doing here will be missed.

If you want to benefit from the time that you will spend here this evening, then do something in addition to thinking and analyzing with the mind. So many words, so many things are there to describe the *other* feelings – for example, the state of prayer. If ever you have been in a state of prayer, or at least you understand the state of prayer, then this is what We are talking about. In a prayer there may be words, there may be thoughts, but of course there is *so* much more.

The words and thoughts are not the primary focus. They are there and have a benefit, but the focus is the mood, the feeling, the desire behind the prayer. It is an internal process; it is a going within.

This "going within" confuses people. As is the nature of the world of duality, the tendency is to think one way or the other: So you have those that go within, and they believe that is the only way; and then you have so-called external processes, such as worshipping the Lord Jesus. Many that practice "going within" consider worshipping the Lord Jesus as something external. If you believe just one or the other, then you are missing something; you are not understanding what is going on. We do say, "Go within, it is within you" – this is important to know. But yet, how is it that when one goes within they start feeling the unlimited love of the Lord? Or indeed, they begin to experience a whole other realm of existence? So there is much confusion, especially now. The western minds have not had this education or understanding very much. If someone from a meditative philosophy who believes that everything is within – which it is – goes to a Christian, the Christian will denounce what he has to say. And in many cases, they are both missing a point, because in fact, when the Christian is deeply in prayer, praying to the Lord Jesus, deeply, he is within – and this is a meditative state.

The question is one of focus. You want to focus your attention *within*, because when your attention is focused within, you enter into another realm, to different degrees. You begin to experience another realm of existence to different degrees as you become more and more adept at this. Until you come to a point where your whole consciousness, your whole attention *is always* focused within. And while you may appear to be in this realm of illusion with everyone else, you are *not*. This has been the case of sages and saints throughout the ages.

Not to put the Lord Jesus in a category with everyone else, but this is an example that is commonly known, of one who was in a physical body, yet He certainly did not exist on this realm of illusion. Even though He may have eaten, He may have slept, et cetera, bodily functions – *never* did He exist on this plane of illusion. *Never!* And this is what He taught: how to find that place, how His disciples could advance in this area. So many instructions, so many hints were there. But the things He asked of them are not possible if they were not situated within.

And there are examples of many Christians who are well situated within. There are different degrees, and this does not mean that illusion still does not cover them to some extent, but they feel that love of their Lord. They have such a connection within with their Lord that even while they still may be plagued by illusions of this plane, they are able to tolerate such suffering.

Of course, the Lord Jesus Himself – what He tolerated while nailed to the cross – yet His only concern was these beings in illusion. And because of His unlimited compassion and love, He wanted them to become free from the illusion and suffering that they were in, even while He was in this state. Any normal man, of course, would only be concerned with himself, but even in this state of terrible suffering and agony, even while the body was dying, He was only there to try to help. And help He did, until finally the body died.

The Lord Jesus turned to the right, but the man on the right would not let go of the illusion; he would not listen; he would not hear. The Lord was right there and could have given him *everything,* yet he would not hear. He would not understand. He persisted in his illusion, even while he was dying. Yet the man on the left had faith. He trusted. He knew in his heart that this was the Lord. You see, both knew in their hearts that this was the Lord, but one *wished* to remain in illusion and suffering, and one *wished* to finally become free from illusion. That is what is going on with everyone. It is as simple as that. One wished to remain in illusion, and the man on the left said, "Lord, remember me when you return to your Kingdom." At that moment he surrendered. At that moment he let go. At that moment he gave up the illusion and his attachment to suffering, and he surrendered to the Lord. At that moment! And the Lord said to him, "*Today* you will be with Me in paradise. *Today.*" And he was.

So the Lord Jesus waged a war against the illusion, even though *He knew* they were going to crucify Him. That did not stop Him. *Still,* He had to show the darkness; He had to expose the illusion. He had to go into the so-called temple and He had to expose the so-called teachers of the truth for what they were. He had to show that while they held scriptures in their hands and they preached the word of God and they made a show of doing nothing but worshipping the Lord – in fact, they were in *illusion, and they were keeping everyone else in illusion as well, under the guise of spiritual process!* So while He was kind to so many so-called sinners like the prostitute, He was furious with *these* so-called teachers. Because of the position that the so-called teachers held, people were coming to them for the light and the love and the truth – but these teachers were in darkness and illusion, and they *helped* everyone to stay bound in darkness and illusion. The Lord Jesus, who was bringing light and love and truth, could not tolerate this. *So even though He knew they were going to crucify Him, He had to go into their own sanctuary and expose them for what they were. And He did.*

But the nature of illusion is that it is never-ending. It never stops. It is unrelenting. It continues to work. It continues to fight the truth; it continues to cover the truth. Just as with the priests, at one point it was truth, but what they perverted it into became a lie, an abomination. In the same way, Christianity today teaches love and light – there is love and light, know that. I am not saying that they are not teaching love and light. And of course many Christians find it, and they feel that love of the Lord in their hearts. This is why they are so convinced. But due to the nature of illusion, over time so much darkness has become interwoven with the *truth* that they will not become free from the illusion, because they have accepted too much darkness. They have accepted too many lies as the truth in order for them to become free from this plane of illusion, from this plane of existence, and go to the Kingdom of God. The greatest example of darkness (which is the opposite of the love, light, truth and compassion that the Lord Jesus taught) is that they preach that if you do not accept the Lord Jesus, you will be cast for *eternity* into *hell,* without hope of ever leaving hell, and there you will be tortured mercilessly forever and ever.

I am also one who cannot tolerate the illusion. I cannot tolerate the darkness. And I have come to expose the darkness to those that are serious about finding the truth. The Christians will be helped, because, if they will let the darkness they have accepted go, they can know so much more love. They can know the Lord Jesus so much more: He is all-merciful, all-compassionate, all-loving. He preached only love and light and truth. And yet in His name, they threaten, take people's lives, and destroy them with guilt and with this threat of eternal damnation if they do not do basically what *they say.* They are saying more or less that the Lord Jesus has promised if they do not accept Him, that He will punish them for eternity mercilessly, without any hope of stopping, *ever! Just see the darkness that is there! What a terrible darkness they are preaching.* The light and love is there, but they have mixed in a *terrible darkness and illusion, which is an abomination before the Lord!* And preaching this lie, holding onto this lie, and propagating this lie is *preventing* them from having a deep and loving relationship with the very Lord that they are trying to have a relationship with.

So this is how the illusion works. It is so obvious. Anyone who has been a parent – even if you have not been, you can just try to imagine a father: He has so many children; let us say he has ten children. And he knows that of those ten children, only three will behave. He knows this. At the most, three are going to behave. And the other seven are going to misbehave. And he will give them all a very short time period in which to prove themselves, either to behave or to misbehave. And at the end of that time period, he will take the three that have behaved with him, and he will love them and cherish them. And the seven of his own children that misbehaved, he will begin to torture them – minute by minute, mercilessly, day after day – for eternity. Here there is such a furor when anyone tortures their children, molests their children; there is such an uproar and an outrage. *And here the Christians are saying that the ultimate Father of love is more or less promising to torture for eternity the majority of everyone that takes birth on this planet, because the majority do not accept Jesus into their hearts as they have dictated!*

What a terrible lie it is they are propagating! A father who behaved like that on *this* plane would be killed. And they are saying that the Almighty Father, who is nothing but love and light, would do this? And this is just one example of darkness. This does not please the Lord Jesus that they are preaching like this. If they wish to continue and increase their relationship, they should stop this lie.

So the pure truth is very, very rare – very, very rare. It is almost nonexistent. Because – even as with the Lord Jesus – when the truth is presented, the pure truth, the pure love and light, before long the illusion comes in and perverts it and creates monstrous things from it.

Until you are free from all illusion, until there is no more illusion, until you only know the truth, the love, and the light, then you will continue to take birth on this plane of illusion. And because the illusion is so strong – there are endless traps waiting for you – without personal guidance, it is very unlikely that you will find your way through this dense maze of illusion – very unlikely. So even those that have the desire, that go out and begin searching, become lost in so many areas of illusion and stay in illusion until they die, and they again take birth and go on.

Because the illusion is so strong, because you need to be corrected, and then again corrected, and then again redirected, without *constant* guidance you would be lost. If there were one hundred people, and the truth were spoken, those one hundred people would go their separate ways, and each one of them would have understood what was said in a different way. And what way they understood it in would be formulated by the illusion that they are in. So even though they just *heard* the direct truth, because of their illusion, they *immediately* perverted it, put a slant on it, contaminated it, tinged it, and there would be a hundred different philosophies. If theoretically, each one of those individuals would go to a separate country in the world and begin spreading the truth that they had heard, within one hundred years you would have one hundred different religions. They would all be preaching something different, and none of it would be the truth – because every individual who heard it was in illusion. The only solution to this is to take you from a state of illusion and guide you into a state of full awareness – a state that cannot be contaminated, a state that cannot be broken.

Like the men on the cross beside the Lord, just as one of them wishes to remain in illusion and one wishes to have the light, so at the beginning, you must *at least* ask yourself whether you want the illusion or the light, because most are choosing the illusion. They are *choosing* the suffering; they are *choosing* the illusion and all that goes with it. That is what they want, so they continue to create their suffering and their illusion. Know that. You hear this philosophy that you are creating your own reality; it is true. You are. Perhaps not in the way they are preaching, *but you are, by your desire.*

Or do you want light? Are you tired of the suffering? Are you tired of the illusion? Are you tired of being in ignorance and not knowing what is really going on and confused by so many contradictory philosophies and statements? This is the beginning. You must ask yourself. *Because the reality is that most people want the illusion, most people want the darkness.* And though they may want a little light, they do *not* want to come to a state of full awareness, because that would mean leaving this plane of illusion, going to the Kingdom of God, as the Lord Jesus referred to it – the true realm of existence. So they accept the Lord Jesus, but they mix in *so much darkness,* so much contamination that they are more or less *guaranteeing* that they will return to this plane of illusion, and they hold firmly on to this, because their *real* desire *is* to come back to this plane of illusion.

What We are doing here is trying to find those that are serious about leaving this plane of illusion for good and not returning – not just a path of light, not just more enlightenment, not just another meditation, another way to advance some more, but to completely become free from *all* illusion, to come to a state of *full* awareness, *and to leave this plane of illusion for good and never return.* This is primarily what We are doing. And of course, even those who do not have enough desire, who will not do enough to totally break free in *this* lifetime, will make so much advancement; they will evolve so far in their spiritual life. So of course, there is no loss.

The illusion is so obvious once you begin looking at it, once you begin seeing it for what it is. It is *so* obvious. And just as I have spoken tonight about this terrible darkness that the Christians hold on to, who of them, when this is pointed out, will change? The ones who will change this philosophy, (which is all it is, a philosophy, a belief, and a lie), those that *will* change, those are the ones that truly want to leave and know the Lord *more.* Those that persist in holding on, under whatever pretense, this is an obvious indication of one who wishes to stay, because at the time of death if you are holding on to an illusion, you will return. As long as you are in illusion, you will come back to the plane of illusion until you reach a stage of full awareness, which means you no longer have any illusion.

This is not just some philosophy, some words to compare and think about; this is something to experience and see. We have just been here a short time and working just a short time, and already some have been amazed. One woman, just this last weekend at our retreat, came to the realization that she loved her suffering. Not through some philosophical belief system, but through direct experience, she entered into a state of awareness where she *realized* that she had been creating more suffering because she loved the suffering so much. It gave her the greatest pleasure.

This is something very hard for people to understand, normally. Yet, more or less, this is what is going on with everyone to different degrees. They are very attached to the suffering, so they create situations where they *will* suffer – guaranteed. So she came to *a stage of realization,* in which she became aware that *she* was attached to the suffering – that *she loved* the suffering! That it was the suffering that gave her *the greatest pleasure. What an insanity?* Is it possible? Yes, because of illusion. This is the nature of illusion. Even while suffering *terribly*, one believes they are happy. This is the nature of illusion.

You can look at a drug addict. This is a good example. If anyone knows or has ever seen a drug addict, they may appear or they *believe* themselves to be in states of ecstasy. They consider that they are at *their happiest state* when they have just taken, injected, or ingested the drug, especially the heavier drug, and are feeling the maximum effects of the drug. But for one who is not in illusion, they can stand back and look at that and *see how they are suffering, constantly!* Not just while they do not have the drug, but while they are on it and consider themselves to be in the highest states of ecstasy – they are suffering *terribly*. So it is like that with everyone in this realm of illusion; even while appearing to *be* happy, even while *you think* you are happy – it is because of the illusion.

What a place this plane of existence is, where people love to suffer, where they are attached to suffering. To some people this may be new; you may never have heard it. It may sound too bizarre to believe. Yet even your modern psychologists, as little as they know, know this is very common – that people are attached to their suffering so much that they will not take steps to stop the suffering because they love their suffering. *What an illusion this is.* And this is practically what is going on with everyone. To be in illusion means you will suffer. To the degree that you are in illusion, to that degree you will suffer. And if you will not seek the love and the light seriously, you are making a statement like the man to the right of Jesus, "No, I do not want it." But if you will become earnest, somehow or other, if you will find some desire in your heart – even if it is not very strong, it can become stronger – you can succeed: You *can* find the truth; you *can* come to a state of full awareness; you *can* feel the unlimited love that is within all of you. You *can* do these things. *If you just desire it, then everything will be there for you! If you will just desire it* – it is *so* simple. Because once you desire it, then the help, the power, and the guidance will be there to take you to the light. And if you do *not* want it, even if the Lord Himself is sitting next to you, you will stay in illusion and darkness and suffer – just as the man on the cross. Even if the Lord Himself is next to you, if you do not want it, then you will stay in illusion and you will suffer.

And this is what is going on. So We are beginning to search out, We are beginning to try to find those that would like to feel this love, that would like to know what true love is, that would like to know the truth, that would like to understand their existence. *Not* just some words, some philosophical understanding, just knowing the words and thinking, "Oh, now I know," but a knowing that is beyond words. A knowing that comes from going within and experiencing the true realm of existence.

And I make a very bold statement when I say I can guide you from this illusion – *but I can.* And I make a very bold statement when I say I can show you the truth – *but I can.*

Each one of you is bound by so many illusions. You have no idea. But if you ask those that have been around, and it has just been a few months, they will tell you already how many illusions, how many misconceptions that they have let go of, and still there are so many to go. And without guidance, how would they ever have gotten around these? How would they ever have seen through these? In such a short time their awareness has grown so much; and it is just the beginning. So this is not a belief system. This is a system of truth: a truth that you will find within, that you will experience. Not that you believe in something and in the future some result will come, not like that. It is something that as you sit here, if you will pay attention, there is a change going on. Some have come now for a little time, and they have not even understood what is going on. Yet in their hearts they know something is happening; something is going on; something is changing, and there is a draw that brings them back.

There comes a point when there is no more need for philosophy, there is no more need for searching, trying to find the truth. There comes a point when it is just time to accept the truth and reject the darkness. We had one man, also from this last weekend, who for twenty years has been searching different spiritual paths, sincerely trying to find the truth. I had a conversation with him, and the discussion was, "Are you ready now to let go of the illusion and go to the light? Which choice are you going to make now? Because you have understood: You have read so many books; you have thought so much about it. You have had experiences in the light; you have felt that love. You know that it is there – you know that the true realm of existence is there. It is not something that you need to experience; you know it is there. Also, you are fully aware of the illusion and its power and its magnitude, and how it binds people. Now which will you choose?" And at that moment he was not certain, because when it came time to truly let go of this plane of illusion, he could not decide. So this was his meditation. This indecisiveness was always reflected in his spiritual search and practices where he would do things that would create failure or setbacks because of the uncertainty of direction – not clear where he wanted to go.

People say, "How is it possible to leave this plane of illusion in this lifetime? You never hear of this. It is unheard of, almost an impossibility." *The main reason* is that the decision has not been made. Finally, by the end of the evening, this man had decided, firmly, that now he's going to leave, and he's going to the light. And it has changed his whole life, because he just made the decision – finally, after twenty years of searching for the truth he came to a point of making a commitment and a decision, "Yes. I want the truth. I want the love. I want the light, and I do not want the illusion any more." And since then, just a few days ago, his life has changed so much, and now his progress will be so rapid.

This is the nature of illusion. It is so strong. It is so binding that even after experiencing so much, even after knowing so much, it comes down to a decision; it is difficult. But for many of you this is not the immediate problem. Each individual has a very individual problem. That's why the blanket philosophies do not work so well. It is just like a doctor giving one drug to everyone in the room, yet everyone has a different disease. By chance, maybe one person gets completely healed because it was the exact drug they needed, but others get only a little better, and some became even sicker. So to say to everybody to do the same exact thing is like giving everyone the same prescription, yet everyone is different. Some need to experience that true realm; some need to feel that love; some need to see that light; some need to have a change of awareness that is perceptible, that they can appreciate – not just some philosophy or some belief or some hope in the future but practically, *now*. And then, ultimately for everyone, even as you advance in this group, there will come a point of decision when you will see. You will know that the light is there; you will have experienced it. You will see the illusion for what it is, and you will decide.

At any rate, I hope this gives you some idea of what is going on.

Generally there is some apprehension about asking questions. So try not to let the false ego get in the way – afraid of asking something stupid or inappropriate. If it is not appropriate or I do not want to answer, I will just say so. Do not let *anything* stand in the way of the truth. If you are one that would like to find the truth, do not let any of the social interactions stop you. If you have any questions, whatever your questions are, no matter how trivial they may seem, do not be afraid to ask them. If it is something that bothers you, it is an obstacle, and it needs to be removed for you to progress. Try not to let the obstacles stand in your way.

Person One: Gourasana, you have spoken so much about having proper guidance to get us out of the illusion. Is this guidance meditating, going within, and realizing that you are in each of our hearts, or is there other, outside guidance, that is needed?

Gourasana: Both. You need outside guidance, but the outside guidance is just to remove the debris that is preventing you from going within and finding the truth, finding the misconceptions that you hold, and removing them. You need both. Although it is possible, if one is determined, to sit alone in a place and go within and find the truth and come to a state of full realization. But practically speaking, who will succeed? It is very rare. Even yogis that have so much discipline that they can sit and go within for hours and hours and hours every day. They do not need to work. They can just go and get some berries from some bush or a piece of fruit or a little rice and they are satisfied. And the rest of their whole existence is going within. Out of thousands of such men, only a few come to a state of full awareness.

But I am not saying that it is not possible without guidance, because that would be a lie. I am just saying that, especially now, there are so many misconceptions, there are so many illusions that are interwoven with the paths of truth, that unless these things are sorted out to a great degree, *practically speaking*, you will not work through them. You see, just as with the Christians, you find a Christian who has sincerely been serving the Lord Jesus for many, many years, yet some area of extreme darkness is still there. So there is something *binding* them. And without outside guidance, without this being pointed out, even though they have been praying and working so hard, they are bound in an area that is dark and in illusion. So without some assistance and outside guidance, they will not become free.

So you need both. Not that you get outside guidance and get some structure, and mechanically do that and find the truth – no. *You* find the truth. But your obstacles, the things that are in your way, the illusions that you are holding on to, that you are not aware of, can be pointed out. And even once they're pointed out, it will be difficult for you to remove them. But what is happening here, what has been happening here, is that the illusion is pointed out, the individual can see the illusion, and then at least they can begin working on it and then become free from it – and then there are other illusions. But without it being pointed out, how will you become free? It's practically impossible – practically.

Person One: Other than yourself, where could someone go to get that kind of guidance and be confident that it's not contaminated? If a person didn't live here or it wasn't possible for them to have that type of instruction, where would someone find that if they were really sincere?

Gourasana: If they are sincere, they will find it. There are not many. It is very rare – very rare. And that is why it is very rare for someone to come to a stage of full enlightenment, because it is so rare.

I'm saying, *here* it exists; and I welcome challenge. There are masters who are fully realized, and they can impart the truth. But I will say, there is something unique that is going on here. But that can be repeated so many times; what is the use? It will only be experience that will convince, and further discussion and further illusions going away until the truth becomes clearer and clearer and the illusions become less and less. That is the only thing *that counts.* To follow something for years and years and not come to a state of good realization – you are doing the wrong thing.

There *is* a need for many paths and many teachers. It is not that one is right or one is wrong, but there are degrees of illumination that come from different paths. That is true. And the number of people that want to leave this plane for good is a very tiny percentage – although now more are leaving, or will be leaving, than have before. It is an unusual time of evolution of consciousness. It is not some imaginary thing that is going on – this evolution of consciousness. This sudden growth in consciousness is very real. And just as the masses will evolve faster in so many ways than they have before, so also a certain few, the ones that simply want to leave, will now be able to leave if they desire it.

Cindy: Gourasana, is a state of health in the body part of this illusion – just a state of mind? What was happening during the experience I had a couple of weeks ago, when I went into a deep state of meditation while I was in the midst of a very bad cold and my body immediately healed, and the next morning all signs of the cold were gone?

Gourasana: The idea that the health of the body is just a state of mind is a misconception. This is proven with tradition. Your traditional seekers of the truth had a very strict physical discipline, strict diet, and strict exercise program. The care of the body is important.

Although what you have described is possible, generally it is not the rule. When one has a disease, it overtakes their consciousness and they are not able to go within, they are lost in the disease, and it becomes everything to get out of the disease. Perpetually they are fighting to get out of the disease. Of course, to continually do things to create more disease, or to never quite get well so one always stays in a state of disease, is another way to perpetuate suffering.

But, at any rate, I just wanted to say that one thing: that this idea that your consciousness, if it is good, will automatically make the body good too, is not true. The yogis do not eat poison like you eat in America. The great meditators and saints from all countries have principles of health and diet that they adhere to because it is important. As your awareness increases, there is an energy that comes into the body that goes through the body; there is a power that comes through you, and if you are sick and weak, then there will be some restriction. At any rate, it is an important area to be aware of, and there are ways to achieve good states of health or at least sufficient states of health. But it is not like some people think: you can just do anything you want, and just have a good attitude and you will be fine. It does not quite work like that.

Cindy: But if you have a good attitude, then is that going to direct the body on what to do, on what would be best for it?

Gourasana: I am not saying that a good attitude is bad. I am just saying that the attitude alone, as some people think, is a misconception. I am just pointing out a misconception. *Yes,* if your attitude is correct, then you will seek health and you will not be satisfied until health is achieved, just as you will not be satisfied until the truth is found. You will gradually do more and more for your health and your physical strength, just as you will do more to find the light. But you cannot come to a state of full awareness and go to these places that serve nothing but poison and eat that poison and put it into your body in a state of full awareness. Generally, this is being done because of no awareness or little awareness. As you become *more* aware, then you will be more careful about what you put in your body, generally. Anyway, it is an important area, I do not want to emphasize it *so much,* but there comes a point when this has to become a consideration.

Person Three: Gourasana, I'll be going through the Resurrection seminar[1] next weekend, and there are a few specific fear blockages that I want to release. I'm ready to release them and it's my honest desire. Are there any recommendations, things I can do, to prepare for this? Any suggestions on how I can release these fears more easily?

Gourasana: We are going to have a special session this Sunday night with those of you that are going through the structure.

Carol: She doesn't know if she'll be able to come.

Person Three: I've had tickets for a couple of months to go to Dan Fogelberg, my favorite musician, up in Irvine. That's Sunday night.

Gourasana: Who?

Person Three: Dan Fogelberg. We've already bought tickets and I've been really looking forward to that, and also my husband. So, I want to go to that. I know that this is important too, but both things are important.

Gourasana: Yes, so that is all right.

Person Three: Is there anything that you can share with me in this area?

Gourasana: One thing is that you can call Carol. She has worked with these structures a long time, and she can help you as difficulties come up as the time comes nearer. What

1) The person is referring to a transformational seminar.

is going on in this structure is excellent, and it is what we are doing here, so I recommend that people go. What are we doing here? We are changing your awareness as quickly as possible, in the shortest time possible, because there is not much time between now and death. And to take you from the state of illusion that you are in now to a state of full awareness, where you feel that unlimited love inside you always, there is so much to be done.

If you are aware of this seminar called "The Resurrection," you will see that there are drastic changes in people's awareness, and there are drastic changes in their consciousness while they go through this structure. Again, it is not a belief system; it is not some psychological formula. It is what we are doing here. It is just that in the seminar you are in a certain structure for so many hours, for so many days that your awareness can change so drastically into the light, you see. It is excellent that you are going, because one thing that most find who go through these structures is love. Some people who have never known love, real love, they go into this and they find such an intimacy and a love that they could not imagine existed. The structure is very hard, and there is a great deal of fear that is attached to it, but you must be assured that no matter how great the fear becomes, you will go *through the fear.* And when you go *through the fear,* on the other side of that fear, waiting for you, will be a love and a light that you have never experienced before. Try to remember that when you come to the fear – and you *will* come to the fear.

We had one man in the last Resurrection who could not stand the fear any more. At one point it became too great and he left. He decided not to return. We sent someone to go and get him and bring him from illusion – very difficult.

He was very determined to stay in illusion. So a great deal of trouble and difficulty was created to bring him from illusion back to the structure. But once he came back, then he found the light. He went through the fear and he found the love and the light. And it is always the case, it is always proven: No one leaves the structure caught in the fear.

That does not mean as you advance on the path, that you will not come across other fears. And it can be incredible fear, it can come to a point of practically terror; it may not, but it can. But whatever fear you come across, no matter how great that fear becomes, have faith. So many have gone through these structures – hundreds have gone through, both in this one and there is another one, they call it "Lazarus"– they come through and the end result is always excellent. So if you can have faith, no matter how bad it seems, no matter how bad it gets, no matter how unbearable it becomes – anything that makes you want to leave or stop is just an illusion. It is just the illusion; it is just the darkness of this world that is begging you, distracting you, trying in any way to get you to stay in the illusion of fear. So the main thing, of course, is that you "stick it out," as they say. You stay with it and you do it. You do not hide in your fear.

If you are going to hide in your fear, then you should make arrangements where you can stay with someone who also is going through the seminar. There are several going through, and they are going to be congregating at one apartment here in Alpine. So I suggest strongly that if your association when you are not in the structure is not so good, if you are going to be with those that will not understand, then as much as possible I would recommend – especially for the second half – that you sleep with and take the association of those that have gone through or are going through, who know what is going on, because what is going on in the structure is what we are doing here. That is the beginning and this is the continuation.

In that structure, *illusions* are being broken. Ways that you are being controlled by the illusion, ways that are making you suffer, are being broken. And the more the illusion is broken and dispelled, the more love and light you will perceive. That is why there is always such exhilaration immediately after this experience. The tragedy is, after finding so much, people again allow the illusion to cover them over and let the illusion control them again. But that is the next step.

First you go through this structure and give your heart to it. You can make so much progress in your evolution in that short time period: more than you probably would in your entire life; you can make so much advancement in that brief period of time. In just a few days, you can make more true evolution than you probably would in your entire lifetime. So it is something to go into with the greatest seriousness and give as much effort and desire as you possibly can find, because it is important. It is not just a seminar, something you go in and out of and, "Oh, that was a nice experience." *It is your life!*

And you can *change your life drastically* in a short period if you will give it the effort. And then if you wish to continue in this vein and get more light and more love, then you can come here. Or, also there are some other ways you can continue. But it is no light thing. It is very serious, but the rewards are wonderful. Do not give up. Remember that on the other side of the greatest fear is the greatest love. Have faith in that. Know that everyone comes through fine.

So no matter how difficult it becomes for you, no matter how great the fear, *do not stop.*

Person Three: Do the blockages dissolve once you make the choice?

Gourasana: The structure will remove the blockages. You do not have to be concerned about the blockages. Once you are there, you will begin removing the blockages; the seminar facilitators will help you to remove them. They know; they can see your blockages. Some are so obvious. It is a beginning. I can see the more subtle blockages. Most here have been through the structure and still there are so many blockages. But once the blockages are pointed out, and what to do about them, then they can work through the blockages. So at any rate, once you are there, you will be able to work through them. That is the structure. That is how it is designed to quickly break through barriers and blockages that are preventing you from knowing your true self. And one thing everyone receives in this structure is they at least learn about an aspect of themselves that existed, which they had totally forgotten, or were unaware of – which is an incredible accomplishment in just a short time, *just a few days.*

As I have said, if there are further doubts or you wish to discuss more, then talk to Carol; she is very knowledgeable in this area and knows. She has helped with Resurrection and she has guided others that do these structures. She has helped them to see. Assistance can be there if you need it between now and the beginning or during the break periods of the seminar. It is good that you are going, because there is incredible value that can be gained. Even if you do nothing else, even if you just go back more or less to the great illusion, your evolution will have been changed a great deal. So there is no loss for anyone to do this.

Cindy: Gourasana, this week has been very intense for me. When I left here last weekend I was with my family. It was sad and unfulfilling. It was like going back to the unreal world and seeing them in their little illusions of what they think of as important. After what I experienced here, I find it very difficult to find peace. I was very saddened. Each day the attunement grows stronger; I feel this unease at not being at peace. It is very difficult for me right now. Will this get better with time? What can I do at this point? I very much feel the duality, and I'm having a real hard time dealing with that.

Gourasana: Well, you see, this again is another misconception about coming to a state of awareness. If one thinks that in a state of awareness they will walk around like they are on some drug and everything is just fine, then they are mistaken. And if artificially they try to stay in this state, then it is another trap; it is another illusion. Yes, after you have experienced the light and the love, after you have seen the true realm of existence and as you experience it more and more, as the illusion that is going on here becomes more obvious, then with the love and compassion that you feel when you go within, you naturally want to help others more and more. So this disturbance is always there for one who is realized.

Cindy: Where I am right now, it seems very difficult for me to feel that I have to live the rest of my life out on this physical plane with this other realization. How can I do this? How am I going to find peace?

Gourasana: Again, it is a conception of what you think peace is.

Cindy: Or sadness, some of the sadness I feel that I did not feel before. I guess what has happened is that I have become very much aware of the illusion and this is very saddening. I don't want to live in that illusion, and on this plane physically. If I am to be *here,* how can I live *here* and not live in this illusion?

Gourasana: First of all, *you* are not in the illusion to the extent that you see it.

Cindy: Right. I know this.

Gourasana: No. No. You should stop talking and listen.

It is what you do *not* know that is the problem. It is what *you think*. You have all heard Me say you have misconceptions or preconceptions of how it will be. You want it to be a certain way, and when it is not that way you think, "Oh, this is not the truth," or "I must be doing something wrong," or "I must get away from this feeling or this experience as soon as possible, because it feels negative." But this is a misconception. As you see the illusion more and more, and as you see that people (as I gave the example of the drug addict) are actually suffering even while they think they are enjoying, your care for them, your compassion for them, will just increase.

You do not get some state of peace, again like on some drug where everything is just fine. Things are not fine at all. The children are suffering terribly. They are confused and lost. Parents are abusing children grossly and subtly. Then the children grow up and they suffer through different stages. There is so much suffering going on. And I am speaking of *here* in this country, which is considered to be the nicest place in the world, not the obvious places in countries where children are dying of starvation before they reach the age of five, where they have no food or water or shelter or freedom from disease, or relief of any type. I am talking about here where practically all comforts are fulfilled. The most *comfortable* people in this country are suffering.

As you become more and more aware, you will see this more and more clearly and it will move you – because an aspect of one who is aware is compassion. And that aspect will increase, and that aspect will motivate you, and that aspect will not let you *be* at peace because if there is someone you can help, then you will help them. This is why all the great leaders that have found the truth, that have known the truth, they give their whole life, they try so hard to just convey to the people in illusion: "Please, look around you. Please, wake up. Please, see that you are suffering. Please."

Again, the Lord Jesus – His existence was not one of just peace, not at all. There was incredible turmoil and trouble, and He knew of His impending doom. Yet His compassion and His care for the people was so great that He could not resist. He *had* to help them. He would *plead* with them. He would beg them: "Please. Follow Me because I know the truth. And if you will just hear Me. Try to hear Me, please! And do what I say, then you can become free from this illusion. If you will just have some faith and some trust."

He gave *everything* just to try to help the people in suffering. This is the nature of one who is fully realized. They cannot sit idly by and just let the poor suffering masses go to hell. This is not a place to find peace or the misconception of peace that is being created. This is a place to become aware. But just as you become aware of the love and the light, you cannot be totally aware in one area and black out the rest. You cannot just be absorbed in love and light and not *feel* the pain and suffering of those in illusion.

Full awareness means just that: You are *fully* aware of *everything* that is going on.

And just as you cannot stop that love, that light, and that compassion that you have from within, you cannot stop these things as they grow, so when you are with those in illusion and you see them suffering – even though you cannot help them, because they will not take it – still, you cannot help but *feel* compassion for them. These poor people, if they would only listen even a little, they could receive so much happiness. They could have so much light. They do not need to leave in this lifetime, but if they would just open their minds and hear a little, they could receive so much. But they will not. So that compassion and that love and that caring that you feel for them cannot be stopped. All of the emotions are there in a state of full awareness.

One who is fully aware does not just sit there like some statue: "Everything is okay." There is a breed of impersonalists that come to this stage. It is called "impersonalism," and they do this. They do not feel love. They do not feel compassion. They achieve an awareness of the illusion so it does not bind them any more, but this is a defective or retarded stage of awareness. But they specifically try for this type of state where they just feel fine. And if there is a child in front of them who is starving and will die, since the child will take birth again and will go on, the impersonalists feel no disturbance or compassion because they know rebirth is true. But this is not recommended. This is not a state to desire to achieve.

So it is painful. So being aware, just as you will learn in this structure, means that yes, you feel the pain too. This is why people stop feeling, because they do not want to feel the pain. They do not want to feel the sadness. They do not want to feel the sorrow. So they stop feeling. But to feel the love, the light, and the compassion, and to know the truth, you must feel it all; you must experience it all.

So what else? This covers some of the things. Is there anything else in this area; do you understand somewhat?

Cindy: I understand very well that I need to stop conceptualizing.

Gourasana: Yes. Everyone can hear this, because this is a practical, specific example of one who is seriously searching for the truth (as she is), and a misconception is preventing her from knowing the real truth – from being free from all illusion. A conception of how it should be or how she wants it to be, a misconception, is preventing her from being free from illusion.

So there is just a little more to say, and that is to continue on in the area of misconceptions. Being in illusion means that you truly know nothing. You have ideas or concepts about what is going on, but mainly they are *mis*-conceptions. There may be some truth to them; there may be something about the idea you have which is true, but the darkness is interwoven so it prevents you from progressing further. And everyone is contaminated with these conceptions. Your desire for the truth must override any conception that you have. What the truth is, what the light is, what the love is, is something far beyond whatever your mind has concocted. The experiences that you will have if you pursue this path are like nothing you can conceive of. Practically all your conceptions are misconceptions. And while there is some truth to things that you believe, they are all riddled and interwoven with darkness. And your determination to find the truth must override your misconceptions – or how *you* want it to be – because the truth is the truth. If you say,

"Oh, yes. I want the truth, but it needs to be like this; I do not want it to be like this," then you will not find the truth. You must approach the truth in a fully receptive state, not mindless where you let any garbage come in. No, you use great discretion and look at everything that is happening with great awareness. Not mindlessly, but yet fully receptive and open so that as it comes, you will accept it, no matter how it comes, because *the way* it will come to each individual will vary – and *the way* it will come will not be something that you could conceive of.

Apparently, this may or may not be true, but it is just an example. One woman that was here left, because she felt that this was a Christian-oriented thing; that we were mainly trying to convert those present to Christianity. Which is of course a misconception and is not true. It's just that I was using this example, because the teachings of Jesus Christ are known more in this country. If I used examples of great masters and teachers from other countries, like for example Lord Ramachandra and Vamanadev and Lord Krishna, you would not understand, because these names would probably mean nothing to you. So I do not. I refer to the Lord Jesus frequently, simply because in this country, even the non-Christians have certain basic knowledge about Jesus.

Yet if one desires the truth, they will not let such a thing stand in the way. Because, you see, what if the Lord Jesus was the ultimate truth? What if the ultimate truth was that Lord Jesus was the *only* way – which is not true – but what if that was the case? The one who left has rejected the truth, if it were the truth – you see. And by not being open or receptive to the possibility, one says, "No, if the truth is that the Lord Jesus is God and I must surrender to Him, then I do not want the truth." In this way as you go on your path, truth will come and you will miss it if you say, "No, I do not like this truth. I do not want it to be like this, so I will not accept it now. I will leave." This is what is happening all the time. We see people come, but mainly they leave because they get to a point where they say, "Oh, well, this is how the truth is – well, I do not like it like that. I do not want it like that. I will not accept it like that." So, you see? In this way you remain in illusion. You must *constantly* be receptive and open to the truth, which is changing, and as you become freer and freer from your illusion, and the truth unfolds before you, you will go through so many different stages. And if you are not receptive and open to the *truth*, then at some point you will say, "No, I cannot accept it." Because, why? "It is not in the preconceived package that I had of how the truth should be. When I find the truth, I want it to be like this." You see, preconception, misconception.

Anyway, this is one way that the illusion is binding most people. So what We are doing here is exposing the illusion. And when you stand back and look, it becomes so obvious – the illusion. It is so obvious. Just like this woman: she formed a misconception that We were propagating Christianity. It's an illusion; it is not true. Yet, she was bound by that illusion and acted under that illusion, and left. You see? So in this way, each and every one of you is being bound by different illusions, and acting in that illusion, and in this way you are forced to act in certain ways, always bound by illusion: never to be free from illusion. And without specific guidance pointing out your illusions – because you have *so many illusions, so many misconceptions,* and you create even more as you go on the path – practically speaking, without guidance it is not possible to become free.

So I hope that those that are serious will come. There is nothing here that is threatening. We are asking you to go within and find the truth. It will be *your* experience. *You* will go within; it will be highly individualized – what you will find and what you will go through. And *you* will know; *you* will come to a state of realization – not accept a belief and just act mindlessly on some belief, but you will act from direct experience, awareness, and knowledge. So We hope that you will take the steps to increase your faith and your awareness and your knowledge.

If there is anything, anything anyone wishes to ask? At any rate, we are here every Friday night.

So now the talking is over and now we will do what we have been talking about – and this is experience.

Stop Settling for this Pitiful Existence

June 25, 1988, Alpine, CA

What We are doing here is beyond the belief systems of normal processes of self realization that exist in the world. In all your systems of belief, whether it be Christian or Vedic or Muslim or whatever, it is always that first you believe like "this," you follow some rules, and then sometime in the future you will begin to get an experience, you will begin to get a result. And for most, that result is not even achieved before death. They are relying on the belief system so strongly that they wait until the time of death, hoping futilely that at the time of death they will somehow or other automatically be saved or come to a state of full awareness – even though their entire life they have been in illusion. It is not that they do not grow in awareness, because they do, but they are still bound by illusion. And there is no such thing at the time of death that just automatically takes you from illusion for good. It is not so simple; it does not work like that.

You might say that here We also have a belief system. But the difference is here We are saying, *tonight* you will see some truth, some light – to the degree that you let go. You could also say yes, this is a belief system, but the difference is that you will have practical results *tonight.* Even while you sit here, your awareness can be moving, and you can begin moving into another realm of existence. So it is not some promise for the future, which is just another trap. You know of the different belief systems that promise – like Christianity: They believe they will die, and then Jesus will save them. Even though they are in complete illusion their whole life, they *believe* that the illusion will all go away at the time of death.

So one could say they are making a promise and I am also making a promise, but the difference is that the promises that I have made are not something far in the future. Indeed, we have seen that practically everyone in this room, within such a short period of time, has experienced *so much awareness and so much light.* This is the difference. Not that you wait for the future to find the truth, not that you have some hope, not that you follow some belief system for years and years that promises love of God, yet after years and years you do not experience love of God, and you still go on almost mindlessly following. Yet We have seen within such a short time here, literally just weeks, people experiencing love of God – a love so intense that tears of joy are rolling down their faces, that they are trembling in ecstasy.

In other words, We are not just talking here. We are not just presenting another belief system: "You do 'this,' and then sometime in the future. . . ." No, you come here, and to the degree that you let go, within a *very* short time you can have *immediate* experiences, *immediate* growth in your awareness – very practical, very tangible growth in your awareness – so many realizations, so many experiences. This is *very* unusual. This extreme rate of growth is almost unheard of: that within a few months, one can go from a state of illusion to a state of so much awareness and enlightenment, and have experiences that you only read about in books of great masters in India, or books of great saints and sages from the past.

But it is interesting, because here also We see who truly wants to leave the illusion, who truly wants to leave this realm of illusion, become free and enter into the spiritual realm, and never return here. So many hold on so strongly to these belief systems, because the belief systems have built-in darkness and built-in illusion, which ensures that the people involved in the belief system will *not* become free of the illusion. And in their hearts, they know this. This is why they cling. So even while in so many religious systems they appear to be endeavoring so hard to find God, to find the truth, they accept a system with built-in darkness and illusion so they will not *become* free. So they actually *cannot* become free. But that is not the case here. When you come here, you come very soon to a point where the philosophy goes, where there is no more need to think about the truth, to search for the truth. You become confronted here in a very short time, relatively speaking, with a clear decision, and that is: Do you want to become free from illusion, do you want to become free from the darkness, and do you want to leave this plane of illusion for good and enter into the spiritual realm, the true realm of existence?

We see that so many make a pretense, or have been in belief systems for so many years, but when finally they came to that point when there was no more need for philosophical thought, no more need for searching, when they became confronted with this clear decision between the light and the darkness, they chose the darkness. They chose the illusion, even while pretending or making a show of wanting the light so much. Yet their actions and their decisions very clearly stated that they really *did not* wish to leave this illusion; that they really wished to stay here and not leave this plane of existence and again take birth after birth – which is the decision that most will make.

It is ironic that most of the people who have come and gone have been so-called seekers of the truth. They came to a point where they did not need *to seek* any more. The decision was clear; they made the decision and they went back into their "searching." But their searching, their belief systems are just an illusion for them to hide in again. And they are back hiding in their belief systems and their illusions because they truly did not want to give up this plane of existence.

Now for one who is searching, this may be very difficult to believe or to understand. Yet those who have been around for a few months have seen it so many times already, so many times, in just a few months. Just as with this woman who has just returned. She took to what is going on here – there is so much power going on here – and she moved *so* quickly; she began to leave this realm. After living in this realm for so many millions of lifetimes, it is unavoidable that you are going to cross some fear, that you are going to cross some turmoil in your existence when you begin to leave. It is not possible to avoid difficulty. Not possible. It is not beyond toleration, but it is very difficult. So at one point several months ago, while moving so rapidly, she stopped suddenly, completely turned away from the light, left, and went into illusion. But because her sincere desire is to leave this plane of existence, because her prayer is sincere and has been for years that she truly *does* wish to leave this plane of existence, it has been impossible for her to go back into illusion – *impossible* – which of course is a great benediction (not to one who is in illusion, who cannot see how this is a great benediction). Once you understand what is waiting in the true realm of existence and how pitiful and miserable this existence is here on this plane of illusion, you can understand what a benediction it is that one can *no longer be happy on this plane of illusion.* And she had come to this state, so for the entire time she has been gone, several months, every day it has been like a nightmare and suffering. Because she is sincere, because she truly desires to leave this plane of existence, because her prayer, in spite of the suffering, was so strong and sincere, now she is back, and she is facing certain things that she needs to face to break free finally from this illusion, to go beyond this illusion into the light.

You must not let anything stop you. If you truly want to find the truth, then it is here. And the assistance is here to find it. This is not a hope for the future as is set up in so many belief systems. This is hope for now. You can ask some who have come. Practically every time they come, they again grow in awareness and experience so much. They move so rapidly, not just while they are here, but while here there is a special rate of evolving that takes place. But whatever it is that stops you, that takes you away from this, whatever guise it comes in, it is just the illusion. It is just the illusion keeping you trapped. Here there is no longer an excuse, because here there is no darkness. Here there is no illusion.

All of your belief systems have built-in darkness and illusion, every single one. How many have come to a state of full realization in your belief systems? So many of you have known belief systems and practices where people have practiced for years and years. How many have you known in these organizations that have sat and cried from the love that they have felt, from ecstatic symptoms, from great growth of awareness, realization? After years and years of following these belief systems, after people have given their lives, when they die their awareness is not so great. And here we are seeing *within weeks and even days, people's consciousness is changing so rapidly.*

I have come not only to give the truth. The truth always has been there, but it is almost always so interwoven with illusion that you cannot separate them, and you become bound. You accept a belief system such as Christianity, where there is so much light; but because there is so much darkness *interwoven*, you are bound in illusion. Yes, the truth has always been there, but the illusion is so subtle – it is working its way in at every opportunity. So the truth becomes perverted so quickly that it is barely spoken before it is perverted, twisted, and contaminated. This is why so few ever achieve a state of full realization.

It will be My main business to expose the illusions, not just the illusions in the philosophies, but the illusions that you are bound by individually. Those that have known Me a little and have discussed with Me a little personally have seen so many of their illusions exposed, so many of their misconceptions exposed. I can tell you frankly, that as far as the truth is concerned, you mainly have *misconceptions*, and you truly understand very little. Even what you think you understand is contaminated with misunderstanding, misconceptions, and illusions. But I will guide you through these illusions.

What discussion, if any? Does somebody have something they wish to ask or discuss? Any issue at all? Who here wants to know the truth? Who here is seriously interested in leaving this plane of illusion? And what will stop you? Embarrassment? "Oh, I am too embarrassed to ask a question, so I will stay in darkness and illusion." How strong is your desire if you will let something like embarrassment stop you?

There are so many misconceptions about what you must do and how you must approach the truth. The biggest misconception, the biggest trap – which is the trap of all the organized philosophies – is that everyone must approach the truth in the same way, practically speaking. Yet your path toward the truth is a highly individualized thing. You cannot say, "Here is one rule and this rule applies for everybody." It is ineffective. It is like you all have a different disease, yet I give you one medicine and you all take the same medicine. But you all have a very unique disease, which needs a special prescription, a special combination of herbs to cure the problem, because you all have a different disease. Yet in these organized philosophies it's like you all have a different disease, yet I just give one medicine to all. That is why, you see, for some it works better and seems to have more of a curative effect, and for some there is very little potency, very little healing, if any at all. They achieve very little. Even those who achieve the most, because the prescription is not exactly what they need – even though they become better and more aware – they do not achieve a state of full realization. Why? Because the prescription needs to be changed constantly. As we have seen with those that have come here, the prescription is being changed. Maybe for one period of time, "this" is recommended for this period – a month or two – and now for this next period another thing is recommended. Like that. It is not that for the rest of your life you just do the same exact thing day after day, day and night, and then automatically at the end of your life, the Lord will come and save you. This is a lie.

And practically speaking, the organized philosophies are all preaching the same lie: that all of you do the same exact thing, and at the end of your lifetime, no matter what, the Lord will come, and He will save you. And it is not the truth; it is a lie. Here We are asking you to believe *enough to try it.* Not that you try for years and years, but you come and begin to experience. And as long as you are moving in your awareness and can appreciate it, then you continue to come. You will move at the rate that you desire to move and to the degree that you will let go of the illusion. Not everyone moves at the same rate, but there is *no one* who has been coming who has not moved. There is not one who has been coming who has not moved in their awareness. And some have moved *a great deal.*

Person One: Gourasana, I need some guidance with my meditation. I feel like my mind is getting in the way too much. I'm trying to let go, but my mind wants to visualize things. I'm opening up to feeling more in my meditations, but I feel like I need some guidance on where my mind is supposed to be. Should it be empty, blanked out? Can you give me some guidance?

Gourasana: One of the greatest obstacles in meditation is that one tries to understand with the mind what it is they need to do; and then they try to execute what they have figured out or concluded in their minds, or from hearing other teachings. Now, while this may give assistance, what is happening here and what you need to do is something different. We use the words over and over, and yet as easy as they are to say and to hear, what they mean is hard to grasp.

First, understand that there is a part of you *that knows exactly what to do.* Know that. Who you think you are is a being of illusion. Who you know yourself to be is all illusion. Your body, your mind with all of your thoughts and conceptions, these things are all an illusion, which will go at the time of death. But there is a *part* of you, *your true self, which knows what to do.* So in one sense, you do not need to *learn* or to *understand with your mind* what to do in order to achieve the result. It is more *with your heart.* It is more an intuitive thing.

Of course, there are obstacles that hold you back. At some point, these obstacles, as you keep running up against them, will become clear. You will have a better idea what it is you are running up against. Then private discussion with Me or in the group will help to remove those obstacles. The obstacles are always misconceptions. What *you think* you should be doing. How *you think* you should be feeling. You see? These are the main things. These are the obstacles.

So you need to practice. Practice and the association of this group would be the most powerful thing. (You have the facility to live close by and come.)

It is not something you understand with your mind. It is a fact that you have to let your mind go, because all of your thoughts and all of the nonsense you have learned is just an impediment. So many have come, and they have read so many of these books on philosophy, and so many things. It is just nonsense. It is just a barrier from the truth. It is just more traps. All of these different things: visualizations, astral plane, astral projections, so many things like that, they are just traps and obstacles. These things must be gone through and left behind.

So when you enter into meditation, you need to let go. When we enter into meditation tonight, I will discuss these steps. So you need to know, as I have said, that there is a part of you that *totally* understands what to do. So the *key* is to *let go* of the illusory part of yourself *that does not understand* and have the *faith* that your true self will be taken to the true realm of existence – which will happen. Practically it has been experienced.

(Speaking to Person Two) I do not think you would mind if I talk a little bit about your experiences?

Person Two: No, it's fine. Anything.

Gourasana: He is a very learned man, much philosophy, a professor. Is it not?

Person Two: Yes.

Gourasana: For so many years, so much knowledge and information. But as you let go of all of this, then the experience came. Did it not?

Person Two: Yes.

Gourasana: And can you say that within just a few months, that you have had extraordinary experiences when coming here?

Person Two: Deeply, deeply moving experiences.

Gourasana: The experiences that he has had are very rare in the realm of so-called spiritual seekers. In their entire lifetime of seeking, they may have one experience of which he has had a number. So again, it is not a promise that if you do this, then in a few years you will have some experience. No. You have it as soon as you let go of your illusion. You have it tonight, and that is what we will be doing. That is what we will be working for *tonight* – that *each and every one of you, each and every one of you go within and move your awareness, move further into another realm, have a direct experience, and stop settling for this pitiful existence of illusion!*

As You Endeavor, Simultaneously There Is a Result

July 9, 1988, Alpine, CA

What We are doing here is undertaking a very serious endeavor. This endeavor is to take those on this plane of illusion, which of course means everyone here, and bring them to a state of *full* awareness by the time of death – so that there is no question of rebirth. Now generally, this type of seriousness repels people, but you can take whatever degree of seriousness that you wish; you can apply to your life whatever degree of seriousness you wish. It is not that, in order to succeed, you need to immediately become one hundred percent serious – which most people mistakenly think. As you advance, as you begin to experience the true realm of existence – the spiritual realm of existence – as you begin to see the illusion that you are in and others around you are in, more and more you will naturally gravitate toward becoming more serious. First, most are not even aware that they are in illusion, nor do they have any concept at all of what is going on.

The main thing that prevents people from making serious spiritual advancement in their lives is misconception.

In your state of illusion, not knowing the truth, practically speaking, you have nothing but misconceptions. Even what understanding you do have of the truth is not correct. So because of misconceptions, most people are repelled by what We are doing here. Just as an example: Generally, on spiritual paths certain things are forbidden – such as intoxication – and there is a belief that if there is intoxication that you cannot advance spiritually. But this is not true. This is a misconception. So many will come and see that some are so serious and are doing so many things, meditating every day perhaps for hours, and they say, "Well, I cannot do that, so this is not for me." But at whatever stage you wish to begin – in spiritual life, of course, the main thing *is that you do begin* – the degree that you move will be determined by your sincerity, by your desire for the truth.

So while it is – you might say – Our main focus to try to take as many as possible from this plane of illusion once and for all, even those who perhaps need to take a few more births can make a great deal of advancement; so there is no loss. Any endeavor that you make in spiritual life is permanent – *it is never lost.* You *never* go backwards in your evolution. This is another misconception – that you ever go backwards. The reality is *everyone* is going forward in their evolution; no matter what their position, no matter what they are doing, they are going forward. The issue is *the rate* that they are going forward. Will they take one million more births, or will they take one more birth, or will this be their last birth? Like that. But ultimately, *everyone* will evolve off this plane of illusion. It is a *temporary* situation; although the time period involved is very vast, still, in eternity your existence here is just one classroom. So whatever you do, eventually you will evolve off this plane of illusion. But there are those who are ready to leave this plane, become more serious about their spiritual life, and do what is necessary to leave. And for these living entities, assistance is always provided. And that is why *I* have come: to provide assistance to those who wish to leave this plane of illusion in this lifetime. But I want to emphasize that even if you are not certain that you are truly ready *to leave* in this lifetime, there is a great facility here to move very quickly, spiritually.

So at any rate, I can discuss so many things; but if you have any questions, we will discuss them for some time before we begin the meditation.

Person One: I have a question. My question is, how can I heal that part of me that still feels inadequate, which keeps me from feeling close with God?

Gourasana: The disease is the illusion, and until the illusion is completely gone, then there is no question of complete healing. That is why I am saying, here We are interested in you coming to a state of *complete* healing. If you heal a certain degree, anyone who has made any progress spiritually knows that when they heal, they become free from some illusion; they feel some "closeness to God," as you say. They feel *some*, but it comes, it goes. So it is a question of degree. And many spiritual paths, many spiritual teachings and practices, will bring you closer, will remove some illusion. But to *completely* heal, to take away *all* illusion, to come to a state of *full* awareness, this is very rare and very difficult; so it requires special assistance, and it requires a great desire upon the part of the individual. So the question is not just how do you become closer, but how close do you want to become? Do you want to know God fully and be in a full state of awareness twenty-four hours a day, or are you going to be satisfied with some feeling of Presence, some knowing in the back of your mind, some security that God is there? You see? It is a question of degree.

Inadequacy is not the way to look at it. Everyone is adequate; it is just that everyone has a disease, and that disease is illusion. And until that illusion is removed, then you will be separate from God. And to the degree that the illusion is removed, you will come closer and know Him more truly, feel the presence more – like that. But there is nothing in you that is inadequate. It is not good to think like that, because it suggests something is wrong with you. Everyone has the same problem, and that is they are in illusion.

The job, the purpose of all great teachers throughout time has been to somehow or other communicate the truth. Of course, the truth cannot be communicated in words; this is very important to understand as you all sit here tonight. If the truth could be communicated in words, if you could come to a state of full awareness through words – so many words have been written, literally thousands of books have been written – all you would need do is go and read the books, and then you would know. But the words are only hints and suggestions: some direction, some guidance. The truth can only be found from direct experience. The mistake *almost everyone* is making is that they are following a belief system; they are taking words and structure, and they are mechanically following it, hoping for an end result. So you have different philosophies with a promise of some reward in the end.

Just like for example, in the Christian faith they say, "You do this: You accept Jesus. You try to follow these rules, and at the end of your lifetime, the Lord will personally save you, automatically" – which is not true. So you see, it is a *belief system.* It is a belief that if you behave in a certain way now, then in the future, a reward will come. This is just another trap of illusion, and though it may be ironic, the fact is that most systems of so-called spiritual paths are in and of themselves a trap. For instance, for a Christian to come to a state of full realization is difficult, because most have accepted something which is *not true* as the truth. They have accepted *words* that have promised an end result, and they *are counting on that end result.* In the same way, so many other belief systems (you can go to India, for instance, where they have hundreds of belief systems) say also the same thing, "You do different things. You do not take drugs; you pray; you chant this mantra; you do this, you do that, and at the end of your lifetime, the Lord, He will come and save you," which He will not.

So here the difference (and this is a very important difference) is though words are necessary to give guidance – because specific individual guidance *is not only necessary but essential* – the main thing that is happening here is *direct experience.* You see, *it is you going within and finding the truth* – not you believing something outside of yourself that is told to you, acting upon it and counting upon it to manifest sometime way in the future, perhaps only at death, which is what most are counting on: the Christians, so many of the Hindus, the Muslims. They are not aware *now;* they are in illusion *now,* yet they have a false hope that at the time of their death, the Lord will just come and save them – which is not true. So unfortunately, while appearing to be *a spiritual* path, it is another *trap* of illusion. Not that they do not make spiritual progress; I am not saying that. This, of course, creates some confusion, because they are *developing* more love; they are *growing* in their awareness;

certain illusions *are* dissipating, but *not enough* to come to a state of full awareness, *not enough* to never take birth again. They will just advance to whatever degree they can with their process and their desire, then they will take another birth, and again. . . .

So. More questions?

Person Two: Gourasana, in the last several months, I've seen individual attachments and misconceptions dissipate, but there are always more to take their place. Is it that I should not be working on loosening myself from these individual misconceptions, but that I should find a general total experience of freedom from misconception? I get confused about that.

Gourasana: You can move through misconceptions. You do not have to *individually* come to a conclusion, come to an understanding about your misconceptions. If you move at a certain rate, if you let go of the illusion at a certain rate, you can bypass so many of the misconceptions. Automatically, *with awareness* so many misconceptions will go – automatically. And everyone has literally hundreds of misconceptions. So every time you grow in awareness, *automatically* misconceptions go by the wayside. The main thing, the main problem is that because of the misconceptions, one is stopped in their spiritual progress or greatly slowed down – because of their misconceptions. This is the *greatest* danger of the misconception.

The ones who are trying to follow the instructions . . . let us say the Christian man: He is married; he has a nice family; he is going to church; he is a moral man. If he goes out and becomes an alcoholic or a drug addict, begins having sex with so many women, and abandons his family, then he is no longer eligible for spiritual advancement. So he gives up.

Now this is a misconception – that this makes him ineligible. And there are so many misconceptions. That is why it is so important to discuss such things.

You can all try to see and understand how many of the millions of Christians, when they deviate too much from the path as it has been laid out for them – they give up. They feel worthless because of their belief system: "Now God does not love me. I am having sex with so many women. I am taking so many drugs. Now, I am no longer on the path." So they give up, but it is a misconception. So in this way, almost every single person gives up. First of all, only a minority are seriously interested in making any spiritual advancement. And of those that begin, that go out and begin to search and go on different paths, they quickly come to a point where they become either stagnant or slowed down because of misconception: either their own misconception or a misconception that is being taught to them – just as on the Christian path.

So the primary danger of misconception is that the misconception *stops you or slows you down.* Just as we have seen over a period of months, people have left, and when you ask them why, their reply will be a misconception. In other words, it will be something that is not true. They have created a concept, *believed* that concept, and then *acted* upon that concept. This is how the illusion controls you. You come to a wrong conclusion, you *believe* that conclusion, and you *act* on that conclusion! And you are doing this in numerous ways, so *you are bound by illusion in numerous ways.* And without *personal guidance,* you will not get free of this illusion in this lifetime; because, while on the spiritual path, you will come to more misconceptions. This is why it is so rare that one comes to a state of full realization, because the paths of consciousness themselves are riddled with illusion.

Person Three: Gourasana, how can we recognize what our misconceptions are? Sometimes it's hard to see, as the saying goes, "the forest through the trees."

Gourasana: One thing is that there must be discussion. If you do not discuss what is in your mind and in your heart, then misconceptions will tend to hold you and bind you. So one must be receptive. "Receptive" does not mean mindless, that you believe anything that comes in. *"Receptive" means that you are always willing to change whatever conclusion you come to.* Because practically speaking, as you grow spiritually, every year that goes by, *everything* will change. Each and every one of you, the conclusions that you have now come to at this point are wrong. "Wrong" means that they are not ultimately the truth, or that there is contamination. So in this way your conceptions, your conclusions, will always be changing; so you must always stay in a very flexible state, in a very receptive state. Because as you go upwards to different stages, you will be able to *understand* more, understand something *clearer* so you can let go of the old way of thinking and accept the new. So you must be very receptive.

But you must also discuss. You must also take guidance. Without guidance, it is not possible – practically. You have come for some time, and you have seen others and their misconceptions. They go on and on and on, and they are compounded. A person may have a firm misconception, and upon discussion and analysis that firm misconception will be built upon a number of other misconceptions. So to open up and to discuss, to become serious, is very important. That is one critical thing.

Also, the main thing is that you go within and you find the truth for yourself; that is how all misconceptions will ultimately be eliminated. That is how you will come to a state of full awareness, because full awareness – as I have said – cannot be given through words. *But your misconceptions can stop you from finding that truth within!* Or slow you down so greatly that you will not achieve full awareness. So the words, the direction, are mainly just to remove the blockage. The words are not giving the truth. The truth cannot be put *into words*. The words are mainly to remove the blockages, the misconceptions, the things standing in your way. Then once removed, *you, yourself* go within and *you* find the truth – not a belief system, not a promise from Me. This would be an example of a promise if this were a belief system: "You come here every day. You meditate for two hours. At the end of this lifetime, the Lord will come and He will save you." And this is what the majority of the organized philosophies are all practically saying. Or whatever end result they are promising. They are saying, "Do this, you do this, you do this, and then there will be this end result."

So the misconceptions, just as in *your* question and in *your* question, they can be bypassed to a great degree. But *certain* misconceptions are holding you back, slowing you down, and in some cases stopping you. Every single person who has come moved to a certain point, knew it to be the truth, went within, moved so far, and then they stopped like they hit a wall. And if asked "Why?" their answer will be a misconception, something that can be logically spelled out, not just a belief that, "Oh, they are wrong," or "They are not understanding." But logically, it can be explained just how they have come to this misconception, and how this misconception has currently trapped them; the illusion has currently trapped them, every single one without fail. It is so obvious. Some who have left *even acknowledge* they are in the illusion. And yet they are satisfied to be in illusion.

So you could say that We also have a belief system here. But it is not a trap, because with our belief system while you are sitting here, your awareness is moving in the moment. Everyone's awareness is moving; it is just a question of degree. And this very evening even while you are sitting here, there is a potential – due to a power that is being brought in and a special guidance – for you to go within and directly experience so many aspects of the true realm of existence: the spiritual realm, what the Christians call the Kingdom of God. The words – do not become lost in the words. So yes, you could say it is a belief, but it is a belief that you can practically experience now – not when you die. It is Our belief, and We see it happening all the time: that if your desire is strong, if you are sincere, if you truly want to find out what is going on through *direct experience, not some words* – "Oh here is another one promising; there are thousands promising so many things" – here We are saying you can go within and directly experience it yourself. And the rate at which you can move is dramatic. So the very few who have not gone back into illusion, who have chosen to keep going, do not even need to discuss very much, occasionally a question or two. They just come, they sit down, and they go within. But those that are not sincere, those that do not care – their misconception, their belief, will not allow them to do this. Whatever the reason, whatever the conclusion someone comes to that takes them away from this internal process, is illusion.

Very few truly want to become free from illusion. Spiritual life, to most, means a little light in their life. They become a little happier in this plane of illusion: relieve some of the anxiety, relieve some of the pressure. So, for them, going to a psychiatrist or going to church or going to temple – they are all basically the same thing. They are looking for a little relief, a little light to make their stay here on this plane of illusion happier. But they are not serious at all about spiritual life. They just would like a little relief. To *leave*, to *leave* this plane of existence is not conceivable, nor is it desired. No. They *want* to stay in illusion. And "searching" for the majority that are searching spiritually means: searching for a process that will give them enough happiness to at least tolerate this plane of illusion. Some drink a little; some take some intoxication; some play some sports. There are many different ways people try to find some happiness in illusion. Also, in the spiritual processes, the majority are just looking for some relief – *just enough to be happy on this plane of illusion.* And once that is achieved there is no need for further searching, because they are satisfied.

But they are bound in illusion with no hope of getting free from the illusion. They have received enough light, enough love, to be a little happy on this plane of illusion. So they are satisfied; they search no further; they question no further. And when approached and discrepancies in their beliefs are pointed out, they do not care to hear. Why? Because *they are satisfied. They are happy to be in the illusion that they are in.* They are happy to be in that state of illusion, and they have no desire to upset their happiness in illusion.

Carol: That's why when they hear something like this, they want to get away from it as fast as they can?

Gourasana: Yes. It makes them very uncomfortable – *very uncomfortable,* because it is the truth. Someone who is serious and they just have a disagreement in philosophy, they would at least take enough energy to challenge and say, "Well, I do not agree. I think that you are mistaken in this area." If they were serious about spiritual life, if they truly cared about the truth, after they spent so much time coming here, they could spend another few minutes challenging. But they are not serious. They are not serious.

Is there any need for discussion?

Cindy: I have a question, Gourasana. I find it increasingly difficult to communicate with people, including several of my friends, outside of this group. It becomes very uncomfortable. They want to know what is happening to me, and they place their judgments on me. I find myself wanting to isolate myself from them. I feel like I'm becoming more alienated, and I'm comfortable with that. But, is this okay to feel this way and to do this? Or should I be talking to them and be opening up and let them place their judgments on me?

Gourasana: No, you should not open up to those that are not receptive. It will hurt you; it will weaken you.

Cindy: What do I tell my close friends about what is going on with me? I do not know what to say.

Gourasana: You say you are meditating to find the truth. And as they begin to know all about Me, eventually you can just say, this is a teacher who is guiding me in my meditations, giving me advice on how to meditate. I am achieving results, and I am becoming happier. But better to say your awareness is increasing. That what you are doing here is you are meditating; you are going within, and you are experiencing another realm of existence. Just state it very simply. You do not have to elaborate; you do not have to preach or to encourage them. You can see, especially when you get to a certain state of awareness, who is interested – not too difficult, because most are not. Even the ones who were here, who are supposedly seeking, are not truly interested – what to speak of just a person on the street. So you just make light of it; it is not important what your belief is. For example, the Christians and people with different beliefs all work in the same place – and you are just known as a Christian, or you are just known as a Hindu, or you are just known as someone who meditates. You do not have to make a big thing of it so that it creates disturbance in your interaction with those around you. You can just say you meditate and it is *very* important to you; you are having good experiences and there is someone there who is teaching and helping you at this time.

Person Three: Gourasana, Carol and I were discussing how lonely it is socially, because people don't understand what we feel and what we go through. Nor do we feel compelled to share it with them, because we understand they really don't understand. In that way, it does make us feel very lonely, interacting amongst many people, even so-called intimate family members, because it's such an internal process.

Gourasana: So you take that loneliness and you go within, and you will find the association of those who will stop that feeling of loneliness. Do not try; do not endeavor at all to satisfy this loneliness from the others around you on the plane of illusion – as you say, even intimate family members. You take that loneliness, *that need* for someone else, for a relationship, for love, reciprocation, and you go within and you will find *full* reciprocation, and you will not be lonely at all. You will find the greatest "social" contact, the greatest. Here on this plane of illusion, at best, you may have a few friends. But if you take this desire and you go within, you have unlimited association – wonderful, pure, unconditional love association. It is a difficult transition, because one is not feeling that association so much at first. But during those times of loneliness, when you feel no one around you satisfies that deep heartfelt feeling of need for someone to understand you and to communicate with, you will *only* be fully satisfied by going within and finding that association of other living entities who understand completely. Even with this group the association amongst members is still only going to be satisfactory to a degree. You see?

Like you say, you cannot associate with others on this plane, because they are in illusion. They have no desire to learn the truth, so you have no grounds for communication. You cannot become close to them; you cannot share with them. Then ultimately, what do you want to share? Not just your experiences, but ultimately *your love*. But you cannot even get past the social barriers created by their judgments, their beliefs, their illusion – let alone share true love with them.

You want to leave this plane of illusion and go to the true realm of existence. *That* is the association that you want to seek, because once you leave this plane of illusion, that is all the association *you will have. And of course, that is everything!* So now, although there may be some sadness and a feeling that it is unfortunate that you cannot share as you would like to with so many others around you – you even lose your best friend, or there is separation from mother, father, brother, sister – that cannot be helped if they are going to stay in illusion and you are leaving.

It is not possible for the separation not to be there. The alienation will be there. You must find the satisfaction from the association of the true realm of existence, because there everyone will understand you perfectly and they will reciprocate with you perfectly. And the more you experience, and the more your consciousness expands, no matter how greatly it expands, they will understand completely. It is the perfect complement, and there will not be *any lack*.

And not only that, because of the state of awareness that you will come to through associating with living entities *not* in illusion, your love and your relationship with those that you now feel alienated from will become better. *Even though these people hate you, even though they reject you and judge you and condemn you and hate you, your relationship, your feeling toward them will be better and better until it comes to a point – as it is with everyone in the true realm – of unconditional love for everyone.* That does not mean that you will choose to be around them, if nothing else because it is a waste of time; you do not have time to waste – but your love for them will increase, and your relationship with them will become better and better and better, but only if you find that love on the true realm of existence. If you futilely try to make relationships work on this plane of illusion with others in illusion that will not move from their illusion – even if you try to find full satisfaction with each other – then you will be stunted in your growth.

Person Four: Gourasana, how do you operate in the business world where so many are in illusion and you feel this alienation, and in order to get business done, you have to play certain games with them? I find that to be difficult. On a personal level, you can choose not to relate with people you're not comfortable with, but in the business world, you have to deal with people constantly and play the game. People want to do business with people they get along with. You understand?

Gourasana: Yes. And that is what it is like. For certain social obligations you feel that you need to meet with business associates and family members, that is exactly what you are doing: You are playing a game; you are playing their game. And you can be good friends with everyone because you are so detached – you see. When you are in illusion, you have a *certain* game that you are playing, but when you see *all* of the illusion, you can play *any* of the games. So you can more easily associate. You can, through seeing the illusion and understanding the illusion, actually associate with a much wider variety of people more intimately, because you just understand their illusion. You play their game with them, whatever their illusion may be. Of course, you are not involved to the point where your activity becomes like theirs, but just in discussion with them, you can play the game.

Person Four: So that is okay, that's part of it?

Gourasana: Of course. Of course. And it is more peaceful. They do not even need to have any knowledge of your awareness, and you can go from one individual to another, and they will all consider you to be a friend and understand them. And your relationship with people can become better and better, simply because you play their game. And the illusions, of course, are unlimited. One man is afraid of the nuclear holocaust, and when you are with this man, this is his prime topic – you can discuss with him, you know. If you need to discuss something, if there needs to be some social interaction, you can play the game: "Oh, yes, I am so afraid we are going to be killed anytime." And whatever he says, you can just say it back. Then there is no antagonism or friction.

You do not go into the church of Christians and say, "You are all in illusion and you will never get out, and it is a lie that the Lord Jesus is going to save you at the time of death." What is the point? If someone is not open to change and the truth, why waste your energy? And why not be friendly with them, because ultimately they also will leave, and the oneness with them is there. They are just in illusion, and you are not in illusion to the same degree. So if you have a Christian friend, you can use the positive side: "How wonderful that you have a connection with the Lord Jesus." Diplomatic. Practice diplomacy. Do not become agitated. If you are going around to people and you are agitating them, then you are not behaving properly. Unless, of course, you are specifically on that mission, like I am. I agitate many people. It is not My purpose to come here to give peace to people's minds. Although if someone comes and is not going to leave the illusion, also, I can behave diplomatically. There is no use in creating turmoil in the world. What is hard in the relationship is if you are trying to break through their illusion, which is almost impossible. If you will let go *of that* and just play the game, things become very easy.

Person Four: You're not sacrificing yourself playing the games; you're just doing that in order to make peace?

Gourasana: Yes, of course. How can you sacrifice? You can use it as a tool to become more aware. You can sit and discuss with someone their illusion and be an observer while you are speaking. Just see how deeply the person is in illusion, and observe all the facets of this person's illusion. You can grow from this experience and walk away from it more aware. What have you sacrificed?

It is not your duty to go out and save the world! You cannot do that.

Now we will have people that will be going and preaching, but they will only preach to those that truly want to hear. But *anyone preaching* is going to create agitation. *My* speaking, the things that I say to those that are sincere, frequently creates agitation. They become disturbed. But as far as in the workplace, social interaction on the job, you are not sacrificing anything.

The reality is, very few want to leave the illusion, so there's no sense to talk to them. They will get out eventually. They certainly do not want to come here. So there is no need to try to preach to them to come here, if they are not interested in leaving the illusion and finding the truth. What would be the purpose? If you want to help someone spiritually, then you can find some other place to send them. If there is some way you want to help, you can try to help them a little bit in some other way.

But there is no requirement that you go out and preach and speak only the truth. That is not required at all. It will be a waste of energy and it will create disturbance. Better to be diplomatic. The misconceptions come so quickly. This is not only a problem with both of you that have raised this, but I know for anyone working with others in illusion, this is always a problem. So you very gently talk to people in very general terms, and you listen very carefully. In this way you become aware – what are they saying, truly? And if they are open to some truth, then you can give them some truth. Not that you have to give them the whole thing, you understand: "They come here; they listen to Gourasana; they become free from this plane of illusion, and they never take birth again." You can just enlighten them, and they can make some spiritual advancement and become a little happier in their life.

As you become expert at this, people will welcome your association no matter what walk of life they are in – because as your *love truly grows*, as your unconditional love truly grows and you really care for the individuals, they will know that in their hearts when you are with them. You can be with someone who is a drug addict or an alcoholic, or a religious, very moral person – all kinds of people you can be with and be best of friends with at work. Outside of work, there is no time for social interaction, and people will just have to know that you are too busy to have that. That is one area that the line must be drawn. You do not carry social interaction to the point where outside of work you are wasting your time, because your time is too precious to waste. And if they are offended by that, you try your best through discussion to work it out – but that is where the line must be drawn. While at work, things can be fine. You can make it pleasurable, actually, and people will look forward to being with you, because although they do not know what is going on, sometimes they may say something to you, and because of *your awareness* you will be able to give true wisdom; you will be able to give truth. And it will strike their hearts: they will act upon it, become happier, and feel a greater bond with you. In this way you can become intimate with someone. Of course, some are just crazy and there will never be a relationship, so you can at least keep things smooth. But do not feel obligated or feel that you are doing anything wrong by not converting them or by not pointing out their illusion. Most do not want the illusion pointed out, because they have chosen to be in it. So not only does it do no good to point out the illusion, it does harm.

This is the rule for preaching: First, you see what areas of illusion this person would like to have dispelled, and then you become expert at gently dispelling those areas. Not that you mindlessly are going out and preaching to everyone to become free from illusion, when practically nobody cares. This is why people who proselytize are so unpopular, because they are talking to people who have no interest at all; they just create disturbance and agitation and become unpopular figures. *Especially* what we are teaching here can create disturbance. The Christian will find many, many candidates that will listen, but for what we are teaching here, they will be very tiny in number – very tiny.

At any rate, do not concern yourself with converting or teaching others the truth. Work with social interaction and *understanding them and their illusion.* Use it as a meditation. Understand each person and their illusion, and your own awareness will grow because of it. And you will become happier in the workplace because of it. This is how many great men and women become leaders. Why are they so first-class and have gotten to such positions of power? (Not that that is our desire.) Because they can deal with a wide variety of people in all sorts of illusions, and whoever they are with feels like they are their best friend or a good friend at least. So they become *so popular* that they have thousands of people who will vote for them, make them important.

Anyway, I have gone on at some length about this; this is one area where the recording should be transcribed, because this is a constant dilemma for those in the workplace. You must learn how to adapt and take something which is agitating or bad, see it positively, and turn it around in the way we have discussed – and there are other ways. But this is the way your awareness will grow. *You become aware.* Not that you go in and say, "Oh, they are all in illusion; they just all want to stay in illusion; they are all crazy; I just want to get out." Well, perhaps that may be what you are supposed to do, but for the majority, you should try to be diplomatic and work with a variety of people. Everyone can benefit from this exercise.

Grace Is When the Momentum Comes from Nowhere

August 6, 1988, Alpine, CA

To come to a full state of awareness, to leave this plane of existence in this lifetime, one must be prepared to give up everything: every attachment, every trace of ego, every desire for enjoyment on this plane. Ultimately, this must be done. This is confirmed by all the great saints, sages, and masters throughout the centuries. But one may think, "I do not want to give up so many things, so this is not for me." To *truly* give something up, one must be totally detached from it; which means that the illusion surrounding the thing must be totally dispelled. If there were no illusions, if there were no attachments, then you would already be in the state of full awareness. But too many stop because they say, "I do not want to give that up," or "I do not want to give this up." But your desire will change as you become more aware, and the giving up will become automatic. You will not need to make such a special endeavor to give up the thing that *now* you cannot conceive of stopping.

Most misunderstand this "giving up" that is talked about in all great teachings, and they stop artificially. So they are constantly unhappy, constantly hankering for the thing that they have stopped, because the stopping did not come from awareness; it came from something artificial – as if when you stop *the activities* of this plane of illusion, *the illusion* will stop. But it has been proven by so many paths and organizations where the members stopped so many things they desired to do: to engage in sex, to take intoxication, to have different types of recreation, whatever. For years they stopped and did none of these things, but in their hearts, the whole time they longed for them. So in actuality, their giving up became an obstacle to truly giving it up.

So you should not worry, be concerned, or think it is not possible to give this, or this, or this up, because once you reach a certain stage of awareness, *automatically* you will be detached from that desire. You will not have to make a *separate* endeavor. *Automatically* as the illusion goes away, your desire for the activity will go away, and you will be free from the illusion.

In all of the great teachings, there is always some discussion, if not a great deal, indicating that it is necessary at some point to be free from sexual activity. Misunderstanding how to approach this, most in these processes artificially try to stop, and of course they are just frustrated because the desire is still there; the illusion is still there. Stopping the activity does not decrease the desire. Of course, it can *increase* it. So one hears this and they look at their *own* desire, and they think, "This is not possible; I cannot even attempt it. I am desiring sex daily, and ultimately I will want to stop it entirely? So I just will not even try to stop, *because I have the desire*." *What a terrible mistake that is,* because once the illusion surrounding the activity is broken, then the desire will be broken. And it will become just one more thing in this world that you will not want to do. It will hold no *special* significance for you. Now this may take many years, but there are so many things, in the meantime, to work on.

The only thing binding you to this plane is illusion, and if you will make a continuous effort in your life, the illusion can be broken. You do not have to stop an activity and suffer because you are not performing that activity. This is the mistaken thinking of most – so most do not even try. They are so attached to this plane that they do not even consider that they might want to leave. If the thought of leaving this plane of existence in this lifetime – even though We speak of this frequently – is inhibiting you in any way, then you should just ignore the words and just advance as much as you can, as much as you desire. Because there will come a point where what is not conceivable to you now will become very conceivable.

There comes a point in your progress where you can let go at a very rapid rate. One may endeavor for ten years and seem to not make so much progress, and then in the eleventh year, give up eighty percent of their material activities. And then be moving so fast that they can see the light at the end of the tunnel. They can *see* that it is possible. At the beginning of the path when one is beginning the search, it seems *impossible*; their attachment to so many things is so great it seems *impossible*, so most do not endeavor. And of the ones who do endeavor, most of them artificially try to give up activities, thinking, "If I do not perform sexual activity for ten or twenty years, eventually it will go away," but the whole time harboring the desire for sex so they are really inhibiting their advancement. It can be helpful to stop activities, but it is not the true way to break free from the illusion. The illusion will only be gone *when you see it* for what it is, when you see the illusion. When the illusion is broken, then the desire for the activity *will just be gone*, and you just will not perform it, because you will have no desire to.

One thing after another will be like this; you will just lose the desire. And simultaneously your desire for the light, for the truth, for the spiritual experiences, will increase. And where once in your life you hankered for sexual activity, you will hanker for spiritual ecstasy, for spiritual experience. But do not *artificially* try to assume that position, and do not let anyone pressure you or persuade you to artificially assume that position. "Oh, you are still having sex? That is not good. You cannot be fully aware and be having sex or smoking cigarettes or taking some intoxication." This is how it starts.

One thing for sure is there must be some endeavor in your life. There must be some continuing spiritual endeavor. Even if one is very young, and just beginning their life – like a young couple who have just been married and who are so involved with material activities – even if at the end of their day their minds would just turn to the truth for a few minutes, it would help their progress toward the light so much. They just need to remind themselves that they are in a plane of illusion – even while they are caught in it, even while they are voluntarily accepting and enjoying the illusion, by being a little aware *that it is an illusion, they will be breaking the bond of illusion.* So one may enjoy the illusion of family, children, sex, and so many other things, but if part of them remains aware and stands back and sees, "This is an illusion. Still I am going to enjoy this illusion, but it *is* an illusion," this will speed the breaking of the bonds of illusion – so fast.

But most teachers will mislead you on this point. They will say, "No, you must break it now. You must not be attached. You must not engage in these activities. These things are sinful, and God is repulsed by these activities." These teachers are suggesting that when you engage in these activities, God goes somewhere else, because He cannot tolerate your bad behavior. Such nonsense; another trick of the illusion.

At the same time, don't let *anything* stop you from progressing. The degree that you want to work on your spiritual life may vary, and of course we encourage you to do as much as possible. But you *need* to do something. For those that are moving quickly, that want to leave this plane of existence, that have made that decision, even if half-heartedly – *there can be no reason, no excuse, why you would stop.* You must let *nothing* stop you. *If you allow anything to stop you, no matter what it is, it means the illusion has trapped you.* You have succumbed to the illusion.

Knowing how much to do, the proper balance, is a delicate thing. So many fanatically over-endeavor. They do more, take on more than they truly desire or can handle, and artificially stop the activities. And then because they have placed themselves in a position that they cannot maintain, eventually they just stop their spiritual endeavor. They become frustrated. They gave all their effort and then became frustrated.

Such a difficult thing to communicate. On one hand I am saying, do everything you possibly can, but on the other hand, *there is a question of over-endeavor.* Give yourself some room. Do not become so bound by the activities that you have taken on that you cannot deviate from them without some guilt or fear that you will not make it. *Only you can decide this,* and it is a very delicate, *very* delicate balancing.

So many times you will see in organizations that people give their whole lives and work day and night, and they become spiritually frustrated, so they enter into some perverted material lifestyle, as has happened with some leaders of spiritual movements. They are trying to behave like a saint when they are not a saint, and because they preach that you have to behave like a saint in order to belong, they cannot lower that facade. So when their desire overwhelms them, and they perform an activity that is against the teachings, then they are finished – and so often they just abandon their spiritual life. Better to have steady progress throughout your life – daily doing something, trying to increase your progress, and continuing to increase every day throughout your whole lifetime – rather than to artificially take on too much.

Person One: Gourasana, what if our largest attachment is to our job, work, in order to support us, give us food and shelter? Eventually, do you have to detach from that and all the things connected with that? And if so, how do you support yourself?

Gourasana: You can perform an activity and be detached from it – but frequently the activity needs to be changed. For instance, many are *over-endeavoring* in the area of making money, because their original desire was for so much money, for so much advancement, because they needed so many things. But as their material desires decrease, there is need for less and less and less money. Your existence can be reduced to something very simple. Frequently there is a need to change or to adjust your mentality. For instance, if one is in a corporation, they may be happy to stay where they are instead of having that continuing desire to constantly compete and go up and up. They can do the work properly where they are and become detached from it, be satisfied with it, and learn how to be peaceful performing the activity. But if the activity is impossible to perform and remain peaceful, then you must look at it; then you must look at your priorities.

But again, care must be there that it is not an artificial change. There are so many factors – the age of the person, the desires of the person. If one has a good position, is making a good income, is young, and has so many desires that have not been fulfilled – they want a family, children, house, and cars – then for them to stop that work and try to live simply could be, *could be* a negative thing to do.

But you see? You cannot give a general instruction. It is so highly individualized. I am not saying that everyone who has these desires should just allow them to manifest and not do anything to check them, or to control them, or to balance them. But no two situations are alike. Where one man will be happy sleeping under a tree and bathing in a lake, another man will only be happy if he has a nice house and a car. Both will be peaceful in that state. But still, the man with the house and the car can advance spiritually if his life is arranged properly. This does not mean that he cannot achieve the same end result as the man under the tree – if he pays attention and is careful.

You see, it can also be the opposite. The man under the tree may desire the house and car, and he may be frustrated in his spiritual growth because he is artificially trying to give up. And the man with the house and the car may be moving spiritually, becoming detached and seeing that the house and the car are just an illusion, and becoming free – whereas the man under the tree is still desiring and locked into illusion.

Or the opposite can be true. The man under the tree can be free, remain free, and move so rapidly because he is not caught up or does not have the danger of being caught up. And the man in the house just becomes more and more caught: bigger house, more things for the house, bigger car, more cars, more money for the house, cars, wife, children. So you cannot just say one thing.

So few achieve full awareness, because while they will give so much thought to their profession and perhaps so much thought to the raising of their family and to all of their material needs, they will not give the thought and the time and the effort to understand themselves and their desires. Rather than coming to a point of understanding, more often than not they will just become frustrated, develop a misconception, and give up. And that is the only way you will not succeed is if you give up. As long as you are sincere and continue, no matter what your position, you can succeed in this lifetime.

Another term for full awareness is *self awareness*. You must begin to be aware of yourself, even your illusory self. How are you going to deal with this? How are you going to work with this? Just like you do not go into the woods, capture a wild horse, and immediately expect to saddle the horse and have a child ride it; there is a first step, a second step, and a third step. You must be aware, be realistic, and understand what the steps are to tame and control a horse. You do not *artificially* try to force the horse to be still and get on him; otherwise it can be disastrous. It is like that with your mind and with your desires. You must understand what they are *and work with them.* Just like with the horse – give it some rein. So you must give your desires some rein.

This philosophy that you stop everything is so disastrous. The examples are endless of people who have practically destroyed their own lives by *artificially* trying to assume a state of consciousness that is not real. They see a saint who is beyond sexual drive, beyond attachment, who is beyond intoxication, who is beyond the comforts of houses and automobiles – who is truly beyond and totally happy with whatever little thing comes his way: a little food, a tree to sleep under. So artificially, they copy the saint, but because their hearts are not changed, then at some point something worse can happen – their consciousness can become demented. Even if they carry on this suppression of their desires up until death, they will take birth again, because they have not freed themselves from the illusion. If they still think there is something wonderful in the sexual activity – even if they have stopped it – as long as they think that, the illusion is not broken, and they will have to take birth until they can see through the illusion.

Cindy: Gourasana, what if you reach a point in your spiritual awakening where very quickly you want to give up so much in your life? Let's say maybe seventy-five percent of everything in your life you want to give up. Is there any danger in giving all that up all at once?

Gourasana: No. But if you do, and it is truly your desire, you will move at a very great rate. If you are going to undertake such a serious spiritual endeavor (which We are trying to at least get a few to do), you must pay *very close attention.* Pay very close attention to your mind, your desires, and your spiritual progress, because there will be so much activity going on.

But no, it is good if you desire it. Mainly I am speaking of outside influence pressuring someone to behave: Like let's say in this group, if several who have totally stopped sexual activity go to one who is engaged in a great deal of sexual activity and they put some peer pressure on them. This is how it happens in the organizations: "Oh, this is just an illusion, you should just stop it." And somehow the person is persuaded against their will, because they do not want to appear to be not spiritual or not serious – whatever. That is what I am speaking of: doing something that is not your desire, but someone else's desire. Like in the organizations they have blanket rules: "You join *this* church, you cannot smoke. You join *this* church, you cannot take intoxication. You join *this* religion and if you perform sex, then it is sinful and God will punish you." Like that. This is what I am speaking of, mainly.

No. If it is your desire, you can give up as much as you can and then more and more and move very, very rapidly. But at the point that you are letting go of everything, of course, that is ultimately the stage that We want you to come to. I am just warning of the danger of doing this artificially. Someone may come, and they may see several people stopping so many activities. And they may feel some peer pressure, or because they are used to social equality, they may feel that to be part of the group, they need to behave like the rest of the group; even though no one verbally persuades them, they try to artificially behave like the rest.

Person Two: Gourasana, in the last few weeks it seems you've spoken a great deal about this matter of sexuality. Is this because this is a major problem or distraction for people on the spiritual path? Or is this a problem for *this* group? Are you speaking of this so much because this household has that problem and that attachment to a greater extent? Or is it something that all people must find a way of accommodating?

Gourasana: It is a great illusion, and all illusion must go. So it is emphasized in all of the great teachings in one way or another. In different teachings, stages are even suggested. One man may not be able to have sex with just one woman, so he has sex with so many. The next step for him may be to become married and have sex with just *one* woman. That is a step toward ultimately becoming free from the illusion. You can take different steps as you are ready to take them. But it is certainly one of the most powerful illusions. *And it is an illusion.* You must become free of it, because it is just an illusion.

But again someone hears this who has great desire for sexual activities and they think, "Oh, this is not for me," because they have the desire. So I am trying to emphasize that that is all right. You have *so many* desires. You have *so many* attachments. You have *so many* illusions. It is just one more. Do not let that stop you. When the illusion is gone, the desire will disappear, and automatically you will cease the activity without such a tremendous struggle. So do not worry or let this disturb your mind on the spiritual path, because when you are bound by an illusion – especially in the case of sexual desire – it is almost impossible to see how you will ever become free and actually not even care to engage in the activity. But once the illusion is broken, then the desire is the same as all the other illusions that have been broken. It is just *not there*; you just no longer *care* to engage in the activity.

How you approach these different things is very important. For one person, one thing is more important than another; one thing is easier than another. One may give up sexual activity early in life, yet have desire for a great deal of money that remains for many years, whereas another may not care for any money, but the sex desire may be more important. So you need to *understand* your desires and the binding influence that they have on you so that you can deal with them accordingly.

But you do not want to become frustrated. This is very important. You do not want to become frustrated. "Oh, I've been meditating for so many years, and I still want to have sex. I still want to make money. I still want a nice car." As I said, you may go on for ten years and seemingly make little advancement, and then suddenly in the eleventh year it will all manifest, and you'll move so quickly. So many things that were not possible to achieve in the first ten years, you can overcome in one year. But there must be endeavor. You must care. There must be desire.

Person Two: You said we never move backward. Is this a form of momentum that we can expect to experience more and more as we continue to practice? Is this what is meant by grace?

Gourasana: Grace is when the momentum comes from nowhere. Suddenly, you are in an intense position, on an intense spiritual search, where perhaps one or two years ago, you were not at all. Suddenly, you find yourself totally involved in an intense spiritual search. That is grace.

But again, one can move so quickly. Then they come to a point where there is something to let go of and they do not want to, so they try to stop their spiritual progress, misunderstanding the situation. You can still hold on to some attachment and advance spiritually. As you advance in other areas, the thing you are holding on to will gradually reduce, and the bind on you will gradually reduce. So those that come to the conclusion, "I can give up everything, but I cannot give up *this*, so I will just resign myself to another lifetime" – it is just a trick of the illusion. They are surrendering to the illusion at that point. At the moment you give up, at the moment you stop, that is the moment you have decided not to succeed.

Cindy: Gourasana, what if you reach a point where you have an attachment you want to give up – you want to want to give it up, and you want to move spiritually beyond the point where you don't want it anymore? What can you do to get over this attachment? In other words, you know your attachment is there and you don't want it to be there.

Gourasana: Increase your spiritual activities. An increase in spiritual activities means a decrease in material activities. So you can pray. You can meditate. As your awareness increases, the thing will lose its hold on you. The illusion will become weaker as you meditate. I am not saying to not endeavor. So many words must be spoken to just try to clarify one issue. I am not saying that you do not make *any* endeavor and wait until everything disappears. There is a need for *some* endeavor at a certain point. In other words, you may be ready to stop sexual activity, which is one of the greatest binding factors, and it may require some endeavor, but self awareness means *you will know* when it is *truly* time for you to stop and you will make that endeavor. You will not feed the fire of that illusion. You will say, "I know I am ready to do without that now. And while there is still *some* desire, I will let that desire die, because it is near its end." So there is some effort. Prayer, meditation, and other spiritual practices, whatever your spiritual practices are, can be there.

Cindy: What if the attachment is a child? If you have a child and you need to care for that child, can you come to a completely detached state and still raise that child?

Gourasana: Yes. You can raise the child better, because you will have the proper vision of who this child is and their true nature. In the state of illusion, you are thinking, "Oh, this is *my* child." From this illusion of trying to control the child, so many negative things can result. So many parents become estranged from their children when they begin to rebel. They become enemies. They cannot communicate. It is good the child rebels against the parents. Because of the parents' attachment and their belief that they are totally responsible and totally controlling the destiny of the child, they can stifle and hurt the growth of the child as well as hurt their relationship.

But from a spiritual, detached point of view they can relate in such a way to the child that the child can grow free. This does not mean undisciplined. But there is a freedom that the child is given that allows them to grow as they should without being stifled. So many are stifled that they leave home. Thousands and thousands cannot even tolerate their parents. The children are so stifled, because the parents have a fixed idea of how the child should behave. And if the children are not behaving like the parents want, the parents cannot tolerate it because of their attachment.

So some *de*tachment must be there. Detachment does not mean without love. Actually, *detachment* brings in more real love. Attachment is a love mixed with a fear. So the more *attached* you are, the more contaminated is your love for your child. The more *detached* you are, the purer is your love for your child, and the purer your love is, the better you can raise the child. So yes, you can be detached, but "detached" does not mean without love. "Detached" means a *pure* love, a more *real* love. "Attached" means that the love can change. Like the parent who loves the child so much, but when the child tells the parent to die, leave them alone, the parent sometimes begins to hate the child. They fight and they become enemies. That results from *attachment*. With *detachment* that does not happen. So attachment can produce very negative results and produce a very bad relationship between the parent and child. And attachment does not let pure love come through. But in a state of pure love, the relationship can be very sweet, no matter what the child is going through.

So if someone is raising a child, they should try to do it from a point of spiritual awareness, not so much from the material awareness standpoint: "They must have this and this and this, and if they do not, they will not be happy. If they do not have this education, then they will not succeed. They will not make enough money, then they will not have the family that they should have, and they will not live like they should. They will be poor, therefore they will be unhappy," on and on. The better way to raise a child is not with material awareness (how to succeed on this plane of illusion) but with spiritual awareness; that is the best way. From spiritual awareness, if the child is inclined spiritually, then you can help them so much. But even if they want the material, if you are spiritually aware, you will also allow that without disturbance, because you will see things from a spiritual point of view and know that yes, so now they wish to engage in so many materialistic activities, but there will come a point. . . . How many parents and children cannot even talk to each other – have no true communication? Most.

Person One: Gourasana, I need to more clearly understand the actual concept of the word "illusion." My mind keeps getting stuck on that "illusion" means "unreal." Is anything really happening on the physical plane? Or is it an illusion? Or is it happening on some other spiritual dimension? I'm confused about exactly what that means. Also how that relates to us creating our own reality?

Gourasana: The most important aspect of your question is that you wish to understand it clearly, and you must give up this attachment. To think that you can understand *clearly* would mean that the factors, the aspects of all that is going on can be categorized and neatly laid out in a way that you can *clearly* see it. This is not possible. On this plane of *illusion*, some things can be clearly seen, like in the construction of a house. You can see there is a foundation . . . this and this, et cetera. Clearly you can understand. Certain laws of physics can be clear. So things on this plane of illusion, the material things can be clearly understood. But when you enter the spiritual realm, you must let go of *this* desire to clearly understand. It is another obstacle. I am just saying, not trying to discourage you, but it is another stumbling block. There are so many.

If nothing else, the stumbling blocks that I have mentioned so far since I have been here – and there are so many more – should just be listed, because *so many stumbling blocks* are preventing your spiritual growth, and for each stumbling block that I've mentioned, there are thousands who are stifled in their spiritual growth. And this one, that is stifling many thousands, is that at first they believe they need to *clearly* understand what is going on, that they cannot come to a full state of awareness unless they *clearly* understand all the aspects. But how can you *clearly* understand what is infinite? How can you understand *clearly* that you can go in any direction eternally, and you will never come to an end, and yet it is all *right here?* The mind cannot even *clearly* understand what is taking place on *this* plane. When it comes to facts – how things are functioning, how things are going on, on *this* plane of existence which you can see, touch, and feel, and which scientists can study – still there are so many misconceptions, so many misunderstandings, and it is so unclear on this plane; what to speak of understanding the spiritual realm.

If you demand clarity, you must be satisfied with – I hesitate to use the word – but it is like a certain "vagueness." If you *demand* clarity, if you demand to *see* it and completely *understand* it as you go through it, or as you experience it – then you will lose it. You must give up *all desire to understand,* because ultimately, as you come closer and closer to the mark of full awareness, *you will not desire to understand it at all.* You will just *be – aware.*

And this frustration of first trying to clearly understand it is stifling the growth of so many. They say, "I cannot understand it, therefore I cannot accept it. If I cannot clearly understand it, then I cannot accept it. First I must clearly understand it, or at some point along the path I must clearly understand it." But I am saying, and it is true, that you cannot *clearly* understand it. Where does this clear understanding come from? It comes from your conscious mind, which is limited, which must be left behind when you enter the true realm of existence. And what is unlimited, what is infinite, what is ever-changing, what is beyond your comprehension, of course, cannot be clearly understood.

When one *tries* to clearly understand, naturally confusion happens; *naturally* confusion is there. So as a result most are confused about spiritual life, and to make it easy and to stop the confusion, they join an organization that makes everything very clear. It may not be the truth, but it is very clear. There is no need to think any more: "Jesus came to save you; you accept Him into your heart, try to follow a few guidelines, and at the end of your life, He will come and save you." You do not have to be confused, or concerned, or think or worry any more. So it is like an easy way out – you think. But of course it does not work.

It is a very good question, and it is a very important answer. You must give up all desires. To try to understand what is happening to you as you grow spiritually can be a *tremendous stumbling block,* and frequently is. Better you just experience. Do not try to understand it with your mind. Better you just experience and let the experience go on and on and on. The more you try to think about it, understand it, and hold on to it with your mind, the more you slow down the progress; the more you slow down the experience. Do not spend your time *dwelling* on what happened, because you are living in the past. Rather, spend your time *experiencing* what is *happening now.* Not trying to understand it, but *experiencing* it. *You try to feel it; you try to experience it.* But to try to *understand* it is a stumbling block.

It cannot be put into words. The moment you put it into words, the moment it goes into your thoughts and becomes words, then it is no longer the truth, because the truth cannot be put into words. You can say it is *something* like this. This is why We are always emphasizing that the words mean practically nothing. They are just giving some guideline, some hint. This is why when we discuss like this, you want to try to hear from your heart, not try to understand with your head, with your mind. To sit here and try to figure it out, and try to see it clearly, and try to understand it with your mind will slow you down. You can spend the time, just as we have spent so much time already, and you may not even remember the words so much – maybe a few key points that were made that are pertinent to you – but more important is an awareness that you can let grow in your heart. You will just automatically have an awareness that will direct your behavior, rather than understanding something with your mind that directs your behavior.

Person One: Can you comment on the concept of us creating our own reality?

Gourasana: You create what you desire. If you want to come to a state of full awareness, that will be your reality. You will come to that reality. If you desire something else, you will come to that reality. Practically, minute-by-minute, you are making changes in your direction – minute changes in your direction that lead you ultimately to different areas. And if they do not manifest in *this* life, they will manifest in a future life. So one may desire wealth his whole life and never have an opportunity to achieve it, but that desire will carry over. Then in the next life, perhaps, or the next life, it may be achieved. Your reality is created by your desire.

Person One: Do we create things on a physical plane? I know my mind just wants to understand it. I just want to know the basics. Is anything really going on out there? Or is it all just an illusion, a dream? Is there nothing that is really happening? I don't know. I'd like to just understand the basics.

Gourasana: Yes. There is a material manifestation of your desires. But the perspective of what is happening is the difference between illusion and not. But yes, the material manifestation is there. The body feels pain, but your perspective on that pain is another thing.

But again, even if it is not real, even if it is nothing more real than a dream, as long as you are in illusion, what is the difference to what degree it is real? In a dream, if you believe you are being killed, you can suffer terribly. So in that sense, it does not matter to what degree this material manifestation is real or not real. As long as you are in illusion, you will suffer or enjoy according to what takes place in this illusion, in this dream. Once you are awake, once you are aware, your perspective of the suffering and the enjoyment will change. But there is a certain density of matter that makes a distinction between this plane and the higher planes of existence.

It is good to question, but be careful of frustration from not understanding and therefore not pursuing. When something cannot be understood, then just let it go. Do not hold on to the desire to understand. It is another thing to hold on to, and anything you hold on to will hold you back. If you cannot understand something, do not become frustrated.

Extreme Happiness and Suffering Are the Same

August 13, 1988, Alpine, CA

What is your desire *now?* Each of you, look at your consciousness, at your desire, *now.* Because you will receive, you will be enlightened, you will become aware depending on where your desire is now, where your consciousness is now. If your desire is unclear and confused, We can discuss and try to clarify it. Although it may take time, eventually you need to have a clear focus, a clear desire.

Generally, it is hard to determine the degree of your awareness or consciousness, but one thing you can see now is your desire. At least your desire must become clear, because desire is everything. To the degree of intensity that you desire to know the truth (or whatever name you want to call it), to the degree that you have that intensity and that clarity of desire, to that degree you will receive what it is you desire.

No matter what your situation, you need to look at your desire. Your desire may be clearly just for more light and truth, or your desire may be to find the answers to make a decision about which direction to go, because you were unclear. Your desires are mixed. Practically speaking, as long as you are in some illusion, your desire is mixed, is tainted. We have seen many come who desire the light, they truly do; but frequently they desire the illusion more. There is no such thing as complete illusion once one has come to *this* point – if one has come here even once there is a light in them that will *never* be covered.

As with everything on this plane of duality, it is always a question of degree. It is not necessary to have a pure desire to come here and advance. Actually, it is impossible to have a pure desire. So if one comes and thinks that their desire is not sufficient for the intensity of what we are doing and mistakenly they go away, then they will miss an opportunity.

Try not to be confused by seemingly opposite desires. Simultaneously you can be, and frequently are, desiring the light and also desiring some illusion. Of course, generally speaking, especially once the meditation has begun, it is Our request that you desire just the light and the truth. The rest of the time you can desire the illusion. But while you are here for that brief period of time that you come to *seek* the truth, your desire and your focus should be as clear as possible – to find as much light and truth as you can in the period of time you are here.

But the mind interferes, confusion is created, misunderstanding is created, doubt is created. Discussion is to quiet – as much as possible – the turmoil of the mind, so that by the time we are through discussing, the mind is calm enough to meditate with some clarity and focus. Those of you who are fortunate enough to not have so much turmoil, as you already are focused, can continue to increase your desire, focus, and clarity even while we discuss these matters.

If there were not doubt, if there were not illusion, there would be no need for seeking or questioning or searching. So do not be intimidated by discussion. Frequently the questions that are raised are questions that come to the minds of men and that have come to people searching for centuries and centuries. Everyone faces similar problems to different degrees. So we try to discuss as much as possible in a group, because what one person needs to have answered will frequently help others. But if there is need for private discussion, then that can also be arranged.

Person One: Gourasana, there seems to be a lot of suffering on this path to the love and the light of God. Is that necessary? Can you comment on that?

Gourasana: The suffering on this plane of existence is unavoidable. It may increase or decrease, *but it is unavoidable.* One can try to ignore or cover up the symptoms of suffering, but suffering is taking place nonetheless to different degrees with different people. Also, on the path of enlightenment, suffering is unavoidable. How can you avoid suffering? It is just a question of degree. But to avoid it, to not have *any* suffering, *it is not possible!* Will you never have a pain in your life? From the mildest of sufferings, discomfort of the body such as hunger, headache, some anxiety, some worry, some concern, suffering from someonc else, feeling too hot or too cold. At any moment, you can look at your own body and find some discomfort – different degrees of suffering. For some the suffering is not *so* great, and for some the suffering is horrible – constant terrible suffering.

Person One: Why would suffering be necessary if you're going toward the light? It seems like that would dissipate it or help to heal it.

Gourasana: That is what the mind would like to believe, but there is no basis for this. There is no support for this anywhere. There is no *example* anywhere to support this. Even seekers who are not sincere or as determined as We are trying to create, *even they* undergo suffering. For instance, when doubt comes, this is suffering. For anyone who has experienced love and light, when that love and light is gone, and all that they can feel is emptiness, doubt, and longing – this is suffering. Who can avoid these things? Who can go from a state of illusion to full awareness without ever having doubt?

What everyone is doing on this plane of illusion is trying to *avoid* suffering. Or because they cannot *avoid* suffering, they try to *compensate* for the suffering. So they work hard all day, and while they are working, they are suffering with anxiety, tension, headache. So when they come home they take intoxication – they do something to relieve the suffering. When there is time, when they do not have to work, then again they create activities to escape the suffering. But this does not stop the suffering. Even while they are trying to escape, they are suffering, although this is difficult to see unless one is a little aware. If one is a little aware – and you can become more aware by observing – watch sometime when someone is in a state of so-called enjoyment. If you see someone who is intoxicated, trying to enjoy, notice their countenance, their eyes, and you will see that there is suffering going on, *even then* – in many cases *more* suffering.

For one who is on the path of awareness, they need to come to a realization, to an understanding, *to an acceptance of the fact that you will not, no matter what you do, be able to avoid suffering in your lifetime.* I am not saying to mindlessly go through life and create suffering, but whatever you do, suffering will come. So for one who is searching and wants to direct their energy to be as focused as possible – to take them as quickly as possible to the light – *they will stop this fruitless endeavor to mitigate or stop the suffering.* They will *give up* that waste of energy, more or less. That does not mean that if it is hot, you cannot come into a cool room. It just means that your main focus, your direction is going to be to go toward the light, even when there is *more* discomfort, even if there is *more* suffering.

In other words, *suffering has got to cease to be an issue,* because going toward the light or going toward illusion, in either case you are going to have suffering. It requires a spiritual maturity to come to this point of acceptance. It is not that you do not strive to create a life that is conducive to spiritual life, and it is not that you mindlessly create a life of chaos just because suffering is there and then have so much unnecessary suffering.

But it is not possible to avoid suffering. Whatever you do, whatever you decide, whatever direction you take, *it will be there.* There is one large difference, however, and that is when you are going toward the light – because your awareness is growing, because you are understanding more clearly who you are and who you are not (mainly you are not this body, this mind, and you are not truly part of this plane of illusion) – even while *suffering* is there, simultaneously a *detachment* increases. So you do not suffer *in the same way* as someone who is bound by illusion and who measures their life by suffering and happiness.

When suffering comes to *one* who is bound in illusion, *it is a terrible disturbance and everything must be done to stop it.* All energy will be poured in that direction

– practically. But for one who is spiritually pointed, there is a certain acceptance, not to the point of deprivation, but an acceptance. You do not fight; you do not resist the inevitable. You do not behave foolishly and create suffering, but when suffering comes, one who is on a spiritual path becomes detached from the extremes of happiness and suffering. They become equipoised: The mind is calm. For one who is spiritually oriented, extreme happiness and extreme suffering are the same thing. They are both illusion, and they are both a disturbance. If you allow yourself the extreme happiness, happiness that comes from the illusion, then you will be unable to avoid extreme suffering. But there is a state of detachment that you enter into as you advance on the path, *that no matter what happens,* you are basically all right.

So one may look from the viewpoint of illusion at someone in this process and see, "Oh, they are suffering so much." But because of an awareness that is going on simultaneously, they are not suffering like those in illusion who even appear to be happy. They cannot be judged by the same standard, because they come from two different mentalities. The most extreme example of this is when they crucified the Lord Jesus: What was His consciousness? It was *love* and *compassion.* In the most extreme state of suffering, practically, that you can experience on this plane – mental and physical, total public humiliation, condemnation by practically everyone, physical torment of the greatest degree – yet what was His consciousness but love and compassion? But you take one who is bound by illusion and put them in the *same* situation, and what will their mentality be? Terror. Fear. Madness. Lost. Those are extreme examples, but they show what I am trying to illustrate here: that no matter how great the suffering may appear of one who is on the *spiritual* path, their suffering is *not* the same. Just as the suffering of the Lord Jesus was *not* the same as one who is bound in illusion.

One who does not seriously take up the spiritual path because they wish to *avoid* suffering (which is not possible) has of course made a mistake and has fallen prey to one of the many traps of the illusion. To someone in illusion looking at those that are on the spiritual path, it does not look good. All one in illusion can see is so-called deprivation in areas of enjoyment, like the many yogis, priests, monks, and saints who have given up comfort: not eating very well, not having good clothing, no security from a material standpoint, suffering public humiliation, rejection from family and friends. Everything that one in illusion *holds dear,* one – as they advance spiritually – *rejects.* From the standpoint of one in illusion, being seriously on the spiritual path does not look very appealing; on the contrary, it looks like something very bad.

Person Two: Gourasana, does this mean that no matter what plane we are on in our spiritual awareness, there will always be happiness and suffering? But the higher you go, the easier it gets to become aware?

Gourasana: The further you advance, as your awareness increases, you see the true identity of the happiness and suffering in illusion. You see the happiness for the suffering that it is, and you are not disturbed so much by the suffering as your awareness *grows.* You see, if you cling on to illusion, it is in *that* situation that you will *feel* the suffering more than anything. And it is *on the path of awareness that you will not feel it, that you will be detached from it,* that you will see yourself as separate. Not something theoretical, but practically *you will be living and experiencing it. See the nature of illusion again. Because people see what appears to be suffering, they are afraid of the spiritual path. But by avoiding the spiritual path they are in fact creating more real suffering, because in the state of illusion they cannot separate themselves from that suffering. And when that suffering comes, it is devastating! It destroys them!*

Look at so many old people as their bodies begin to go. The young people, when they are in a relatively healthy state, they can sit back and pretend that this illusion is all right. But as the organs begin to fail, as the brain begins to disintegrate, as the real suffering of disease sets in – then they are *devastated,* and the only way they can deal with this is to become *mindless,* become *unconscious.* And you see, they call it senility; when it is too much to bear any longer, there is senility that is created by the body, but also it is created by the *mind;* the mind cannot face *any more.* The suffering has become *too great,* so they have to become *very unconscious,* because they *cannot* face the suffering. So there is *no happiness.* Their life becomes practically *nothing* but suffering, and the *only* way they can deal with this, is by becoming completely unconscious. And you can go and see thousands and thousands of these people in convalescent homes, the homes for the aged. They become lost. Someone may argue, "Oh well, not everyone has this state." But everyone is doomed to suffer. Who does not suffer as they grow older, as their organs begin to fail – the inevitable suffering?

So you see, this is the trick of illusion. This is always the way it is. If you choose illusion, it means you have been *tricked.* You think you are choosing something easier, something with less suffering, something with more happiness. *Something is better about it so you choose it, but it is a trick! Illusion means a trick. It is an illusion!* And of course, most fall for the trick; most fall for the illusion. They embrace the illusion. But the reality is, as one who is on the spiritual path becomes older, not only are they not in the convalescent homes, but they are becoming *more* aware, and *real happiness* is there. *Ecstasy* is there, and you can *see* that these aware people – even in the midst of so-called suffering – are in states of ecstasy.

Again, the example of the Lord Jesus: He endured the most terrible suffering, and yet He, of course, was in a *state of ecstasy, feeling the greatest love, the greatest compassion* – so that His own suffering was not even of consequence. What was His concern? Was He saying, "Oh, I'm suffering. This is so terrible. I should never have done this. I should have stayed in . . . ?" No. He's thinking: "Father, forgive them, for they know not what they do."

He has so much love and ecstasy that He is *praying* for the very people that are *crucifying* Him. Yes, the suffering is there, but because of His *awareness*, because of the focus of His *consciousness*, what is it that He is *really* feeling and expressing? It is *His love and His compassion,* not the torment that He is going through. That is not His concern.

So it is like that on the spiritual path as you progress. Even though there is suffering and it appears to be great at times, because your awareness is growing, you are detached from it in a way that makes it unimportant: not the issue. This example is there with so many saints. Many books have been written about so many saints who have voluntarily suffered so much in deplorable living conditions (especially if judged by standards in this country). Yet they are in a state of spiritual ecstasy.

Person One: Gourasana, is there any suffering in the spiritual realms? Or is it just limited to the physical plane?

Gourasana: The true reality is there is no suffering, the suffering is just an illusion, and it is only in illusion that you can suffer. That is why these saints, these masters that have come to a state of full awareness, truly they do not suffer anymore, because there is no suffering. The suffering is an illusion. The sooner you can *get away* from the illusion, the sooner you can *get away* from the suffering. It is by holding on to the illusion that you hold on to the suffering, because the suffering is part of the illusion. That is why when one comes to a full state of awareness, suffering and happiness are the same thing. These things that I am saying are ancient truths and can be supported by many different teachers from all over the world throughout the centuries. That is why they do not pursue happiness, that is why they do not pursue suffering, and that is why their consciousness stays the same no matter which comes – because both happiness and suffering on this plane are just an illusion.

Try not to understand these things so much with the mind. How can you understand? If one is seeking seriously, they only need observe those who have gone before them that have been *recognized* as achieving enlightenment, and look at the example of their lifestyle. It will support what I am saying. They do not care to pursue happiness at all; they do not want to give *any* energy to this pursuit, because it is just an illusion. They just live as simply as they possibly can so they can devote their time to more and more awareness.

Just see what We are trying to do here: to break this illusion that has you fooled – tricked. We are trying to break you free from this to take you at least far enough so that you can know enough to continue. *But most will not go that far.*

They come, they experience a little, they experience some discomfort; they associate that with suffering. It is the duty of one in illusion to avoid suffering at all costs, so they avoid *this* at all costs. And they pretend to be in the light. They are like a child, and like a child that cannot face reality, they pretend that everything is all right.

So the criticism is: "Oh, here they are preaching it is all suffering, everything is so bad. It is *all* suffering." But these people do not stay. They do not question. They do not care enough to pursue it to learn the actual facts. So *quickly* they pronounce judgments. So *quickly* they come to a conclusion. *Where is their sincerity? Yes, I talk about the suffering, but the suffering is just an illusion, and you will only become free from the suffering when you become free from the illusion!* But they come and they hear the discussion of suffering, and what do they do? They go into illusion and they continue to suffer. They reject the way to become free from the very suffering they cannot stand to *hear about, and suffering becomes their reality!* And as they go more into illusion, their suffering increases. The *very reason* that they run away is because they are *afraid* of the suffering. Unfortunately, they are running into the *arms* of suffering; they are running into the *arms* of illusion. They have been tricked because they were not sincere. They accepted some *cheap facade of truth*, but that facade will not hold up against the onslaught of suffering that will come. *And in their state of illusion, they will identify with and feel that suffering in a way that is not possible for one who is aware.* So the thing that they think they are *avoiding*, they are *creating*.

Who can be so foolish as to say there is no suffering? Yet this disturbs them so much – that here is a way to stop the suffering.

Person Two: Gourasana, when the trick of the illusion is overcome, does that mean that what you are getting is a focused beam of truth and spirituality?

Gourasana: Yes. You are getting a beam of light that dispels the darkness of this plane. If one will only hear, if one will only try to hear, if one will only endeavor a little – we meet once a week – if one can come once a week. We are not asking that you give up all the illusion; it is not possible. You can hold on to the illusions that you wish to, gradually advance, and let go as you feel comfortable, as you feel able. It is only because of the illusion that it is so difficult to understand something that is so easy.

Let me give you another example *to try* to help you understand. *You* must try to hear, and *I* will try to use the words that you can relate to. If you take this little baby here, and you take a pin and you stick the baby with that pin, then due to the awareness of that baby, the suffering will be enormous, will it not? Screaming, horror, terror, yet for everyone else, practically, the same prick is nothing. You may say, "Yes, there was suffering, but what was it? A prick." Just like a mother who is cooking in the kitchen and accidentally cuts herself. There is blood, but she is not hysterical. It is a small thing. You see? *It is almost meaningless.* Maybe she needs a Band-Aid, whatever, to take care of it so she can get on with her business. You see? *It is almost meaningless to her.* But you take a child and the same knife and the same cut – *ooy!* So what is different but the consciousness? What is different but the awareness? So it is something like that.

I am not saying that when you reach a state of full awareness and someone comes and cuts off your arm, that there is not pain. *But because of your state of awareness, it only has a certain amount of meaning to you; it affects you only to a certain degree.* Just like for the mother, her cut is something that hardly made an impression on her consciousness. It practically is meaningless. But to the child, it is devastation and terror – the same thing, the same amount of pain – so it is something like that.

One in illusion is just like the little child, and they hold on to that childish mentality, pretending. From that childish, immature mentality, they are looking at what is going on here. And in that immature mentality, they are like the child who sees his mother being cut and thinks, "Oh, it is too much, it is unbearable." Their fear is overwhelming. They will not even consider what is going on here. They will get as far away as possible, and label it as bad because of their immature, childish mentality. They will go and play and pretend everything is all right, until the suffering comes again and they cannot pretend. And then they will suffer like the child – deeply.

Person One: Gourasana, it seems like a baby or a child would be more aware because they have less time to live in this illusion. You know how a baby seems like they're much closer to God and less inhibited? It seems like they would be more aware and less affected by a pin than an older person who is further away from God and deeper in the illusion. Is a child not closer to God and more aware when he is born?

Gourasana: Again you use these words "it seems," but again there is no evidence that supports this. It may seem like that, but nothing bears out those facts. A child has a certain purity and innocence, but their consciousness is not developed. They are not aware. You see? They have childish fears. They are afraid to go into the dark, because they have not reached the state of awareness where they know yet that it is safe – as safe when it is dark as when it is light. There is no difference in the room if the light is on or off. It is the same room, but because of their consciousness, they are afraid.

This is important for you to observe, because the common trap of illusion is that individuals form incorrect conclusions. So the conclusions need to be examined. Just as those that have come and left, they have come to a conclusion, and those conclusions are based upon facts that are erroneous. So they can only come to an erroneous conclusion – which they have. And almost everybody does this. It is important to be careful about conclusions.

The reality is that as one grows older and older, they are able to endure more, because they have come to understand it for the significance it has. When the child receives a certain injury and their conscious mind is new to this pain, they cannot think this pain, this particular pain will be over in seconds or minutes. All they can focus on is the pain. But one who has learned, one who is aware, when the pain comes, they will feel the pain, but they will know that within a very brief period it will be gone and there will be some discomfort. So it does not affect them. They have learned this from experience, but the child has not learned, so when the pain comes, all they know is that "Here is the pain." And as far as their consciousness is concerned, it's going to be indefinite.

One characteristic that one must try to hold while they are searching is humility. If you knew, you would not be searching. We are not asking for blind acceptance, but from a point of humility, one will always remain open to all of the possibilities. The ones who have closed their minds and who have turned against this – this comes from the ego and from a lack of humility, or of course from a lack of desire.

Because philosophically, I do not think you can fault the teachings that you hear here. On the contrary, if you will compare them to teachings of great masters, yogis, and saints, you will at least find certain similarities, and in many cases, identical statements.

Do not be fooled by the illusion any longer. Do not let it control your life. You can start from where you are, and you can progress as you desire. But do not fall victim, as so many have, and totally reject this. They say, "Oh, yes. We can find the truth elsewhere." That is true. But then why are they so against this? Why do they label this as darkness? Why are they so militant in their stand against what is being spoken here, when what is being spoken here is just the truth? So I am not contesting that they can find the truth elsewhere, but the fact that they leave here and are so militant in their stand against what is going on here – the truth – makes the likelihood of their finding it elsewhere not so good, because they cannot accept the truth where they have already found it. So they may find it somewhere else, but they cannot accept it when they do find it.

Do not fall victim to the illusion. You have to take it on faith from the masters that this is better. *It is wonderful! It is ecstasy! It is everything!* That is why some have given up everything that is held dear to those in this plane of illusion. To achieve this, they have given up *everything!* Why? Are they all insane? Or have they *found something* which is so great that it does not even matter to them that some suffering may come or not? It is not an issue. Even if they know they are going to enter into great degrees of suffering, it is not of consequence to them. It is not something that they weigh or even consider, because of what they have experienced, of what they know is waiting.

Most do not have to plunge into some terrible disturbance immediately, but it would be naive and childish to say that you will not have to go through *some* suffering when you *will* have to go through some suffering, whichever direction you choose. Try to keep that in mind. If you choose the illusion or if you choose the light, in either case it is childish to think that you are going to be able to avoid some suffering. But in one case, just like the mother cutting her hand, the suffering will become meaningless. But in the other case, the suffering will become overwhelming until the only way you can deal with it is your mind has to go, and you stay like that until your death and your next birth.

So any more questions, more discussion?

Let us prepare for meditation.

The Principle of Degree

August 20, 1988, Alpine, CA

So much confusion comes from all teachings of truth, because there appears to be contradiction – opposing statements. As I have discussed in the past, the path to full awareness is *highly individualized.* While there are certain truths that apply to everyone *all of the time,* there are truths – or things that must be done – that will apply to each individual *at different times.* Depending upon your consciousness and what your particular difficulties are, a certain practice may or may not be recommended, an area of endeavor may or may not concern you. But it is never all one way or another: it is some degree. But people do not like this; they do not like the vagueness. They think that the truth should be something that their mind can grasp with a certainty, that they can know: "Yes, it is this way; this is right and this is wrong; this is sinful and against the Lord, and this is saintly." These people are restricted in their consciousness to limited perspectives of right and wrong. And to say that there are those who according to common moral standards are considered the most sinful are actually closer to a state of full realization than so many who by the same standards are considered saintly, would confuse these people.

You do not know how deep in all of your hearts this goes: your misconceptions about *how* things should be, about what is moral, what is immoral. Of course, in this country, due to the incredible propaganda, generally you lean toward the Christian standards of morals, and you believe as the Christians – generally. But just as they, the Christians, have limited themselves, have closed doors, so have all of the major philosophies closed doors. In the Hindu philosophy – of course that encompasses a great many beliefs – but generally, to kill or eat any animal or aquatic life, or substances from their bodies, like eggs, is sinful. The Christians do not believe this. So just as the Christians judge by their "right and wrong" standards, so do the Hindus. Therefore, for the Hindu, if someone is eating some substance of this nature, then automatically they are rejected as someone who could possibly be aware – automatically. Just as to the Christian, the prostitute cannot be a true Christian and continue to engage in the acts that she does.

Now, there are reasons why these beliefs have become prominent. It is not that they are totally wrong in their conceptions. There is good reason behind some concern about sex and eating flesh of animals. The difficulty comes in the rigidity of *thinking*, the "right and wrong" *thinking*. Generally, if one is caught up in the lust of sex (as some are so captured), for the most part they think of nothing else – it is their goal. Lust is a very binding force, and in a state of lust, consciousness does not come through. But again, you must remember in all areas the principle of degree. One who – occasionally – desires sex and engages in the act is not stopped from advancing. There is some disturbance in the consciousness, it is true, because ultimately sex is an illusion – ultimately. Still, even *that* is not so rigid. So the conclusion that one *cannot* engage in sex and be fully aware is not true. But most will think, "Oh, so let us make a checklist of what is right or wrong to make it clear." Can you see what would happen then?

So in the pursuit of clarity, most are missing the point. They have their checklist, no matter how subtle it may be, of what is right and wrong, what can and cannot be, who is qualified, who is not qualified, who is saintly, who is not saintly. *You all* have these checklists, and automatically you are "writing people off." You see an alcoholic, a "bum" on the street; automatically, on your checklist, you write off this man. How can *he* be aware? You go to the big city's downtown area, and you see the "bums," as you call them: "Oh, how can these people be aware?" Yet there are some amongst them who are far more aware than all of the thousands and thousands of businessmen in their suits working in the office buildings for big corporations. Some of these businessmen are little better than animals, and some of these so-called "bums" are saints by comparison.

But you have your standards that you have set. You have your checklist of what is right and what is wrong, and your society reinforces this. It is so *ingrained* in you. You must *rebel* against the propaganda that has been *filling* your ears since birth: the *garbage* from your parents, and then the *garbage* from your teachers, and the *garbage* from your friends. I can tell you frankly that practically there is nothing but garbage in your minds, to different degrees. Like everything else, it is not all the same degree of rottenness.

So you must open your mind. But opening your mind does not mean more garbage can just come. Great discrimination must be cultivated. After every conclusion you come to, there should be a question mark, because there is a very good chance that in *any* conclusion you've come to, there is something about it that is wrong or contaminated. It is *never* clear. And then you have the continuing pressure – not just what has filled your mind already – you have the continuing pressure and propaganda of society going *against* the truth, forcing you to be like everyone else. And if you are not like everyone else, *immediately,* from the time you begin deviating from normal standards, there will be something coming at you from society to get you to stop, to change, to be normal again.

So you go down the street and you see the police; they are harassing a bum, but this is normal. This is their business. You can accept it: "This man, he has no rights; he is a bum. Certainly the police must be behaving properly." Everyone accepts it; no one is questioning. But if it were the businessman in the suit and tie who the police were treating in a similar fashion, people would stop and think, "This must be a great criminal. Perhaps he murdered somebody," because the police would not touch such a man *in this fashion,* unless he had done some terrible thing. They would be very careful, because they are being controlled by the dictates of society: not just the rules that are in the books that they learned, but by the constant current of propaganda and beliefs that are reinforced daily and hourly by those around them, by society, until they truly believe it is all right to treat the bum in a certain way and it is very bad to treat the businessman in the same way.

So this analogy is important in searching for the truth, because this just shows how much the mind is influenced. It shows how much you have inflexibly accepted certain things as right and certain things as wrong, not to mention how you accept more and more subtle things.

Just as with every teacher that has come along, any teacher of the truth, there is so much fierce criticism. See, society is against teachers of the truth. But, society *has* to be against them. Just as there are a few trying to preserve the truth, likewise it is the duty of the society of people on this plane of existence to preserve the illusion, although they are not doing it consciously. So when someone comes with the truth, then that person is the enemy of those who wish to perpetuate the illusion. This is why when someone comes with the truth, there is sometimes so much fierce propaganda against them. People in illusion wait for opportunities to attack teachers of the truth. They wait for the teachers to make a mistake, or what they think is a mistake, so they can attack. And they do attack. And they are constantly attacking.

If you ask your average person, they will be against what they do not even know. They will be firmly against the beliefs of groups coming, like from India. Yet, if you ask them, "What are their beliefs?" they will not know. They will just know that those beliefs are *very bad,* just like the bum in the street; they are bad. They have been *told* it is bad and they *believe* that it is bad.

It is a similar situation here, except there is no proselytizing going on, practically speaking. The ones that are aware of what is going on here are not what you call your mainstream society. They are usually people who are considered to be open-minded. They themselves, generally speaking, are deviating from social norms, and the activities they are engaging in would be pronounced "bad" by the general public and society of this country. Yet, so many are viciously against this because it is a threat to the illusion. And more particularly, it is a threat to *their illusion,* and the illusion is dearer to one than life itself.

It is easier for one to die than give up an illusion. When there is a war, for example, an American soldier will go and fight, and he will believe that it is worth dying for because he is told it is. Now it may or may not be. Of course, there are cases where it is. So he will give up his life for an illusion that is so "critical" that it is worth dying for. That is an illusion. Even though he has a wife and children, he will die to preserve the illusion. You see? They will die to preserve this illusion, to keep this going.

In the same way they will fight just as hard – and they do – to preserve the illusion in a war of propaganda. And because they have the superior weapons of propaganda, mainly controlling the information that goes to the people, of course they are winning the war. A number of great saintly men have come from India and begun organizations, and they have been commonly denounced and condemned by the American society, by people who themselves are totally unaware and in illusion. And the news reporters claim to be giving unbiased news reporting, yet have any of the major television stations or any of the major networks supported any of these saints, who in India are worshipped? No, of course not; they are all commonly against it.

So freedom of speech is also an illusion – more or less: "Yes, you are free to speak as long as you speak like we want you to speak. But if you speak against what we want you to say, then we will attack you." These saints will be thoroughly attacked and defeated by the media. The minds of those in this country are filled with so much propaganda – just as you have your checklist, everyone in this country has their checklist of who they are against. If they were so fortunate to come across one of these saintly men, they already have their checklist, which has been made up from the propaganda they hear: "Oh, this is a yogi from India – on the list, bad, evil." So they miss an opportunity to find the truth. And several saints have come to this country who are very great.

Many who are educated, worldly, not so narrow-minded, they are aware of these things to some degree. But why I am spending so much time talking about it, is that it goes much deeper than the obvious things like this, the obvious prejudice, the irrational thinking. So in your search for the truth, you must open your mind as well as your heart and observe things for yourself; and if you do not understand something, then do not come to a conclusion, a hasty conclusion. And to some degree, by necessity you must come to *some* conclusions, but even those conclusions should be considered temporary – with a question mark after them – because as your awareness expands, the perspectives on those truths will change.

How important is it, what I am talking about? This one thing is stopping practically everybody on the path. You have all built a wall that you will not go beyond. The Christians have built a wall: "If you do not accept Jesus, you will go to hell." This is a huge thick wall that they cannot get around; they are stopped in their tracks. The Hindus believe if you eat certain substances, you cannot be aware. They have erected a wall: "You cannot take any intoxication, any form of drug at all, and be aware, and if you do, then you cannot be aware." Yes, there is an underlying reason – generally, the drug, the intoxication is not good and it will disturb you. Generally, preoccupation with sex is not good and it is an obstacle. Generally, consumption of animal food is not good. But to become rigid in these things is an illusion.

At any rate, it is an area to begin to open up. But when we discuss these things, remember the hearing is with your heart, not so much with your mind. So time after time after time, try to keep all of the things straight in your mind – what is important. With too many words the mind becomes confused. There is an essence going on that you must try to capture – an essence of awareness. If you came to one hundred sessions like this, at the end of the sessions, what you could repeat in words would be a very small percentage compared to what had been said. Yet your awareness will have grown. You will just know – a true knowing – so many things that you did not know before. You will be able to see. You will have a vision that you did not have before. And the real vision, the real knowing is beyond the words.

But society will be against you. This is one wall that most people cannot get around. Since you have been raised, generally, to be accepted by society, to behave in such a way that society will accept you, that your family and friends will accept you, this can be a very difficult first obstacle to overcome. Not, of course, that you need to overcome that before you can advance in other areas. But as you advance spiritually, and become more and more sincere (and you may take years and years), you will be fighting more and more against the current of society and the pressure of society, and you will have to come to a point where those that have known you will reject you. Perhaps even your own family will reject you, because everything you stand for is against everything they stand for; because they stand for illusion, and hopefully you will stand for the truth, so you will never see eye to eye again. Unless, of course, you decide to go back into illusion. So some of you will be more affected than others, but this is a powerful pull that you need to be aware of – *a very powerful pull.* This is why many seekers either choose isolation, such as in the forest of this country, or they go to other countries where there is not the pull or the propaganda, because the pull is so great here, they find if they are here they cannot resist the pull. They cannot, even though they are aware of it and are trying to resist; they are unable to. They find that when they are here they are swayed.

But ultimately, when you will do anything for consciousness, for awareness, then you must be prepared to be totally ostracized by society, to be attacked, to be the object of ridicule. Who can tolerate this? Only someone who is serious. As I say, few can get beyond the first, *this* first test: coming here to be with Me. There are so many who are aware of this who will not even come *one time,* because they are well aware from others around them what is generally thought of what is going on here: that it is something very bad. And they know that if they come even one time, that there will be a lot of criticism from others going on about them, and perhaps ridicule. And if they come two or three times, they may possibly be ostracized from the society that they hold so dear. So they are so cautious, they will not even come one time. Not because they don't want to, but because of the pressure of those around them to not come, because they want to *be accepted.* It is so important. This has been drilled so much into your mind: to be accepted is so critical. After all, a handful of people searching for the truth against millions and millions – it is easier to go with the illusion and feel secure. And if you are not sure what is right or wrong, rather than deciding for yourself, there is safety in numbers – so you think. So better to side with millions than to side with a few.

Even those of you that are aware of this to a great degree, should also be *more* aware of this, because it is a constant force, a constant pulling, an important aspect of the illusion to get you to change, to leave the path, and to rejoin society. And though you may not feel it so much day-to-day, after some time, several years, it becomes a wearing influence if you are not guarding yourself properly. And you can give in.

So, any question? Discussion on this area, or any other area?

Person One: Gourasana, is the attachment to the illusion the main reason we reincarnated, or are there valuable lessons that we learn in this illusion that help our consciousness grow?

Gourasana: One thing is you do not have to be concerned about leaving prematurely: that you would leave prematurely and there would be something that you did not learn, so you would be incomplete. It is not possible to come to a state of full awareness and be incomplete. One who is not ready to leave the illusion, who still has something *to gain* from staying in illusion, will do so. That is most everyone. Yes, there is a purpose to the illusion, but for one who is endeavoring to leave the illusion, this can become a trap. So this cannot be allowed either. Again, sometimes it appears that the teachings are opposing, saying two different things. Yes, ultimately there is a reason for the illusion, and in one sense you can stay for millions of lifetimes more if you wish, and it will be all right, because there is a purpose to this existence after all. But once you are on the path to leave, once you have opened the door and are getting ready to leave this plane, then this thought just becomes illusion, just something to keep you captured, and it must be resisted. When it gets too difficult, one can think, "Oh, I have more to learn. I'll go back into illusion and learn some more." So once one has decided to become free from the illusion, to fight the illusion, then all aspects of the illusion must be fought.

Yes, there is a purpose to the illusion. But if you want to become free from this illusion, if you want to leave this plane of existence, then you must begin *fighting* the illusion. Because yes, the illusion is what holds you here life after life. It is the force that binds you to this plane of existence. But the path is different for everyone, and the time frame is different for everyone. Some that are not ready today to begin will be ready in ten years to begin – seriously, or in twenty years to begin – seriously, or thirty years to begin – seriously. You have so many years ahead in your life. It is not the same for everyone.

My specific purpose in coming is to take *out* those who are ready to leave in this lifetime. Therefore I preach in a certain way and encourage in a certain way, because those who do want to get out in this lifetime must do things in a certain way, with a certain intensity. But even those who want to get out in this lifetime do not all have to take the same steps at the same time. What is in your heart, that is what must be somehow understood. If it is not clear, if you are uncertain, then you can progress spiritually; there's certainly no harm in that. Ultimately, if you do not want to leave, you will not. There are many that search their whole lives, and toward the end, practically speaking, change their minds and decide: another lifetime, two or three or four. So there is no harm in moving spiritually, in practicing, in becoming more aware. There is only benefit to be achieved by this.

Just as I was talking before, there are many who are aware of the general propaganda that is going on, and how artificial and bigoted and narrow-minded it is; but they are in the minority. So, better to become at least aware so that you are not just a mindless follower of society's pressures. You may still follow society's pressures, but mindfully is much different then mindlessly. And you can choose the rate that you wish to go. If you wish to spend so much time every day or every week, then you can choose how far you wish to go, how much you wish to advance, how much of your energy you wish to put into this area. Again. So many see such a black-and-white picture: either they will come here and advance, or they will have nothing to do with it – like that, black and white. Those who are working on becoming aware, who are taking pains to meditate, they could come and meditate with us and make advancement and get help in the areas of spiritual life in which they are endeavoring.

And it may not become clear for some time that what they want is to truly become free from the illusion. Some here are much older than others, and when they were your age, they did not have any idea like this, and now it has become everything to them. So in the same way, you may not feel like this now, but this does not mean that it is written in concrete and that you will never feel like this. Yes, of course, you have certain things that you will need to go through in your life. And if you do not feel a great drive to do anything and everything to give up your life to become free from this illusion, then you are just not at that point yet. But that does not mean that you cannot take truth, apply it to your life, and increase your consciousness and your awareness. There is never any harm in doing that.

Cindy: Gourasana, can you tell us about complete and total surrender in our lives – what that means?

Gourasana: Yes. First you must give up everything as you would have it in your lifetime: all your plans, all your conceptions for the future. How you *want it to be;* how you *think it should be.* You must give all of this up – *even* as you conceive spiritual life to be. Some have certain conceptions of how spiritual life will be, and they must give up these conceptions. Whatever the conceptions, they all must go. You have so many conceptions. A turning point comes in your spiritual life where you have so completely given up your plans that you are prepared to die; you will gladly give up your life for awareness. Attaining awareness has become that critical that you will not only give up your plans and hopes for the future, but *you will give up your future in this existence.* To come to that point is essential.

And then the next step, *the harder step,* is to continue to live, but live as you *need* to live to become aware, without considering – is it pleasurable or not pleasurable, is there fear or not, is there suffering or not, is it increasing my distress or not? You just *do* what another will has you do. You give up your will, and you do what the Universe would have you do.

That is all. If you can take these two steps, then you will succeed. *That is serious. That is complete surrender: to give up your will, to surrender to a higher will.*

Person Two: Gourasana, what is the purpose of your plane of existence?

Gourasana: Purpose? We do not exist on a plane. It suggests limitation. Although I may use the word to distinguish.

One thing that is going on is that every living entity is in a constant state of ecstasy. I don't know if you could call that a purpose. But it is everything that is.

Person One: Gourasana, are you doing any other things besides being in a constant state of ecstasy? It's hard for us with our limited minds to conceive of what you do all day. *(Laughs)* I know that that sounds silly. Do you assist, do the entities assist us on this plane or assist each other on your plane also? Do you all feel a oneness or do you feel a separate identity? Do you feel separate consciousnesses?

Gourasana: Yes. All of those things.

The separation is created by illusion. So you cannot say that there is a separation, yet there is a distinction between entities. As far as the entities that deal with this plane, there are some that are more directly involved with assisting – a minority. And while there is oneness with them and other living entities not on this plane, there are other living entities that, practically speaking, have nothing to do with this plane, or are not concerned with it. Not so easy to describe. But what *to do?* – to try to take the principles of your plane and where you derive pleasure from, and try to describe the true realm of existence by those standards. . . . So what is pleasurable here? Something visual: You see some colors, but the colors in the true realm of existence, even if you would just see one color. . . . Now, if you could just see one color, even very densely like in a fog – which you are in – you would enter into a state of ecstasy and rapture. And there are endless colors and hues. Then shape. . . . Here you become bored because you see something and basically you say, "See, the same thing over and over." What are the most beautiful things on this plane that you have ever seen? They stay basically the same. If it is the forest, if it is the ocean, whatever it is you consider to be beautiful. Basically, you go back and it is basically the same. It does not change, much. But in the spiritual realm, it never stays the same. So while you are seeing, it is changing so much that you cannot even "capture" one picture – as you would say. If somehow or other you were able to take a photograph, it is changing so much that you could not capture it. And then, it is filled with a life force; it is filled with an energy of love and light. If there were no color or form, just the light, which cannot be separated from the love – but there is so much more. Every aspect is so unlimited, and if I were to talk for hours it would do nothing, but if you could just see for a second. . . .

And there is a sound. At first, it appears to many to be silent. But as this so-called "silence" continues, you begin to notice more and more, like a music that never stops, that is filled with a life and a love and a light all its own. It is endless melodies interwoven, constantly changing, and each melody enough to ponder and explore – but there are endless melodies. And still, I'm just trying to describe the stage of the true realm, just as one here may try to describe the forest or the ocean.

No. You never have to be concerned with boredom because *you are eternal.* You will never cease to exist. And all aspects of the true realm of existence, which are unlimited, are ever increasing, ever changing, ever *more* beautiful, ever *more* ecstatic. You cannot compare the two. This plane *is dead.* It is lifeless. It is *without* beauty, it is *without* light, it is *without* love, it is *without* awareness. *It is dark!* Some things only appear to be beautiful, because there are some things that are so much darker, that by comparison they appear to be beautiful, but in and of themselves. . . .

That is why when someone comes to a certain stage of awareness, even with their conscious mind they cannot retain these things that are going on in the true realm. There is something in their heart, a force so strong that there is nothing else for them in existence, because they have seen, they have heard, they have tasted, they have smelled, they have felt – if even for an instant – the true realm of existence, and they cannot be satisfied any longer with this plane.

Person One: Do any, once they're in the true realm of existence, ever choose to come back to this plane?

Gourasana: No. It is not possible that you need to be in illusion again. As you say, you are learning something, but once it is learned, there is no sense in repeating. Once you come to a state of full awareness, there is nothing to learn. There is nothing to come here for.

Gayle: Gourasana, I don't understand your answer to the previous question about whether there are some who come back to this plane of existence to help us out.

Gourasana: No. She didn't say that.

Gayle: What did you say in your last question?

Person One: *(To Gayle)* Do any, once they have advanced to the spiritual realm, do any of them get bored or want to come back to this plane? He said, "No."

Gourasana: Yes. It is as if you are living comfortably in this part of the world, then if you live for some time in the worst part of the world – in the most hellish condition filled with disease, so many types of torture, lawless countries, no security, like some of the prisons where any kind of torture is frequent and allowed – after you came back to California, would you want to go back? For lack of something pleasurable, I am saying. Like you say, suggesting that once leaving here, perhaps it becomes boring because there is no longer the suffering and the torture that you endure on this plane of existence. There is no desire to come back into suffering.

Gayle: I'm still confused, because what about the teachers who claim that they are incarnations and they purposely are coming back to help us? Like Sai Baba?

Gourasana: One thing is to distinguish *your* question from *your* question. She *(Referring to Person One)* is asking, do they not become bored? Do they lack something to do, so they come back here – as if they need something from this plane? This is a different question than what you *(referring to Gayle)* are saying. Some who come to help or assist is an entirely different matter. It is an entirely different question. Do not confuse the two questions.

Her question *(Person One)* is very specific: "Do they not desire to come back? Will they not miss something here?" No. They do not miss something here. There is nothing to miss, so they do not come back because they miss or desire something from this place or need something to do.

Now, your *(referring to Gayle)* question: "Do they not come and help?" Yes.

Person Three: To take form?

Gourasana: Yes. But even then, they are not on your plane, because your plane is an illusion.

Person One: So is it the individual's desire to come back to help, or is it by some higher authority?

Gourasana: Yes, it is by *their* higher authority. They are not ordered to come back. Then there are also different degrees or different personalities you can have. You say that each individual is the same personality. You say when someone is an Incarnation, that suggests that they are here and not there. But – that is not true. Their existence in the true realms does not lessen any by their making an appearance here.

But this is all useless information. What value does it serve, to try to describe what is impossible to describe? There are many attempts at describing, and they are all misunderstood. You cannot understand. How can you understand? You cannot even capture with words *this* plane of existence, *you cannot.* Some are better than others at capturing – writers. But still they cannot capture. You go to another country where no one in this room has been, and you come back and you try to describe it so they can grasp it. Of course, here there are so many points of similarity that you can use, where there are none between this and the true realm; still they will try. How can you describe a smell? How can you describe a sound? Yes, you can say one characteristic of the sound: It is beautiful. But until you hear the sound you cannot understand it. It is so beautiful that you go into a state of ecstasy. You can hear the words, *but until you hear such a sound,* what meaning do the words have? They are just words, practically empty.

Person One: It helps us to get a better idea of the real realm; even a vague description helps us. It helps me have a better understanding of what's to come – that it's so much more beautiful than this realm. It helps us want to drop the illusion that much more.

Gourasana: See, this is nothing. This existence here is terrible. Pathetic. There is nothing here worth staying for. Nothing. If you had the best of everything that this plane of existence has to offer, it would still be nothing.

But, it's all right. It's hard to understand a constant stage of ecstasy when you have not experienced any ecstasy.

Person Four: Is the experience that each individual experiences in this state, is it different for each individual or is it the same? Is ecstasy just ecstasy? Does each person or individual experience it the same, or will each experience it differently according to the varieties of the ecstasy? And is it unlimited?

Gourasana: Yes. It is unlimited and it is ever changing. It is not possible for you to even experience the same thing. You cannot experience the same as another, identical. Similarities will be there, certainly, but the same? No. You could not even experience the same, because it is ever changing, ever increasing. Here you can go to the ocean and the ocean is basically the same. It may change a little, color – like that – but basically, the same. But nothing is like that in the true realm. Nothing stays the same. It gets better.

Person Four: It seems that for most people, they want that sameness. They are afraid to accept there is a constant change.

Gourasana: They do not want *any change.* Not only do they not want change, but they do not want any uniqueness, individuality. They want everyone to dress the same, to think the same, to look the same. They are so concerned about this that it is even against the law to look and act in certain ways that are harming no one else. But all that stops when the illusion goes. At the same time, there is a true oneness that satisfies that to some degree, that springs from the desire for a oneness with everyone, but you do not become one by looking the same and wearing the same type of clothing. So to some degree it springs from that desire – the oneness. But of course, that is perfectly satisfying, there is no dissension – but everything is highly unique.

Still, there is another reason that not too much is said, because whatever is said is misunderstood and people become afraid. But one thing everyone can usually relate to is that it is just love. It is unlimited love that is permeating everything. The word "love" is so limited. You want a description, but yet everything is permeated with love and light. How can you appreciate a color unless while seeing the color, you also can see the light and the love that is in that color? Or the *sound* that permeates it? It is filled with *love* and *light* and *ecstasy* in itself. There is nothing that is not permeated with love and light. Nothing. Even if you could reduce the sound to something – like on *this* plane you have different instruments and they make different sounds. Some are very beautiful; some are very bad. I do not know why they play them *(laughter)*. But some are very beautiful. Yet on this plane, it is *just a sound* made from an instrument. But you can just try to use that as a comparison: The most *beautiful* sound you have ever heard, a sound on this plane that an instrument played, a melody played that carried you, that *moved* you – it is something close. But add to that sound, *love* and *light* and *ecstasy*. And then, of course, sounds like no instrument – then endless sounds, endless melodies – interwoven.

The thing is, you cannot sit in illusion and understand the true realm and then once you have understood it, move from the illusion. The only way you will know it is by letting go of the illusion and entering into the true realm. So you must have the trust and the faith to do that. And the trust and the faith will increase as your awareness increases.

Do not judge yourself too harshly, because you cannot judge yourself how long it will take from where you are. You may think, "Well, I do not see the illusion so clearly," or "I am very attached to so many pleasures that will be gone; I must not be very advanced." Do not judge yourself, because you cannot tell how close or how far you are. You are as close as you want to be, and you are as far away as you want to be. If you want to break free of this illusion, you will break free; if you do not want to, you will not.

And you see, most do not. It is very obvious. They come and they are against, viciously against, because they do not want this; they want to stay. So it is more than a threat to their life, because, again, *the illusion is dearer than life itself!* You have endless lives that you can stay – millions and millions of lifetimes. So life itself is not so precious *as the illusion.* The illusion that binds you and keeps you here for millions of lifetimes, that is the precious thing. Life itself: That can be given up, and is, many times for many reasons. People can die, that is not such a difficult thing. *But to give up the illusion,* that is a great deal. This is truly why people are so opposed to this and any teaching of truth, because any teaching of truth will destroy, or at least expose to a great extent, the illusion. And there is a consensus by the majority on this plane to perpetuate the illusion. Understand? *Everyone wants the illusion. They are choosing the illusion, and they are against anyone that is going to spoil or ruin or threaten the illusion.*

And it has always been so, and it will always be so. *Only when the truth has been properly perverted, and the illusion and darkness has been properly interwoven into the truth so that it is of no use any longer to get out, does society permit it.* Then it is accepted by society. It is accepted because it has been made safe. It will not destroy the illusion so it is accepted – only then will society accept it. In many ways it will help perpetuate the illusion. But the pure truth, not contaminated, is not accepted. First it must be changed to fit the needs of the illusion. To the degree that that is done, to that degree it is accepted.

So one thing that everyone can practice without needing to give up the illusion, the pleasures of the illusion, is to be aware of what is illusion and what is not. This would be a tremendous stride forward. In other words, one can begin to increase their awareness that the act of sex is just an illusion, but they can still continue the act. They need not be afraid that they will come to a point where they will be forced to stop it. If they stop it, they will have come to a point – just as an adult no longer has any desire to read certain books, like comic books, or play with dolls – because they have found something better that they enjoy more. So for that reason they will stop. So in the same way from awareness: As you become aware, then you may achieve a point where you stop it. But it is not something that is forced upon you.

In fact, many continue to engage in sex even once they have understood that it is an illusion *and* that it is not even pleasurable. Still, they engage for some time, until one day they just stop. But the fear is in any process, in any path, "Oh, if I do this, then I will have to stop everything." Well, ultimately, when you leave this plane of existence, yes, you will have to stop all of these activities, but there will be no problem with it. There will be no pull any longer, because the illusion will be gone. And once the illusion is gone, then all the attraction is gone; because the only way you can be attracted to these activities is because of the illusion.

At any rate, the contrast is so great you need not worry. It is not that you leave and there is some regret as you leave. Not at all. Not at all. I cannot think of an extreme enough example to show you the contrast of awareness. But as long as we have the baby here, I will give one example to show extremes. Those of you who have been parents know, or maybe you remember as a child, that children have a peculiar desire to pass stool and to put it on the wall. So who of you now that you have grown, wants to do this? *(Laughter)* Is there any regret that you no longer are smearing stool on the walls? Do you wish you could do it again? Does it tug at your heart sometimes? *(More laughter)* And this is not enough of a contrast, but it is to just give you an idea. It is like that. You will leave and you will look at the activities: what you took pleasure in doing as an adult and what you did as a baby. There will be no longing; there will be no desire to repeat the activity. On the contrary, to get away from the activity as far as possible, is the desire. But because of the illusion, which is so great, most again will be smearing stool on the wall and taking pleasure in their next life. And again. So those of you that do not want to leave, you can look forward to repeating the pleasures that you have already enjoyed. Anyway.

Person Three: Gourasana, have there been any creative people, painters, poets, composers, who have had sufficient glimpses of the light that their works can be a help to our spiritual practice? You do seem to favor certain music, certain fragrances, certain colors. Are these things that would be helpful for us to know about, or is our spiritual practice to be limited to meditation? Is there music that would help us?

Gourasana: Yes. Like the music we play in meditations. There is something there, what you call inspiration. Why is it they call one musician "uninspired" or "no talent?" Why is it that they play, and they play nothing that anyone wants to hear? And another musician plays something that is so beautiful that for centuries they play it, and you can listen again and again and not tire of it? So at the very least, it is coming from a higher source, higher than this gross plane of existence – many things are. The inspiration is coming from a higher source, although perhaps not pure or even spiritual in the true sense of eternal. There are different degrees in this plane of illusion, also – which is a whole other thing.

But yes, something that inspires you. There is nothing wrong in playing some music that inspires you, or in taking pleasure in the fragrance that inspires you. Or, as we have discussed, even in nature you see some beauty that inspires you; there is nothing wrong in that. It does not have to be a distraction to take pleasure in it. It's when *it is* a distraction that you need to be concerned. Even, for instance, the act of sex, which is considered to be very pleasurable: One does not have to be immersed in the thoughts and the lust. They can occasionally engage in the act for the brief period that it takes, and the rest of the time not be even thinking of the act, you see, so it is not such an obstacle. When they can think of nothing else, when it is occupying their consciousness, their sleep and their waking hours, and so much energy and concentration is going into that – then that's another thing. But a brief exchange does not necessarily need to be much of an obstacle. But certain things are hardly an obstacle at all.

Person One: Gourasana, you mentioned that we need to be aware of what is illusion and what isn't illusion on this plane. It seems like most everything is illusion. What on this plane isn't illusion? What is real love?

Gourasana: What isn't illusion, or what isn't contaminated with illusion, is something that again is beyond the words, but by seeing the illusion, the reality – what is light or love – becomes more apparent. This is an example to try to illustrate: the love between a mother and a child. There is undoubtedly a feeling of love there, but the love is contaminated. It is contaminated with fear. If the child is suffering, like when the baby is born – is the baby all right?

If the baby becomes sick with disease or is in danger. . . . So, not just when it is in danger, but the apprehension that it will come into danger or become sick. Or as the child grows, other dangers will come and the parent is suffering and afraid. And this contaminates the love.

Also, the parent wants the child to be a certain way. And as the child does not fulfill the expectations of the parent, this also creates suffering (you can see it, it is common on your plane), because the "love," as you call it, seems to increase or decrease according to the acts of the child. If the child becomes a drug addict and a murderer, the parents' love generally decreases. And as the child fulfills the desires of the parents, the love increases. So this is not real love. But it is love; it is close.

But better than that is unconditional love, where the illusion of mother and child is not there anymore, and there is a purity of love between you that can only come from awareness; where from a level of ultimate awareness, no matter what the child does, the purity of love does not decrease or increase. But because of the illusion it is contaminated and it fluctuates, because of the attachment, because of the illusion. So you need to see what is illusion. You are thinking, "This is my child"; well, this is an illusion. It is part of the illusion that is going on. And why are you so concerned about this one living entity when there are millions and millions of children all the world over? Because you are in illusion that this living entity is yours; but that is just an illusion. And in so many years, in one hundred years, all the characters will change partners, you might say: new parents, new children, and another illusion.

Person One: You mean by illusion, temporary, that it's not lasting?

Gourasana: Yes. The illusion is always temporary. That is one characteristic. It is always temporary. It is doomed to be temporary. It is destined to be temporary. And because of the temporariness of it, it is like a movie in its unreality. You may say, "Yes, but there is suffering," yes, but even that is fleeting. You cannot hold on even to your suffering, because that will change and will be gone – as well as your happiness.

The thing is that you can talk and talk forever and never understand. We had a man here who was well trained in theology. He went to these seminars where learned men of religion sit and discuss the truth for days and days trying to decide what is true and what is not true, what is of God and what is not of God? But at best they can only come to some intellectual conclusion. Similarly, there are meetings of great leaders of churches in America, and they discuss issues like whether homosexuality is all right with God or not. So they will talk and they will talk and they will talk, and they will come to some intellectual conclusion – but no real awareness. They need more experience.

So we want to get to the experience part, unless you want to stay up all night. Just begin to see the illusion. Do not worry too much about it. Just begin to understand that this *is* a plane of illusion and that everyone is being controlled by the illusion. You cannot come to a state of full awareness and completely understand it in the beginning. You get there by practicing, seeing it. So you can only begin by at first recognizing at least the possibility that everyone is controlled by illusion. Your awareness of the fact will increase as you observe, as you observe the illusion and how it works, as you see others being controlled by the illusion: how they are being helplessly taken and practically forced to behave in so many ways against logic and reason. Any man of the mind, the psychologist and the psychiatrist, they can tell you that people seldom even behave logically or rationally. Their behavior is so illogical. Their motivations, their reasons for doing what they do in life are based upon such illusion. A man may have been very small and frail as a child and no one would pay any attention to him, so his whole adult life he is trying to become important so everyone will recognize him – his whole life. What an illusion! He is trying to fulfill a desire that was not fulfilled when he was a child. And his existence as a child is an illusion.

Anyway, it goes on and on, but you must begin somewhere. So just begin seeing how the illusion is working. Look and examine the people around you. Look at your own self. See how you are being forced to do things you know are not good or you do not want to do, but somehow you end up doing them. What is this force that is propelling you? How are *you* being controlled? Like the main part of talking tonight was just how the society and the propaganda has control over you, and you are currently being controlled by what society has already done to you. And if you were in another society, in another country, you would behave in another way, according to their propaganda, and their beliefs, and their society, and their religions.

Just begin to see the illusions. You must begin to see the illusion. And as you begin to see it and observe it, it will become more and more obvious – until you come to a state of full awareness. Because once you see an illusion and truly understand it, it no longer can have a hold upon you. Once you completely understand it, you are beyond it; it can no longer grasp you or hold you.

So the beginning is just to observe it. Begin to observe your whole existence, everything you do. There is an illusion, let's say a common illusion that you go out to dinner and you enjoy. Now, many people enjoy this illusion. So the next time you go out to enjoy, observe, and see just how much pleasure there really is. Just observe. I'm not saying to stop it, but observe it, the illusion: the illusion that you are enjoying, that you are having a pleasurable time here on this plane of existence. So look at the things that you consider to be pleasurable. Just observe them. Do not look at them in a negative way. Just simply pay attention.

Drug addicts – they think they are enjoying. But when one stands back and observes, one sees the drug addict's life is one of misery and suffering, *while they are on the drug*. It does not take a very aware person to look and see that they are suffering *while they are on the drug*. And they think it is so pleasurable.

So these are all ideas you can see. This is all illusion working in different degrees, in different ways, the different ways people think that they are enjoying pleasure. And by observing, you are increasing your awareness. That is all – just observe; pay attention. Do not go through life mindlessly. Even if you do not want to get out in this lifetime, at least lead your existence with as much awareness as possible. By doing this, you can at least avoid the areas that definitely *are not* pleasurable. So many people are constantly doing things that give them no pleasure at all, in fact, give them suffering. But because they are so unaware, they cannot distinguish, and they just know sometimes they are suffering. In one sense, you can increase your happiness on this plane by being more aware and avoiding at least things that are truly suffering – like drug addiction.

But if you are not aware of the illusion and how the illusion is working, then you can be captured by any illusion. People are so surprised. They see someone who seems to be so aware: Perhaps they were on a committee against drugs, and they see them later and they have become a drug addict – someone who has written the propaganda against drugs. How is it that they were taken from that point of awareness, where they were dedicating their life to preaching against drugs and have become a drug addict? That force, that energy we call illusion can do such a thing: can turn a person's life around, can make the saint the sinner, and the sinner the saint. This is a very amazing thing; if nothing else, it will be interesting and add another dimension to your life, like watching a soap opera. Because what is going on around you is so incredible, and the intricacies of the illusion are so amazing, that if nothing else, it will be an added dimension of amusement to your stay here on this plane – to watch and see how the illusion is working and capturing people and forcing them to behave in certain ways, so beautifully, so artistically, that they are not even aware what is happening. One day they are a promoter against drugs, and the next day they are taking the drug and they have no idea how it happened.

So if nothing else, it is a good mental exercise. It will add some dimension to your life, and of course, from Our point of view, ultimately, how will you become free from the illusion unless you see how the illusion is working? But whatever your desire is, you cannot lose by beginning this exercise. Understand that everyone is in illusion, and just begin to see how the illusion is working. And as you go on, it will become clearer and clearer.

Person Two: Gourasana, as you develop more awareness, will you also have less resistance?

Gourasana: Yes. People resist because they think there is pleasure. But once the illusion is gone, where is the resistance?

Everyone is smearing stool on the walls. And once you begin observing it, once you come to a point of understanding that *that* is what is going on, and that there is as much pleasure in the things that they are doing as in *that* activity, then you will not resist giving it up. And gradually you will see in all the activities that are going on, that once the illusion is gone from them, there will be no more desire to engage in the activities. Many activities *will become repulsive* and you will not want to engage in them. You will avoid the activity. Just as with the illusion of drug addiction: One who sees it, if they are not too covered over, is very afraid of it and repulsed by it. So yes, as you begin to see it, your resistance will go.

It is not something unnatural. There is a feeling like you will be torn and forced – but that is not the case. As you become aware, you will just naturally gravitate toward more pleasurable activities, just as children growing up. You see they go through different phases, but they outgrow them. But at a certain point, people begin to stagnate in their growth and they stop growing. And they stagnate and they do not outgrow any more illusions. That is why certain people, after certain ages, do not change very much. They basically stay the same; they change very little, whereas children growing up, every year are so different. Their desires are so different. They are such different people than they were a year or two ago. But once you reach a certain age, you stay the same, year after year, practically, until you die.

But there is that feeling that you are giving up something, that you are giving up something pleasurable, that it will be forced away from you. But it is not like that. *You will just see it, and once you see it you will stop it, and you will have no desire to do it anymore.* The illusion is so strong; however, as your awareness increases, not only do you not want to engage in these activities, but you begin to take pleasure and feel pleasure from other things. Someone who can sit down in a room, as we do, with some music that most would consider boring, unentertaining music, and just sit there. . . . "What's going on? Nothing is going on." You should commend yourself for just the fact that you can sit there and take some pleasure and even perhaps *look forward to this time,* some not even understanding why, but somehow they feel some pleasure, something is happening. They look forward to this time, and this increases and increases and increases. So not only are you becoming detached from these things of illusion, but simultaneously your attachment to the real pleasure increases. And while these things of illusion can stop, and your total happiness can be totally destroyed and devastated to the point where there is nothing to live for, the spiritual things do not go away. And in times of trauma, the spiritual things even increase, because your desire increases; your intensity increases. Because while you may be more easily trapped while it is all very nice around you, if they were to drop a nuclear bomb in the vicinity, suddenly it would not be so nice; the illusion would not be so great. And if you were practiced at going within or meditating, your desire to find truth would increase.

Yes, there is a pleasure in spiritual awareness. It is a great pleasure and it is motivating. Even while it doesn't *feel* pleasurable, even while you are going through difficulties on the path, still there is something that is so compelling in your heart that you cannot stop.

So this is what meditation is. It is tapping into another force. Here on the material plane, the dominant force is illusion. So you want to tap into another force and let that force move you. Let that force control you and carry you.

On this plane, the illusion is dominant, and *it is allowed* to be so. It is like there are certain rules that must be obeyed, because the illusion has its purpose and must be perpetuated for its purpose. So while We come and take those that are ready to go, the illusion is actually being reinforced by many things. Many people's faith in the illusion increases by what we are doing here. They are more convinced that their life is the way to go, by what we are doing here. So it is serving a double purpose. We are taking those out of illusion that want to go and, ironically enough, We are reinforcing the illusion of those that want to stay. They take strength by what We do. So hopefully, you will take the truth.

We should begin meditation.

Let Go of Who You Think You Are

August 20, 1988, Alpine, CA

(This chapter is a conversation Gourasana had with Carol, Gayle, and Jim right after Gourasana spoke the talk "The Principle of Degree.")

For many people, even their spiritual search is life as they would have it. It is the path as they would have it, as *they* want it to be. They want to find God, but they want to find Him *in a particular way.* They do not know they are holding on to something, and then after one, two, or three years at the most, they became stifled in their growth. One of the reasons for this is they would not let go of how *they* wanted it to be. It is another type of attachment. It is another concept, and to go from illusion into the light, you must give up all concepts, all attachment – especially as to how you will get there. So they are practicing seriously, and of course they are advancing, but they want it to be a certain way; so they are constantly trying to adjust their life to fit the conception of how they think it should be. And so many become stifled, frustrated, and give up. You will see this pattern in many paths: where they have a good system – maybe not perfect, but still very good and they could make good steady advancement – but they become totally frustrated and stop the process entirely. Much of this is because of the way they want it to be or conceive that it should be. And when it becomes apparent that it cannot be as they had conceived it should be or they wanted it to be, then they stop in frustration.

Carol: Well, one thing that happened this weekend is I realized that I can't figure anything out. I just have faith; I have faith. I wanted to say that I have to have faith, but *I do* have faith. And now I'm just going to have faith and let go without trying to figure anything out. It feels weird to try to talk about it, because so much really went on with me this weekend and to try to say anything is just. . . . Can you see something else? Maybe something else happened to me. Maybe I'm crazy, but I feel like something happened to me, and it feels really weird. I don't know anything except that I want to be surrendered and let go now. I went through a lot of fear this weekend and I'm not afraid of the fear so much now. I have faith in what's happening here, even though I have no idea what's happening – I am just here.

I would like to move much faster now. I don't know exactly what I can do to speed things up, and I don't even know what that means, to move faster. See, I don't know what any of this means. I just know that I want to find, I want to be with God all of the time. I know that I can be with God right now. I can feel it. I feel like He's right here. I know that He is. I know that *you are.* I can't explain it. I don't know how to let go. I don't know what to do.

Gourasana: You are doing very well for someone who has no idea of what to do. The mind cannot grasp it. The mind cannot understand it. For the mind to understand it means that it has been reduced to words, and it is not possible to reduce it to words.

Carol: That's why I can't explain it. I can't understand it. I can't say what it is.

Gourasana: You cannot put it into words. The mind is just a large storehouse for words, different combinations of words, which have different connotations. But it is obvious that understanding is going on.

So all you need to do is give up all your attachments to trying to understand with your mind what is going on. You said, when you first began speaking, that you have changed so much in three days, that you are a new person. So what does that mean? It does not matter how; your mind cannot understand how, but somehow or other you have latched on to the energy and it has moved you and it has changed you. So you've let go of the mind, and you just let that energy continue to move you and change you. And you trust it.

You need to clarify or distinguish between two personalities: your real self and your illusory self. Again, the difficulty with most people is they want their illusory self to become enlightened, but the illusory self cannot become enlightened because it is illusion. All that can happen to the illusory self is that it will disappear. You cannot bring light into darkness. Your illusory self is darkness, and you cannot bring illumination to the darkness, because the darkness will no longer be there to be illuminated. And so the illusory self, which you have so strongly identified with for so long, will not become enlightened; it will just disappear.

Naturally this confuses people on the path, because their focus of attention is in the true realm to different degrees, which means that they are existing in their true identity to different degrees. When you go to the true realm, the real you – the true identity – goes there, not the illusory self. So when you come back, or when you lose that focus and you come back to the illusory self, there is such a contrast that sometimes it can feel like: "Did it ever happen?" Because when you are totally in illusion, or back in your illusory self, you are lost in that identity, and that identity only knows illusion. It appears that the true realm has disappeared and the experience seems like a dream. So anyway, this is another way to see it and understand it.

The obstacle is that they want to take the illusory self and have that illusory self come to a state of awareness, but that is not possible. That is why you must let go of who you think you are, because once you let go of who you think you are and truly enter into the light more and more, who you used to think you were is gone. It has disappeared; the illusion is no longer there. One symptom of this obstacle that is common is to try to understand it with the mind, and the mind merely is a collection of words, like a large computer. It is beyond the mind and the words.

Carol: What's happening with me right now is that realizations are coming so fast. Something just came from what you said and I wanted to catch it so I could say it, but everything is happening so fast that I can't stop to think about it, even though I can feel the realization. I have to let it come and then let it go without trying to catch it. I can't remember what the realization was just one minute ago. I'm having to let go because it's happening really fast. So I feel like I'm in a fog, like things are just passing by me. I can't explain. There's not a problem. I want to try to explain something but I can't explain it.

But Gourasana, I met this woman on the airplane and it was just the most incredible experience. I was going to get on the airplane, and I turned around and in back of me was this woman, and she looked exactly like me. As soon as our eyes caught, our hands reached out for each other. She looked at me like we knew each other. It was the most incredible experience. To try to put it in words would ruin it.

It ends up, she's coming down to see you. She does seminars. She has a sister who's trying to leave in this lifetime; she wants to find God in this lifetime. I started to talk to her and there were many incredible similarities: We're the same age, her birthday is just two days after mine – same year; she has a daughter who's the same age as Kristine, who has a name almost like Maha; and she also changed her name to Kristy the same time Kristine changed her name. It was pretty wild. Everywhere I went today, I had to be careful about looking at people, because I felt like there were going to be millions of people that I knew. I felt like I knew all these people.

I want to preach Gourasana, so bad, that's all I want to do. I want to find God fast, because I want to help other people, and I know I can't do that until I find Him myself. But there's a drive in me that wants to preach more than anything. If I have to give that up, that's okay too, but it feels very natural. It's hard for me to keep from looking for people. Everywhere I go I'm constantly looking for people.

Gourasana: So this was an excellent stage to reach. Just as you say you hear the words and they change you, but then you move on and where do the words go? As We have said before, the communication is not the words, it is something else. It is an energy, an internal power. So the words are just words, but when you *hear,* then you can forget the words because *your awareness has changed.* So you can move that fast beyond the words. As I have said, when you begin to move faster, you do not even stop to think about it or reflect on the words.

What came to you while the words were being spoken – that energy – you just continue to tap into that energy, that awareness, that communication that is going on beyond the words. And of course, this is very hard for someone who has not experienced it to understand. But as you say, you've just experienced it. No words were spoken and something changed, something happened. So something can be constantly changing and happening, and trying to understand what is happening slows it down. Trying to remember the words slows it down. So there is a point when remembering is good and certain things are always helpful to remember, but at the same time the fast movement comes when you go beyond the words, and you just feel that energy. Just as you have experienced so many times, when you have heard certain words – not just those that I have spoken but what others have said in different books – you *feel* that it is the truth. You have a realization; there is something besides just empty words that goes on, so that something else is perpetually going on. If you can just let go of your mind and of trying to understand, then that energy can just move you more and more.

How do you think these yogis come to awareness? They sit alone in a cave, and who is speaking to them? Yes, there is a communication going on, but not like this, verbally, with the mouth. So they sit there and are quiet and let go of their minds, and then communication comes. And they come to a state of awareness. But who is speaking to them? I have said it many times: The true communication is not in the words – the true communication is going on beyond the words if you can just trust that it is happening.

But as this happens to you more, you become more familiar with it, and you can identify it. It is a type of sensation. It is something that is perceptible, but it is only perceptible as long as you do not try to hold on to it or understand it. Actually, it is only perceptible as long as you do not try to perceive it. You will just *be able* to perceive it. And then there will be times when you cannot perceive it. Or you may not think that you are moving and yet you are still moving, because once you get to a certain point spiritually, you automatically move at a faster rate. Just as I have said: Everyone in evolution is moving, everyone. There is no one that is not moving forward toward the light. Everyone is moving. It is just at different rates.

So it is not just when you are focused that you are moving, and then when you are not focused you go back to the same rate of evolution as everyone else. No. Once your awareness has come to a certain degree, once your consciousness is moving at a certain rate, once you have let go of your mind and how you want it to be, then your evolution – *automatically* – is moving at a much greater rate. So even when you cannot perceive that you are moving, still you are moving at such a rapid rate.

Sometimes you can look in retrospect and understand what was happening, but not while it is happening. Just like David: the one period where he was watching extensive hours of television – practically all of his waking time – he did not try to understand it, yet he knew he was moving and it was something beyond his mind. But even so, it took some retrospect; after maybe one month or more of this period, he understood that his mind was engaged with the television, but he was somewhere else. Something else was going on that was beyond his mind and the television. So to a normal person, it may have appeared that he was just watching television, but while his mind was engaged in the television, his consciousness was not. So he just trusted while it was happening. He knew that those on the spiritual path, if they learned of this behavior, they would just simply deem that he was just watching television – that he could not be very aware. So anyway, it *is* beyond the mind. It is beyond the mind. It is even beyond the activity, but activities can become more difficult to perform.

You want to know how to move faster, so just continue moving as you are moving. The only question of slowing down will be that you try to understand it. You try to talk about it too much, and it will bring you back into that state. It will invite the habit of trying to understand with the mind. It will invite that habit in by trying to explain too much or talk too much. This is why I say, people who just keep going may not perceive with their conscious minds that they are advancing, but there comes a point where it manifests and it appears suddenly – like suddenly you caught on. But in reality, everyone is constantly evolving and increasing the rate of advancement. It is just that certain points are reached where it becomes more perceptible, but you are always moving – especially around Me.

(In the following section of this talk, Gourasana is discussing with Jim, Carol, and Gayle a question he was asked by a woman in an earlier session concerning what it is like in the true realm of existence.)

Gourasana: She was wondering if there is a problem with boredom: "Because on this plane there are so many things to do, but in the true realm, what do you do? You do not have to work for a living. You do not ski or surf, so what do you do?" And also you could see, it was obvious, because then the question was, "Can you come back if you want?" As if you will become bored in the true realm and become tired of the ecstasy and want to come back. But there are so many more direct areas to discuss. But that is all right. After all, the true communication *is* beyond the words. So while sitting here, no matter how much nonsense the talking was, everyone was evolving and their consciousness was growing because they were here, listening, and they were intent and making an endeavor. So both things are necessary. Some who especially cannot meditate or do not have enough faith to *just* meditate can make more advancement during the discussion, because that is at least something that they can focus on – words. And by focusing on the words, they are focusing also on the spiritual energy that is going on.

But at any rate, what I was saying was that the first step – giving up how you would have it, giving up how you want your life to be – everyone must do this. It is just as critical for the spiritual seekers, because they are in another trap: how they want their spiritual life to be. When this first step has been truly completed, then the illusory self is – if not totally destroyed – so beyond repair that it cannot be recovered. It is virtually dead. It is as if it is in intensive care and not able to be revived. So, you cannot go back into that state again. You see?

As you've seen in other organizations, people were able to go back into their illusory self. They kept it around like an alter ego that they entered back into. They did not let go of it. They did not take that first step. They were practicing, but they had concepts on how they wanted it – so all the time they were holding on to the ego and that illusory self. So when they gave up their spiritual pursuit, they just slipped back into their illusory self and it was just the same.

And many just became as they were before. Of course some were changed, but still – you understand. But there comes a point when the ego is so destroyed, the illusory self is so destroyed, that there is nothing to go back to. In other words, there is a point that you cross where you – practically speaking – cannot go back into illusion.

You may try. You may remember what it was like, or some of the things you did when you were in illusion, but you will go back and you will do those things and the pleasure of doing it will be gone. Everyone has had this experience. They go and do something that they did in their past, and they do it and no longer is there any pleasure. And they wonder: Why did they do that? Or how is it that they could have done that? Or at least they know there is no pleasure now. So the illusory self becomes just a memory, and they may try to recapture it, but it is gone. So they are stranded like a living entity without a body – what you call a ghost. They have the body, but they do not have the illusion, so they are stranded, because to be in the body is not enough; you must have the illusion in order to take pleasure from activities of the body. So then there is no alternative but to go on spiritually.

It is really quite simple. The seemingly impossible task of getting out is really quite simple. You just have to desire it. It is that simple. It truly is that simple. Even those that are aware, for instance, like her father[1] – he is very aware – yet even in his aware state, he has come to a point where he has said that he does not care if he comes back. And he will not let go of how he wants his life to be. But that is all right. Still it is just so obvious – that is why he will not get out. And not many attain his state of awareness. But he is still in illusion

1) Gourasana is referring to the father of one of the members of the Core.

and will be forced at the time of death, which is not all that far away, to give up the things he is holding on to, the way he wants it to be – his children, his family. In a very short period it will all be taken forcibly away, but because of the illusion, he cannot give it up now. That is why the first step is so significant. It means that one has understood enough to not be led on by the illusion anymore.

Basically, the first step is just giving up before it is all forced away from you at death. So if you are going to live another forty years, basically what are you giving up? You are surrendering forty years of how you want your life to be. Not such a big price to pay, but one in illusion hangs on until they are forced at death to let go. This is not logical; this does not make good sense. Of course it is illusion. There are so many intelligent people who are endeavoring so hard, but it is these things, these are the reasons that they fail.

Actually, the only words that you can always use are words of prayer. You do not even need to use many words in a prayer. You can just say, "Lord," and your desire is understood. You do not need to spell it out. But also you can do that, you can express your desire in words.

But if you want to preach, then you must use the proper words.

Carol: When you get to maybe a suitable state for preaching, is it possible that you can just surrender and the words just come through you? It seems like I've experienced sometimes that I don't even know what I am saying. That's when preaching really seems to work, is when that's the case.

Gourasana: Yes. You just speak from the heart, as they say. And if you really care for the person you are speaking to, then the words will come. But if you do not care, then do not speak. If you find yourself not caring, better not to speak. Something is telling you not to speak, because the chances are if you do not care and you are aware, no matter what they are saying, they really do not care and you will be wasting your time. This is the biggest danger you must look out for. When you find one who is sincere, you will not need to be so concerned about saying the right words.

We could present it in such a way that we could attract so many, many more people, without lying; simply we would just present it in a certain way, if it were our desire to help a lot of people a little. But the reality is we will help a few a lot. Those that come and go along the way, of course, will be helped, but this is the main area of concern we must look out for: is giving your time and energy, preaching to those that are not hearing. Of course, there is never a question of a waste of time, because you are continuing to evolve. And even those that are not listening so well, they also are evolving by your speaking, but there are just others that will benefit so much more.

So when is the woman you met coming?

Carol: She lives in Santa Cruz, but she's coming down here in October. And she said that she's going to call her sister. Her sister lives in New Mexico. Because after I talked to her for a while, she started to think about who else would want this. She started thinking about a lot of people, but then when she really thought about it, she could see it was only for a few people. She was sure her sister would come down. She said her sister was coming to town next weekend. I'm going to send them some of your tapes. We have some good tapes from the past few weeks that are really nice.

Gourasana: One thing I am happy about is that the consciousness of the group has been protected fairly well. I know in the new place it will be protected better. And you must always strive for a better and better standard. While you *(talking to Carol)* were gone this weekend, David and The Lady and Jim discussed more at length. I think The Lady, however, brought up the best point of all, and that is that one criterion for those who come must be that "they can stand on their own two feet," as she says. This cannot become a rehabilitation center for physically or mentally disabled. This is only a place to come for enlightenment. As you say, your mood is to preach and you want to help, but there are some who you can spend so much time helping and give so much energy to, but your energy can be spent so much better – even if the time that you give to help these disabled people is spent instead in thought on how to preach and how to reach those who are sincere and are not disabled mentally or physically. Of course when I say "not disabled," I simply mean that they are not a burden on the group, that when they come they do not need more than simply spiritual guidance and assistance. At this time, we cannot be a facility to help them with their physical and mental handicaps. If later on there are generous donations and there are some that wish to help in this area, then something can be done, but not now.

Now it is important that the ones that are coming become more focused, much more than ever. I am not interested in bringing so many people part way and then having them cast back into illusion like what happens in organizations that are structured so that a lot will receive a certain amount of enlightenment, but it is not possible the way they are structured to bring them all the way. Not possible. No hope.

So the end result of these organizations is that *no one* becomes fully aware. Many become much more aware, but no one becomes fully aware. So the standard must always be maintained that those that wish to leave this plane of illusion *in this lifetime: they* will have the facility; *they* will have the environment; *they* will have the assistance to do so. And if others can be helped, that is all right, of course. We are not refusing help to those that just wish to advance as long as they are not burdensome.

Again, the concentration will always be on those that want to go back *in this lifetime.* And if that is all that can be done and no one else can be helped, then that is how it will be. But if there is opportunity to help the general population, then it can be done as long as it does not detract from the group that is leaving in this lifetime. We must never focus on numbers, quantity. We must always focus on the seriousness and the advancement of those that are ready to leave.

So you have taken the first step, you see?

Carol: Yes.

Gourasana: Maybe a little shaky.

Carol: No.

Gourasana: And what about you, Lady?

Gayle: Yes.

Gourasana: And you?

Jim: A little shaky.

Gourasana: You just need to contemplate what this means the first time. See how not taking the step is a trap, no matter if you take another teacher or whatever you do spiritually in your life, until you take this first step you are more or less holding on to illusion. Of course, there are many illusions built around spiritual processes. So just as when you hold on to the illusion, you are missing the real pleasure, so when you hold on to your life as you would have it, then you are missing the life that is *truly* glorious. So as with all illusion, it is what you hold on to that causes you to miss everything.

Giving up your life as you would lead it, requires first that you recognize your state of illusion, and that in that state you are not qualified to set the standard for how you should lead your life if you wish to get out. Now of course, also, many times, how your life *will* be led coincides with how you *want* to lead it. It is just the surrendering that is the key. Just as I said also, one must come to a point where one is willing to die – one will say, "Yes, if what I need to be free from this illusion is to leave this body now, then I am prepared." But you do not leave the body – you see? You know, you have heard David; he came to this point: He was prepared to die, but he did not die. So it is the consciousness again – it is having the consciousness of surrender, not that the thing has to happen. So also, when one gives up how they would have their life, it may be that some of the same basic concepts they had will be fulfilled much better. But it is that act of surrender that is necessary, the flexibility, because of the areas that need to be changed. So the majority of the areas may be the same, but there is certain to be some change. Certain.

At any rate, you know Me a little now. If I so desired, I could speak in such a way that I would not drive away so many. But the things that I say weed out those that are not very serious. So just as when one is mining for jewels, they go through so many tons of rock before they find one gem. So we have found a few precious gems and we must guard against their being stolen by the illusion. We must protect the gems that we have worked so hard to find. We have dug through so many tons of rock. So much endeavor just to come up with a few precious gems. We must protect the gems.

After we move, this new household must be like a fortress against the illusion. Here there was so much learning, and now that learning needs to be applied, and the new establishment must be like a fortress against the illusion. And as with any fortress, those that live in the fortress must all be secure. The fortress must be guarded carefully so the illusion, which is always trying to attack, does not get in and create damage.

When you are talking to each other, you can spend time increasing your awareness in this area. Because if you examine these organizations – frequently, even where there is just one teacher and maybe one hundred disciples – there is so much disturbance and corruption. You must safeguard against contamination.

So right now in your presence there are the most ecstatic things going on. The most ecstatic beauty, the most ecstatic love and light – and you are in the midst of it.

It is the most amazing phenomenon that right now you are in the midst of such incredible ecstasy and love and light. But the illusion is such an amazing phenomenon that you can only sense it to different degrees. But you are all aware enough to sense it. Just pay attention.

Why do you think you all have had the faith to become so dedicated? Because even though you may not understand with your minds, a part of you is aware and can sense that there is a whole other existence.You have already experienced it. You cannot say maybe a time or a day that you recognized this, but the culmination is there – in your awareness.

You can get your bed now. I will sit up for a while.

Final Journey Meditation I[1]

August 20, 1988, Alpine, CA

(This talk is called "Final Journey Meditation I" because Gourasana spoke another version of this meditation on November 5, 1988. Gourasana explains the significance of the Final Journey Meditation in a later discourse:

> The Final Meditation is significant, because when practicing this meditation with your heart, completely going into your consciousness, you will see what you are hanging on to. You must practice it sincerely. You must not practice it as an intellectual exercise. You must enter completely into the mood as if it is your final meditation and it is time to let go of everything. And if you do this deeply enough, then you will see what you are holding on to. When you practice this you must truly be ready to leave at that point. And when you see something that is holding you back, that you are hesitating about letting go of, then this you must work on. Because there will come a time when you will do the Final Meditation in earnest and you will leave, and if there is still something that you do not want to let go of, then you will again take birth.[1]*)*

1) This quote is from *Time is Too Precious to Be Wasted*, September 17, 1988, which is the next chapter in this book.

Gourasana: So we'll call this the Final Journey Meditation.

Even your conception about what a full state of awareness is, was wrong, and you are all in a full state of awareness. You do not need to do any more. Nor do you need to stay here any more. Your business is finished. Well, let us say almost finished.

Now you just need to let go of the last few things that you are holding on to. You are going to give it all up now. There will be no more eating. No more need to work to feed the body. All the endeavor and troubles and things that you have done to keep the body alive are finished. So you can let go of all those last things.

And letting go has to be gentle.

You should feel the beauty and the wonder of the place you are going to.

Feel the love that is waiting to enfold you.

Feel the ecstasy that is waiting to carry you away. It is there. It has always been there: the love, the beauty. The satisfaction so great that you are fully prepared now to leave this plane of illusion.

Now let go of the few things you are holding on to: your son, your daughter, your husband, family, friends. These are all connotations of illusion. These beings will be with you. Their time for full enlightenment will come and then they will join you. There's nothing to lament. There is no feeling of separation.

All the things that you have been hanging on to have just been suffocating these feelings of love that you have been seeking; they have been suffocating the ecstasy that you have wanted to experience. So while there is still need to let go, you gladly let go because you know that these things are just illusion and they no longer have any meaning. They no longer have any bearing on your existence. And as you leave this body for good, you will be leaving this plane of existence once and for all – for good, never to return.

Feel what this means. Feel it, because it is a reality. You will not eat again. You will not sleep again. You will not feel pain again. You will not suffer again.

Turn your back on the illusion and turn to the light; it is there. You are in the midst of it; it has just been covered by illusion.

There is nothing but ecstasy. Let it grow and enfold you.

Feel the beauty of the place. It is Home. And you have come Home. And you have left the illusion. The love is so great. There is nothing but unconditional love. You have never felt it so purely before, because here there is no question of contamination.

Like a newborn baby, you need to gradually acquire your senses in this realm. Otherwise you will be overwhelmed. Still, you are being overwhelmed. There's such an incredible beauty. You cannot yet see it but you can *feel it: it is so great.* And it is so sweet because the beauty is filled with love.

And there are others around you – so many. And you feel such love coming from them, the dearest of friends. You have just arrived, yet the greatest of love is already being exchanged.

And there is a sound difficult to identify, but the very sound of the place is filled with love.

Here, there is no more striving. Here, the illusion of time does not exist.

There is no more worry. Just knowing that you have come Home is enough. You have all eternity to let all the unlimited beauty and aspects of the true realm manifest.

Yes, what will manifest is very glorious, but *mainly* I want you to capture this moment – your final meditation, your last few moments in this body, the last of millions of bodies. And what it will be like to finally be leaving this plane for good.

You see, none of this is pretend. As you do this meditation, *you are* leaving this plane of existence; *you are* leaving this illusion; *you are* letting go; *you are* reinforcing the fact that this is your last life.

It is just another way to take your consciousness away from the illusion and probe the true realm of existence. Because just as you are doing it now to different degrees, there will come a point *very soon* when it will be to the *full degree.* And you can experience it *now* to a great degree.

Another way to fall asleep at night: As you fall asleep, you focus on the fact that this is your final meditation, that you have come to the end. Now you just let go of the few remaining things. And now that it is the end, you see how petty and trivial they are and it is very easy for you to let go of them. So you gladly let go.

That last bit of effort, with that last bit of effort you let go of your body and now you are free. You have finished your business. You have ended your existence for good. You will never return to the plane of illusion. And now you can just immerse yourself in the love and the light – fully. And relish the never-ending ecstasy, the ever-increasing ecstasy. And become lost in the beauty and the splendor of the place.

This is a meditation of just pleasure. There is no striving to this meditation. There is no struggle to this meditation.

There's just a feeling of satisfaction in this meditation, of accomplishment. You have reached the goal. You have come to the end and you are happy with it. There is no longing. It is easy for you to leave. Now there is nothing but ecstasy and love and light. Your final meditation. Your most glorious meditation.

This final meditation is a reality. When you are even too tired to pray, too tired to try, and it is the end of the day, then you can practice your final meditation, because this meditation is one of no effort. This meditation is just finally giving up, finally letting go. No more effort, no more. . . .

Feel the significance of this final meditation. Feel the magnitude of it.

Become so successful at this meditation that you do not return. You lose yourself; you go so deep into this meditation that you do in fact leave your body.

Perform *all your meditations* with the greatest seriousness and presence. There is no practicing for the future.

Time Is Too Precious to Be Wasted

September 17, 1988, Pacific Beach, CA

So by now, those of you who have been coming for some time are realizing more and more what it means to let go, what it means to give up. Individually, you can see things that you were hanging on to in the past and were not letting go of, and how that was an impediment. And how those around you would not let go, would not give up. Indeed, you have seen many move to the point where there was something that they needed to give up, to let go of, which they would *not* do.

To leave this plane of illusion in this lifetime, you must be prepared to let go of *everything*, including your very life as you would have it. You must come to the point of surrendering your will. You must give up how you want your life to be, because how you have formed your future is based upon illusion, your material desires. So when one seriously begins this path, no one can stay the same or continue to behave as they have in the past. So many things must change. Someone may have even formed a relationship in illusion and once they begin on the spiritual path, and they see that that relationship is only conducive for illusion, one may be required to give up the association of a mate. Indeed, your relationship *with everyone* will change – your friends, your family.

As your awareness increases, as you realize more and more how precious the time is, you will have less and less time for *useless* social interaction, which is mainly for some entertainment value. As you begin to strive less and less for happiness on this plane of illusion, certain activities will decrease naturally. But because of attachments developed between family and friends and possibly a mate, sometimes extreme effort must be made to sever the relationship, if they are a bondage or a basis for illusion.

Those that are serious must at least have the desire to become free from the bondage they are in. They must be willing to let go *of everything*, even if at the moment they are not able to. They must at least understand that they will have to let go *of everything* before they will be free. And while they may prolong the bondage if they wish, they will have to give up everything before long; because as you have seen, you progress to a certain point, it comes time to give up something, and if you do not give up and move when you should, then you can become stagnant in your spiritual life. You find those who have searched seriously but have not given up or let go become stagnant in their spiritual life. They are no longer growing; their awareness is staying approximately the same. Because of endeavor, there is evolution, but it is a fraction of what it could be. On the other hand, one who will let go, one who will give up as rapidly as possible, no matter how frightening – their awareness can change so much every week.

So look at what you are hanging on to. Look at what you will not let go of. See your attachments, see your illusions, and then you must begin letting go. You must practice letting go. There are so many things to let go of.

If one is going to come to this group, then they should consider whether or not they wish to leave this plane of illusion in this lifetime. They must make that decision and know what the decision means. If they decide to stay, then birth is there again and again. But to leave is very difficult. Your life must become absorbed in this endeavor. By necessity *you have to* come to a point where there is nothing else, because in order to leave at the time of death there must be no attachments. You must have let go of everything, given up everything, so that when you leave the body, there is nothing holding you back.

But the illusion is so strong. Those of you that have been endeavoring in this way for some time have seen how you go from one illusion to another, and how by habit you take up another illusion and believe it and live it. Without correction, without illumination of your new illusion, it would not be possible to become free. So to come to a certain stage of awareness, it is necessary that you have guidance. If you do not have guidance, you will not succeed. The traps are too endless and they are too subtle. You will not be able to perceive that you are in a trap, nor what that trap is. But I have pointed out so many illusions and still they cannot see; they will not acknowledge; they will not hear. So even with outside help, if one will not listen and act upon what they know to be true, then what is the possibility of becoming free in this lifetime?

So what are your questions? Or would you just like to say something to Me about what is going on with you?

Person One: Gourasana, the "Final Journey Meditation" tape is the next best thing to being with you in meditation. It is the one thing that I've been able, in the last few weeks, to use to keep in focus. But in trying to follow your instructions on awareness, I find that the more awareness I seek, the harder it is for me to stay focused. I'm finding myself more easily distracted in the last months than I have been for years. Is there anything that will help me to keep the thoughts from constantly intruding, and sounds of people making music, and other things from destroying my focus? I thought I had it and I've lost it.

Gourasana: When you see that something has distracted you, has taken you from the path, then you must take whatever steps are necessary so that it does not happen again. Even though the steps may be a little artificial, whatever it is that is necessary for you to do, that you must do. If one finds that they are in a place where there is too much outside disturbance, and they cannot focus with this going on, then find a way to soundproof the room and you can sit in that room and be quiet. First you see clearly what the problem is, what is the beginning of the problem, and then come up with a solution. You do not allow the same problem to distract you over and over. Somehow a remedy must be there. *Whatever it is*, a remedy must be there. But *first* you must see the problem clearly. Then the solution should not be too difficult to see. To execute the solution may be difficult, but to know what to do should not be so difficult once you understand what the problem is. Usually there are several problems that are distracting you, and endeavor must be there to come up with a solution. *You must be careful* when you look at what the distraction is, that simultaneously you are in the frame of mind to let go of everything, so you do not reject the solution because it is not something you wish to do. Rather, you see what the solution is, then you may take time to execute it, but you must not avoid *what you need to do* because you do not see how it is possible or because it is too painful.

The reasons to stay in illusion are many, but the end result will be that you are still bound by illusion at the time of death no matter how good your reasons are. There is *no* excuse that is sufficient. If one is serious, they will find a solution for everything. In this way your life will gradually change until it is more conducive to advancement. So you must look at your situation and see what it is that you could change to make it more ideal, more conducive. And then you must act.

Generally everyone is adjusting their living situation to be *more* comfortable, to make their living easier, but this cannot be a criterion. What you need to do may make your life *more* difficult, *harder* to manage. You cannot do things upon the basis of increasing your happiness in this illusion. You must act solely to increase your awareness. You must work constantly on creating a situation that is more and more conducive to your advancement. That is the *only* criterion you should have: *Is what you are doing the most conducive for your advancement?*

The Final Meditation is significant, because when practicing this meditation with your heart, completely going into your consciousness, you will see what you are hanging on to. You must practice it sincerely. You must not practice it as an intellectual exercise. You must enter *completely* into the mood as if it *is* your final meditation and it *is* time to let go of everything. And if you do this *deeply enough*, then you will see what you are holding on to. When you practice this, you must truly be ready to leave at that point. And when you see something that is holding you back that you are hesitating about letting go of, then this you must work on. Because there will come a time when you will do the Final Meditation in earnest and you *will* leave, and if there is still something that you do not want to let go of, then you will again take birth.

Cindy: Gourasana, can I ask a question?

Gourasana: Yes.

Cindy: Gourasana, why is it that some yogis remain in their bodies for hundreds or thousands of years? Why did they choose this, instead of leaving this plane? Is it because they have work here to do, or is it a choice that they want to stay here?

Gourasana: Some have the power to stay until they are ready to leave but it is rare. But you do not have that power, so you must become ready to leave within the time period that *you* have. And as that time period is very short, you need to move as quickly as possible. No matter how many years you think you have left.

Cindy: I do not understand why somebody would choose to stay here when they could leave.

Gourasana: It is not something *you* have to worry about. When I say, "leave," I do not mean for good, necessarily. I just mean when they are ready to leave their body *this* lifetime, they have some choice. They also are attached and will not let go.

Cindy: Gourasana, I have had many difficult situations come up in my life in the last few weeks. Extremely difficult situations, where I can see myself attached to emotions and to the outcomes. The only way I could see to get through the situations was to completely surrender all that I wanted, in terms of the outcome. I've continued practicing this in everything that I am doing, by giving up and surrendering all desires and outcomes in all situations. Is this a good thing to do, to practice this in all situations?

Gourasana: Of course.

Carol: Gourasana, I was wondering how to let go when there are some people that you are close with, and you know that they are having a difficult time and they won't receive help or ask for help. And they even insist that they're okay, and you can tell that they're not. I have a real problem with that, not so much that I want to help, but I can feel it inside. My insides are in total turmoil when someone close to me gets like that. I know I have to let go and let them go their own way. I know that with my mind now, and it seems my mind is getting more under control about it and letting go. But my insides feel like they're ripped apart when I see that happening, when I feel it. I think I need to let go of that feeling. Maybe you can give me some guidance on that? Some practice or some way to begin to let go of even having that feeling inside.

Gourasana: Just examine the feeling and see if it is something that is inhibiting your growth or not. If the feeling is compassion, then it is not inhibiting your growth. If someone will not receive help, it is natural for one who is aware to feel bad. Not that continually you feel that way, because yes, you must let go. But still, the ramification of their not hearing, of their determination to stay in illusion, is to take birth again and again. One who is aware cannot help but feel the depth of the decision this living entity is making. When one who is serious about leaving in this lifetime sees someone consciously choose to stay in illusion, it naturally creates so many emotions. Just as it is difficult for one in illusion to understand why they should give up the illusion, so also for one who is giving up the illusion, it is very difficult to understand how one could consciously stay in illusion. But this will be the choice of most.

So again, the only criterion that you need to be concerned with is if it is something that is an impediment. Certainly, trying to convince someone who will not hear, who is not listening – that is an impediment, if for no other reason then you are wasting your time. Better you talk to someone who is serious and who *will* listen, maybe resisting, but will listen. This you can distinguish. But for one who will not hear – time is too precious to be wasted.

Carol: I think I'm mainly trying to deal with the feelings that I'm having. I don't know what the feelings are, but they don't feel good and they make me want to cry. It's not that I even want to really say anything to the particular people or help them, but I guess I feel bad when I see somebody having a hard time. It feels really bad, and I don't know if that's a feeling I need to learn how to control, because the feeling seems to get worse all the time. Sometimes I can hardly stand it, so I just want to know if I need to control that feeling or do something to let go of it or do something so it doesn't happen. It seems to be coming up more and more.

Gourasana: You let it take you where it will and you see where it takes you. You must learn to distinguish what is beneficial and what is not. But *you* must learn to distinguish. Certainly as you become more aware, your compassion grows. When you see someone choose illusion and you see that illusion for them means suffering, and you know they will die in illusion and suffering, and that their suffering will not end when they die – how can you help but feel compassion? And compassion needs to grow, continually grow so that as time goes on and more and more serious people come – those who are ready to give up the illusion

– this compassion will motivate you to help them. And helping in this way *is not a burden*. Indeed, it is gratifying and will enhance your awareness.

If your helping another becomes a burden, then you need to look at it. Then you are doing something wrong; then you are not doing it out of compassion. You are doing it for some other reason and that reason is contaminated if it is a burden. It becomes a burden when you try to convince someone to do something *other* than what they truly desire. If they truly desire to leave this plane of illusion in this lifetime, then they will act upon what you say to some extent. They will listen.

Carol: So if I don't say anything and just observe what's happening to the people and different feelings come about in me that don't necessarily feel good, that's not something I have to fight against or necessarily try to get rid of them? It seems when those feelings come, that my state of being equipoised is disrupted because those feelings are there. I don't know if it's disturbing my mind, because it feels like it's in my body and my emotions.

Gourasana: If you don't know, then you should find out.

There seems to be too much disturbance in the mind to have a normal meditation. I think it would be good to go to the ocean for those who wish to. If someone wishes to stay and meditate then they can do that.

Carol: Are you going to go to the ocean?

Gourasana: Yes.

Carol: Should we prepare now?

Gourasana: Yes, if there are no more questions. Actually there are *many* questions, but they are not being asked. So perhaps in a more informal setting we can talk more freely.

Somehow this type of arrangement seems to stifle some people.

Carol: It will take a few minutes for everyone to get the proper clothing. If anybody wants to stay and talk for a few minutes while everybody is getting ready, they can.

Person One: In looking at the things that I'm wanting to be willing to give up, to surrender, I find there are several things. The one thing that seems the hardest for me to give up or to surrender (and this is not a philosophical question, it just seems like maybe a very big hurdle) is that sometimes I feel I want to go to the light and not come back here too much. In other words, I'm attached to that. Is that an attachment? Do I need to also be willing to say, "But if I have to come back, I will?"

Gourasana: No.

Person One: Wanting that is not an attachment, it is not an impediment, wanting that with all my heart?

Gourasana: No, only if it becomes an obstacle: If when you meditate, you want to go to the light, as you say, yet, there is something else you *should* do. So again, if it is a conception about how your meditation should be, then it is an impediment. To have *the desire* to go to the light is not an impediment, but what you need to do *to get to* the light, that you must be ready to do.

Person One: I know one of the things that seems to keep haunting me is criticism from people that I thought knew me: that I'm simply trying to escape from life, that I'm running out. I don't believe that I am trying to escape from life, but I'm haunted by the idea that this is how it seems to others. I don't want to be moved by their feelings and opinions.

Gourasana: It *is* trying to escape. Trying to escape from repeated birth. Trying to escape from this life of illusion.

Yes. When they say you are trying to escape from life, they mean life *as they know it* and life as they know it is a life of illusion. So you can say, "Yes, I'm trying to escape from a life of illusion." And automatically by trying to escape from a life of illusion, you also escape from life itself, life as they know it in the body. So yes, you are trying to escape, to not take birth again, to leave once and for all. That *is* escape. This is a prison and you wish to leave the prison. So yes, you are trying to escape.

They think that it is bad that you are trying to escape. But you should ask them, "Why do you wish to stay in prison?" A little challenging of their illusion *will help you, give you more confidence.*

Person One: You have described any of the emotions as either capable of helping us or being impediments. Is that also true of guilt? Because as I find myself focusing more on this spiritual practice, I find myself occasionally feeling guilty about those who I'm neglecting or leaving behind. And I don't see that guilt as helpful to me. I don't see it as a healthy emotion.

Gourasana: Guilt must not be attached to what you must leave behind.

Person One: Even obligations that I have voluntarily entered into: my work, my family, my ailing parents? I find that I'm putting those things at the bottom of my list of priorities as I find myself looking forward to Saturdays to come to San Diego. Nobody understands that. I don't mind that they don't understand, but I still feel some guilt that I'm neglecting my obligations to them. You once said I must be spiritually selfish. Does that also mean selfish with regard to other people – to not have them be in first place in my life?

Gourasana: Absolutely. Nothing must come before this. Nothing.

Person One: You've spoken of how important it is to not be attached any longer to our body's indulgences, specifically sexuality. As I try to free myself from my sexual desires and needs, I can't help but wonder why they're there. Are they there to test me? To see how sincere I am?

Gourasana: No. You just must give up in this area. It is very dangerous, so you must be careful about giving up completely. And guilt must not be attached to giving up sex. If there is need for sex, then have sex, and observe what happens. Do not do it unconsciously. I do not mean just the act, but be aware how your consciousness changes around the whole phenomenon of sex, before, during, and after. See how it affects your awareness.

Person One: I see how it can become a distraction.

Gourasana: You can become lost.

Person One: Yes.

Gourasana: So you must stay aware. But you do not want to go beyond your point of tolerance, which is a common mistake in spiritual life. So many who practice celibacy go beyond a level of tolerance, then they lose complete control and they become lost in illusion. As long as you recognize your illusion, you are relatively safe compared to one who becomes lost and no longer thinks they are in illusion. These are two categories of illusion. One is *in* illusion and they are *not* aware of it, and one is *in* illusion and they *are* aware of it.

So yes, the desire may still be there, but it is not a desire that you can just stop so suddenly. It must gradually disappear through awareness. So through awareness you must conquer the desire; but one way to conquer it may be that you continue to engage in the act, occasionally. Better that, and realize it is illusion and see it. See how the illusion causes so much difficulty, see how one day the illusion is not there and then it comes upon you and you are practically forced to act and go out and seek a partner. And then see how your overall consciousness is affected.

Person One: I didn't know if this was something the entire group was wrestling with or just myself; that's why I didn't bring it up before.

Gourasana: *Everyone* should be aware of this.

Person One: You have mentioned it many times and no one has asked about it. I assumed that they were not troubled by it.

Gourasana: Everyone is silent and yet everyone has so many questions. Privately or informally, discussion is there. So often we meet like this and everyone is quiet. But to be quiet in illusion is a mistake.

Person One: I won't assume anything in my questions; I'll bring them up as they come to me.

Gourasana: Yes. Everyone can benefit from everything we have discussed. Yes, this is one of the largest problems, yet how many are facing this issue?

Person One: It is not that I am bedeviled day and night by desire. It's been two years since I've had any sex with a woman, but I am so much more aware of the women around me. The women in our group, for example, are all very attractive to me. I see them as women. I see them as sexually attractive, not only as sisters in the light or searching together. I feel bad that I look at them this way. Maybe I have, by not engaging in it, made it too important.

Gourasana: Yes. Yes.

Love Is Everything

September 21, 1988, Pacific Beach, CA

To say that there is no hope of leaving this plane of illusion in this lifetime means that one does not really want to leave in this lifetime. After all, to believe that you can leave means that you have the faith, and you cannot leave without the faith. So if someone *believes* there is *no* hope, then there is no hope. But if you *believe* there is hope, then there is.

One who truly wishes to leave this plane of illusion will never give up. They may try a process and when it does not work, then they will try *another* process – but they will never give up.

And those that wish to stay will *never* take the serious steps necessary to leave. They will *mimic* the masters; they will copy the great teachers and go through similar motions – but they will not allow their hearts to change. And they judge: They say that the masters have lost their power, since they cannot change these people. But these people do not change because they refuse to let go; they refuse to change their hearts.

While they may appear to be searching for the truth, in reality most are doing everything to hide from the truth.

When they come to the brink of letting go – those who are *that* fortunate – they refuse to let go. They practice a process that takes them to that point, to the brink where they could let go, but once they come to that point, they refuse. They do not want it. They do not want the truth. So they stay on this side in the illusion and continue a pretense of a seeker of truth, a pretense of an aware person, a pretense of a propagator of consciousness. Yet in reality, the only thing they propagate is illusion.

It is such a simple thing. There are so many teachings, so much philosophy, so many practices, and yet everything leads to one point. That is where you make the decision: Will you let go? Will you give up this illusion *or not?* And if your decision is to not let go, then whatever you say after that is meaningless – illusion. At that point, the philosophies and the teachings become twisted to fit the illusion that everyone refuses to let go of. So you have millions of people following different masters, *refusing* to let go of the illusion, yet still propagating the teachings – but in such a way that does not truly encourage you to let go or to give up the illusion. But that is all right, because those that want to be trapped in illusion, those that want to stay in darkness, are happy to be in this situation because their desire is fulfilled.

But if one sincerely wants to leave this plane of illusion, and finds themselves in a process that takes them to this point, to this brink of letting go, then they will not let *the process* hold them back. They will not let *anything* hold them back. To give up everything means to give up the very processes by which you have come to this point. And there are some who come to this point without any formal process. But to hang on to a formal process means to hang on to illusion.

The processes are just created so that those in illusion can come to a point of letting go, come to a point of awareness where at least they see the illusion; they know for certain they do not want to be a part of the illusion; they know there is something greater; they see this place for what it is. This is the purpose of the process. But once you have come to this point, then the process must be let go of, because after all, it was just words, and they were just a hint of a direction to take.

You cannot leave this plane of illusion thinking that you are a Christian, or you are a Buddhist, or you are a Muslim, because these are connotations of illusion, and you must let it all go when you leave this plane of illusion. To move further and faster, you must let all of the philosophies and all of the teachings go, because they become a bondage instead of a help.

But people become attached to the process, to the religion – another attachment. They identify with a temporary condition. But one who wants to leave will not be trapped by this; they will let go *of everything*. And you must let go *of everything*. Everything that your mind has conceived about the way it will be, practically, is a misconception. You must come to this point where you know you cannot understand the way it will be with your mind. And that means that what you *have* understood with your mind, *you have misunderstood,* because the truth cannot be understood with the mind. If the truth could be understood with the mind, then everyone would be enlightened that read the scriptures, "the truth." They would hear the teachings of the masters and they would be enlightened. But the words cannot convey the truth; they can only direct you to where the truth is.

The teachings take you to a gateway, but in order to go through that gateway, you must leave everything behind, including the teachings. The teachings that took you to the gateway are no longer relevant. Now you must step through the gateway in a totally receptive state, with no conceptions, completely letting go of everything, giving up everything. In this state you step through the gateway and the truth will come.

But of the very few *serious* people who come to this point, most stay looking at the gateway, looking through, trying to see the truth. But it does not fit the conception that they stand there looking with. They do not *see* what they expected to see. They do not feel what they expected to feel, and they will not let go of that conception. They will not let go of how they want it to be. But that is all part of the illusion. In every faith, there is an illusion created about how it will be, and none of them are correct, because they are all illusions. So the Christian has a different illusion from the Buddhist, but they are both illusions. They *both* do not understand at all how it will be. So most will then turn away; they come to the brink and they turn away.

So it appears that the processes are not succeeding, but that is not the case. The fact is the processes *are* succeeding and they're taking the people to this point, but when it is time to truly let go and give up, they will not do it. For those that come to this point, their life has become immersed in the process. And they identify with the process so strongly, that they continue to stay in the process, or attached to the process, even while not practicing because there is no further to go. The process took them to the point where it was meant to take them, and they would not let go. So at this point the process just becomes another illusion.

From then on, they are just going through the motions of the process, but *their heart* is no longer in it. You can see whose heart is still in the process, because they are moving to the gateway, they are going ahead, they are advancing. And you can see whose heart isn't in it, because they have come to the gateway, they have seen the truth, and they have rejected it. They have decided to stay in illusion, so they practice the process from then on heartlessly, without feeling, without advancing. Ironically, they practice even without consciousness. They are just trapped in another illusion.

But out of so many in the processes, there are those, who when they come to the gateway, their desire to leave is so strong that in spite of the incredible attachment they have developed to the process that took them to that point – *they let go of it* because they will let *nothing* stop them. They will see their fear and their doubt just as that. And they will plunge through the gateway in spite of their fear, in spite of the fact that they cannot comprehend it with their mind – so they have to leave their mind. They have developed enough faith in the Lord to know by the time they have come to the gateway that they are in His hands. So *in spite* of the fear, *in spite* of the unknown that awaits them, there is the faith, the belief, the trust that allows them to go through.

This is rare. You see so many people in processes, yet they do not have the faith, the trust, or the desire to leave. The desire to leave means that you desire the truth. The desire to stay means that you desire the illusion. It is that simple. Those who wish to stay, no matter what their statements are, they simply wish to stay in illusion. They may say they need to continue to evolve, so it is not time for them to leave – but this means *they want* to stay. They are making the decision. It is *so important* for everyone who is serious to understand this. *Everyone* in all the formal processes and informal processes is making a decision at a certain point to find the truth and leave or to stay in illusion.

So how will it be possible for someone to leave when so many millions are not leaving? *Because you can decide to leave.* You can *decide* to let go and to give up once and for all. Your desire will carry you through the gateway. But most are too terrified to give up their process; they have become secure in their process. It is unthinkable for them to give up their process. They have so little faith, so they let their fear stop them. It is that simple. And that is why in all the processes (formal and informal) you have a very rare few *who will let go.* You can have it if you just desire it. If it is what you want, then you will have it. It is that simple.

To turn your back on illusion means to turn your back on those determined to stay in illusion. Turn your back in the sense that you no longer seek their association. You no longer desire it, because you have understood that the consciousness that they display is just a trap for them. And you turn toward the association of those who are not in illusion. And once one comes to this point, they will *never* feel alone again, because feeling alone is just an illusion – because you are *never* alone. You are just cut off by your illusion, and once you let go of the illusion, then you can embrace the unlimited spirits that are there.

If one is serious and they have come to this point, then the process just becomes letting go of everything, giving up everything – which means letting go of everything in illusion, giving up everything in illusion so that the truth may come, so that the light may come where there was darkness.

So when will you let go? When will you truly give up your attachments? When will you stop dwelling on this plane of illusion and dwell with Me?

I am calling. Will you make the decision to come? Will you make the decision to leave this plane of illusion? Or will you, like most, decide to stay?

Person One: I'm trying to leave. Is trying really doing?

Gourasana: You continue to let go. You continue to give. You continue to let your desire to leave grow, and you do not do things to stifle it or to stunt its growth.

Person One: Sometimes I'm with other people and I have fear. It's a fear of just letting go around them. I'm afraid of their judgments. I don't even bother to explain to others any more, because there are no words to explain what is going on here.

Gourasana: Words to someone who wants to let go will be beneficial, but who wants to let go? So you may speak but they will not understand. They will not hear. Those whose lives are so-called dedicated to consciousness are just as trapped as the others in illusion. They are just trapped in another form of illusion.

Person One: I don't want to be trapped like that either, and it's easy to become trapped. Even if your desire to leave is strong, it's still easy to become trapped.

Gourasana: *If you do not let go*, it is easy to be trapped. But if you let go, continue to let go, and continue with your desire to leave, then it is not easy to be trapped. It is not easy for the illusion to trap you *while you are seeing the illusion*; it is when you close your eyes and begin dreaming that the illusion can take you.

Person One: That's when I catch myself. I catch myself being unconscious in how I interact with the illusion and how I think it's real. Then I wake up and see it for what it is. This frightens me, how in my unconscious state I was relating to it and interacting with it so thickly. But something always wakes me up, and then I see it for what it is and I know it's not what I want. It's your love that I always want to feel. Is that illusion too, that conception? Is that also a misconception, wanting always your love?

Gourasana: No, it is not a misconception, but the way you think the love will be is a misconception. You see, even what you know as love is an aspect of love, so you must not limit yourself to an aspect of love. It is all right to desire that love, because it is something different than the illusion. But as you move, the love will feel different than the one aspect. Love is not a constant unchanging emotion; it is an unlimited dimension. *Love is everything.* But understand that what is considered love on this plane of illusion is a limited concept, and it can also be a trap. So many people need to face fear and let go. In that state of letting go, they will no longer feel the "*love*" that they are used to feeling. Perhaps the feeling that they will have is predominantly fear, and they do not want that. So they will reject where they are going, because of their conception of how it should feel the entire time. Only in that sense is that one aspect of love dangerous.

But *you* know where what you call "the love" comes from; you know it is not from this plane of illusion. *You* have seen the difference between real love and this pretense of love that goes on here. Again, that is the direction that you want to go. But you must not become confused or bewildered by the change in feelings that comes from going in this direction. You must trust and have faith in where this love came from, that whatever else comes from there is for your benefit. You must have faith that it is only benevolent and that where you feel this true love coming from is not a place of illusion. The only darkness, the only evil comes from the illusion.

What you have been experiencing is not bad, because you have been distinguishing the truth from the darkness. As you say, you become trapped in the darkness, but then you wake up and see the truth. This is an excellent stage to come to, where you clearly see the difference, because most are lost. Those in the processes are lost in the illusion, and it is just one continuous frame of mind. They do not distinguish. They do not see the duality in their consciousness. To *see* the duality means you can become *free* from the duality. How can you become free unless you can see it? So yes, you may become, again, caught temporarily in the illusion, but this temporary state is not the same as it is for others. To be truly trapped, you have no way out. You cannot see the light. You cannot distinguish. You are caught in the illusion, *and you think everything is fine* – even to the extent that you think you have become aware, that you have found the light, that you are immersed in the light, that you are feeling only love and light, while the entire time you are in illusion. Then you are doomed. Then you are truly trapped.

What is happening to you is more a fluctuation of consciousness. Sometimes it is in illusion, and sometimes it is in the light. It is not trapped. "Trapped" suggests you stay there. It is just a word, but I am using it like that – that you are trapped and you cannot leave it. *But you are leaving it.* Many times you leave it. When you leave it, you see it for what it is; and in order to leave it this is essential. So at the time of death, when you will leave every aspect of the illusion behind – your body, your mind, *everything* – there will be *no* doubt, there will be *no* remorse, there will be *no* hesitation, and you will know for certain what you are leaving behind. You will know that it is just darkness, illusion, and suffering, and without hesitation you will leave this plane of illusion for good.

So do not think that these temporary states of illusion are necessarily something bad, and that you will be lost until you can completely be in a state of light. For you, they are a vehicle to further your progress. As long as you continue to let go, as long as that desire to leave this plane of illusion is cultivated, then you will succeed. Those that have stopped, those that have turned away, have made a definite statement that they will not continue. They will *not* let go. *They refuse, completely refuse to let go.* They *completely refuse* to have their illusion exposed. As long as you do not hide in your illusion permanently and refuse to see the light, then you can succeed. The others *are not* succeeding because they will not truly see the light.

Yes, give up your concept about how it will be. It is not that you are lost because you continue to go back into illusion. In your case, it is a misconception. Just as one who is in a prison, is escaping the prison and he has a map. It may appear that he is in the prison, but he is escaping the prison. (You have to expand your vision of a prison and see this world, this illusion, as a huge prison.) So on the way, the prisoner may need to sleep; he may need to eat; he may engage in activities that are part of the illusion, but he is becoming free. On the way to becoming free, one may engage in activities of the prison, but because their desire is to become free, that is the direction they are taking. Their activities are not the same as those in the prison who are happy to be in the prison and have no desire, intention, or serious pursuit of leaving the prison. You should not become confused by this. The activities of the prison don't necessarily *bind you* to the prison. So do not be distraught by certain necessities that you still have. As long as you desire to leave, as long as you continue to let go – then you will succeed. As you let go of your attachment to the activities that you continue to perform, then they will not be binding you even though you engage in them. It is *the attachment* that holds you, not the activity.

Person One: Everything is so simple. Why do I make it out to be so difficult?

Gourasana: Making it difficult means a longer path, because it is a way to avoid confronting what is going on. By making it so complex, almost impossible, one can avoid taking this step. It is made to seem hopeless. Why? Because unknowingly, even unconsciously, most want it to appear hopeless. So they emphasize this. Still, coming to this point and letting go is not easy. It is very difficult. It becomes simple, yet when you are confronted with what you must do to leave it is not easy, because there is no more philosophy; there is no more mindless endeavor.

Person One: I don't like to discuss philosophy anymore, because I can see how my mind and my intelligence gets caught up in it. I'm trying very hard to let go of everything and feel with my heart. There's a knowing inside me, and I know this is it for me. There's a part of me that completely rejoices. I'm so relieved, and I'm so happy. Then there's another voice that says it's just my false ego thinking, "Okay. I'm doing it. I'm getting out of here. I'm the doer." I know that's what my desire is. I know I do not want to stay here.

Gourasana: Yes. Well, you are at least the "doer" of this – deciding to stay or deciding to leave – at least. You can see those that are *in the illusion* that say they are "going to leave," while they are doing nothing to leave, while they are not letting go, while they are trapped in a process. They are in the illusion of believing that they are going to leave. This is another thing. The illusions they are hanging on to are so obvious. It is an area to be careful of. But *you* have an idea, more than most, of the illusion you are hanging on to. As long as you can see yourself separate from that illusion, even though you do not understand it completely, it will continue to lose its substance – until it is gone. So you continue to look around in your daily activities, in everything you do, and you see the illusion. You understand how when you leave, these things will be gone.

Person One: Yes, I understand that.

Gourasana: Confusion comes with many who try to see their illusion, because they consider all of their philosophical conclusions to be the truth, and they do not look and see how *that* could be an illusion.

Person One: I've also come to the point of seeing that. That's why I don't want to discuss philosophy.

Gourasana: You can see how it is binding them.

Person One: Yes, very much so. And I feel I know nothing. And as you uncover each binding conclusion and become unbound, then there's a new experience that takes you further. It's unlimited, so how can there be any conclusion?

Gourasana: That's good.

Person One: Gourasana, who are you really? When I meditate with you, meditate upon you, I'm filled with this incredible love. I don't know who you are. All I know is that there's this incredible love there. I just want to focus my whole being on this love. Sometimes it's bittersweet, sometimes it's all encompassing and warm, and sometimes it's just out of my reach and I'm hankering. Yet it's wonderful.

Gourasana: You cannot understand who I am. Every word that you know that may describe Me is contaminated by your conceptions and by the conceptions of others. But My presence is everywhere. Simply one has to turn their attention to Me, and there I am. And while I may appear different to others, it is because of their contamination that I appear different. So the Christians feel My presence and they say it is Jesus. That is true, because when they pray to Jesus, it is I who hear them. How is it that someone here is feeling this love and this presence, and someone on the other side of this world is feeling the same love and the same presence? How is it that people all over the world, to different degrees, are feeling this love and presence? It is because it is everywhere. There is no separation. Separation only exists on this plane of illusion. Once the illusion is gone, there is *no* separation. To feel alone means you are in illusion because you are *never* alone. It is not possible to be alone. Though your body may be isolated, your spirit cannot be separate. But the illusion is created that there is separation. It is all an illusion.

Person One: I experienced that last week. I couldn't come on Saturday, so I just meditated on you, and then there was no time, no place, no separation whatsoever. And I really understood at that moment, all of these things are just an illusion. But I only get glimpses of this. I guess it's like the carrot dangling in front of the donkey. It entices me more; it increases my desire.

Gourasana: There is a purpose to everything. Even for the process of leaving this plane of illusion, there is a purpose. Just let the trust grow. Have complete trust. Have complete faith. Pray for these things. Pray to be free from the illusion once and for all – become immersed in this consciousness, because while you are desiring, you *are* leaving. This is not something that you are planning to do in the future; it *is* something that is happening *now*. You do not let go in the future; you let go *now*. You do not give up in the future; you give up *now*. It is a moment-by-moment experience. Once you have captured the truth, it is a sensation *that you can feel*. It is like a flow, and your conscious mind will not understand what is going on. It will only understand to this degree: that you know you are in that flow, which means you are leaving, and in order to continue the flow you must let go. When you feel the flow stop, then you must look at what you are hanging on to *and let go*. It is a continual thing, to let go.

It is your desire and it is your trust that will carry you. Trust that the energy is benevolent. It is that simple. If your desire is truly for the light and the love and to leave this illusion, then that desire will carry you, just as certainly as the desire to stay traps and seals the prison of those that wish to stay. They are sealed in; they are bound in an inescapable prison. They are trapped in a maze with no opening.

You have felt this love, and that is good. So feel that more and let this increase your trust and your faith so that when the difficulties come, you will know, you will remember. You will have the faith and the trust, because *you know* that the energy is benevolent; *you know* that it is love and light that awaits you. And while what you may need to go through may be so difficult – and at times there may be so much fear or doubt – still, part of you will always trust. Part of you will continue to go on. That part of you is spirit. The part that is afraid, the part that doubts, the part that does not trust, *that part is the illusion*. As you let go, you will totally become the part that continues to move and you will just move. Once you have captured that, then there is no need to pray; there is no need to trust; there is no need to have faith, because you have already let go and you are situated in truth.

"To be here now" means to be here now in the truth and let the truth carry you. Not "to be here now" in illusion. You will know the true meaning of "now" when you have finally let go completely, because there will be *no separation.* There will be no need for you *to trust* the energy any more, because you will have become *part of the energy.* There will be no need for you *to have faith* in the energy, because you will have *become one with it.* And you will no longer fear or be in terror of being swept along by this energy, because you will have let go; you will have given up; you will have stopped struggling. It is then that you will have achieved what everyone in any serious process is looking for: *being in the now.* But only when you have let go can you come to that state.

But for now, you need to deal with the duality. Do not think that dealing with the duality is something bad. As I have discussed, it is a necessary part of the process for you. Just see the illusion for what it is, and then see it more. You deal with the darkness in that way: by seeing it continuously, by being convinced that you want nothing to do with it. That even though you may engage in activities of illusion and take *some* pleasure, you know they certainly are not worth staying on this plane of illusion for, so you become detached from the activities. You may eat something, and you may take some pleasure in it, but as your detachment progresses, it will be nothing to stay for. If it were your last meal, there would be no attachment – happily. See your activities for what they are; do not be *so* concerned that they are illusion. If you see the illusion in the activity and no longer are attached to it, you will become *just as free* as you will by stopping the activity.

On the other hand, seek the light: you pray; you increase your desire; you pray for more desire; you trust; you have faith. What all of these things will culminate in is a state of being where you are moving; and when that begins to happen, you just let go and let the energy *move you where it will. Letting go means so much.* Everyone wants to be certain with their minds that they are making so much progress. You must let go of that. You must have faith that you *are* moving even though your conscious mind cannot perceive it. You can appreciate that you are moving at times with your conscious mind by memory, because you can remember where your consciousness was a few months ago, and then a few months before that. You can see how it has changed, how you have moved from one place to another in awareness – *and you have moved continuously.*

Conversely, you can see with others how they are *not moving*, even while they are practicing so many processes – they are *not* moving. They are *not* changing their consciousness. Their awareness is *not* changing. They *are* practically staying in the same place. For Our purposes, they are moving so slowly. It is just a question of the degree that you move. And you will move to the degree that you let go, that you give up, because to that degree the energy can take you and move you. Yes, it is so simple, but you must have the desire. And as most do not, most cannot. *But you have the desire, so cultivate it.*

It may appear sometimes that I am just repeating the same words over and over, but as I have said before, the communication is not in the words. What I am communicating to you is not limited to these words. There is a constant *fresh* communication going on. More and more information is going on that you are receiving. Those who become trapped in the words and try to understand with their minds are missing everything. The words are hints, yes. They give some direction. But the *real* communication between you and Me is going on *beyond these words. But the words help you to focus upon the communication – the real communication.* The real communication is not in so many words, but *a feeling, a movement, a knowing.* You may leave hardly remembering any words, so many words have been spoken, yet you will have captured a feeling, a knowing that you did not have when you first came. *That* is the real communication, and *that* communication *continues* after the words stop. The communication continues and the feeling that you have may fluctuate, it may seem to have an ebb and a flow, but it is there. And that feeling, after we stop, will continue. The communication, along with the words, *will stimulate* this ability in you *to perceive the true communication*, but it is a communication without words, so *trust* comes into play, *faith* comes into play. But it is something *you can feel – and it is love!*

Person One: When I came today I was feeling so much. I've been feeling so much in the last few days. I had no intention of even coming here to Pacific Beach at all, but as soon as I got in the car I felt you calling me here. For my benefit, I needed to hear these words to help solidify my own faith in my own self, in the feelings that I've been having.

Gourasana: Yes. Trust. Have faith in where you are heading, because you are going to the light, and you are feeling the Presence *and it is love.* It is unlimited love and light. *Just trust it, let it grow.* Almost no one around you will understand. This will become truer as you go on and trust more. They will understand less. And when they are completely lost in trying to understand you, then you can be assured *by this* that you are making good progress. Because what you are experiencing is beyond their comprehension, because *their* comprehension only extends to the illusion (a little light, perhaps, but not this).

So yes, what you have learned could be put in so many words, but can you see how it comes down to one thing? One communication? One experience that has been going on; and now you can let it increase?

Person One: Yes. Thank you *so* much.

Gourasana: As long as you do not stop, you will succeed.

Person One: I surely don't have any intentions of stopping, only going forward and increasing this.

Gourasana: And will you let go of everything?

Person One: Yes. It is essential.

Give Up the Processes

September 24, 1988, Pacific Beach, CA

For one who wishes to stay on this plane of illusion, the phenomenon that is occurring here[1] *is a terrible thing*. If one wishes to stay in illusion, then they should not come here, because by coming here, their illusion will be broken. It is not just an influence that stays with you while you are here – but when you leave, the connection is not broken. Even when you sleep, the change is going on. It is a deep change. So many have come, and when this transformation began, they ran in fear, because they did not wish to give up their illusion. The only way they could stop it was by rejecting everything that is going on here and having nothing further to do with it. For one who wishes to stay in illusion, this is a terrible thing. It is *worse than death* – because death does not stop the illusion, and following death, birth comes again, and again death, and again, life after life. Death is not so bad by comparison, because you do not have to give up the illusion. But if one sincerely follows these teachings, opens their heart, becomes receptive, and voluntarily lets go

1) "Here" refers to the gatherings of the group Gourasana is speaking to.

of their illusion, then if they continue with this process, they will not take birth again. They will leave this illusion at the end of this lifetime, and be free from it before that.

It is not a philosophy that one can take up themselves and practice, and let go or not let go. If one comes here, a change happens that increases in speed and takes them over more and more, and at a certain point it will not be possible to turn back. So many have come, and they have felt this power. (Those here that have been coming for some time have seen it.) They have witnessed people entering into stages of ecstasy, having experiences that people only read about – that great mystics have. But they come to a point where they have to begin to truly let go and give up their illusions, and even though they have seen so much light – more than is usual in a lifetime – it terrifies them. It disturbs not only their minds, but their hearts. Their very being becomes distraught by what is going on, because what is going on is so serious.

To give up this illusion, finally, to never again be in illusion, is such a serious step. So they do not just leave quietly; they leave with fear, and that fear turns into anger. Even though nothing *has ever* been said here that has not been the truth (philosophically they could not fault it, not a point could they fault), yet they are totally against it with all their heart. *They cannot tolerate what is going on!* Many who have not even come cannot tolerate it, because somewhere in their hearts they know what this means, and their attachment is so deep after so many millions of lifetimes. *Try to understand.* Their conscious minds cannot understand, but *in their hearts they know the depth of what is going on, the seriousness of what is going on, and they cannot tolerate it.* Even the thought, they *cannot* tolerate.

But look around you. There are so few here, and there are hundreds who are against this – hundreds. Not that they are just not interested, but they are against it. They cannot tolerate this, because it is something that they have not experienced before.

You can practice the processes of yoga or the religious processes and still not let go of your illusion at all – or perhaps just a little. Most all of the processes that people are practicing are to just bring a little light, a little so-called happiness into their illusion, make their stay on this plane of illusion nicer. That is the extent of what they desire, so of course, that is all they will ever receive, if they even receive that.

But *this* – this is not about how to be happy in this plane of illusion. This is how to be free from illusion. To be free from illusion *you must see it, and in seeing it for what it is, you must give it up*. You must let go of it – not only not take pleasure in it, but give it up completely. So while they use words like consciousness, awareness, love, and light, they basically want illusion. They want enough awareness to be happier in illusion. They want enough consciousness to be happier in illusion. They want to feel some love and some light, but nothing that will take away their illusion.

It is ironic that the majority of the hundreds of people that are against the phenomenon that is going on here, are people who have practiced serious processes of *awareness* and *consciousness*. And they *profess* to be in processes now, and are currently practicing to *increase* their awareness, to *increase* their consciousness, to *increase* the love and the light in their life. So why is it that they cannot tolerate this? It is because here, it is the intention to take those that are ready to a full state of awareness. But to go to a full state of awareness, to achieve that state, you must give up *all of your illusions*. You must let go of *all of your illusions*. And because there is so little time to do that, we are moving very quickly. Everyone who has come has at some time experienced moving *too fast* – and for those who have left, *way too fast*.

It is difficult sometimes for one to believe or to have faith that it is possible to leave in this lifetime. If you will look around at these people who are so-called endeavoring (some are even engaged full-time in so-called processes of awareness), you can see how they are not letting go of their illusion, how they are hanging on, clinging desperately! Then you can begin to understand *why* they are not going to succeed, *why* they are not going to leave. Even though they are engaged in processes of awareness, they have turned those processes of awareness into illusion, and they desperately cling on to them. So it is just another illusion that they are bound by. They are no longer receptive; they no longer will change; they will not let go of what they are clinging on to. So they stay in illusion.

When they hear these words, they become very angry. Why angry? If they know the truth, if they are aware, why would they become disturbed? If indeed this were illusion, if indeed this were darkness and they were in a state of awareness, why would they be disturbed? But they become very disturbed, afraid and angry – unreasonably; they don't even understand why. But *this is why*: It touches some part of them that becomes deeply disturbed, because that part knows that they must let go of their illusion.

To leave this plane of illusion, you must give up the processes. In order to enter fully into the realm of truth, you must let go of the process that took you to the gateway. If you do not let go of the process, then you are still bound, because the processes themselves are something of this plane.

Person One: Gourasana, is the little bit of love and light these people still in illusion are settling for real? Is it helping them grow in their consciousness, but at a slower rate?

Gourasana: Yes.

Person Two: So it's okay? They are going at the rate they need to?

Gourasana: They are going at the rate *they desire*. Yes, it is all right, in one sense, if one wishes to stay in illusion. But what is going on here is assistance to help those who wish to leave this plane of illusion in this lifetime, so We do not speak that it is all right to be in illusion, to be trapped in illusion. They are trapped in illusion, but that is their desire. They are in prison, but they wish to stay in prison. *This* is for those who wish to become truly free from the prison.

Even those not practicing formal processes are also evolving; their consciousness is increasing; their awareness is increasing. But there comes a point in evolution when one will leave this plane of illusion. It was never meant to be permanent; *it is not permanent*. It is just a matter *of time* before you leave this plane of illusion, and when you are ready to leave this plane of illusion, assistance is there for you.

This is assistance for those who are ready to leave, and naturally the number is very small – *very small*. Because this is *too much* light, *too much* awareness. To come here means to see things *too clearly*. Once you begin to see too clearly, then the things that you are attached to will begin to disintegrate. That is very disturbing to one who wishes to continue in illusion. As this will destroy the illusion, those who wish to stay in illusion naturally have a strong aversion to what is going on here. That is natural. But it is important for those who are serious to understand this. Why are so many against this, most of whom have never even come? They are *so disturbed* by what is going on here. Yet what are we doing? We have meditations; we go within and find the truth within – the love and the light that is within. Does this contradict any of the great teachings? We are not inflicting some dogma. No. We are asking you to give up your dogma.

You must come to the point where you give up the process and the dogma. To not do so means to some degree you are still in illusion. It means, for the Christians, that at the time of death, Jesus will not be there to save them. It is a false hope. So it is with the other processes. This belief or hope that they can do some process and automatically they will be saved, is not the case. The process can take you to a point where you can let go and give up, but if you do not keep moving, if you do not let go and truly surrender, then you are trapped in another illusion. The process becomes an illusion. So the Christians *are trapped* in an illusion. People in different processes of yoga *are trapped* in their various illusions. They believe some aspect of God: some great personality will come and automatically save them at the time of death. How many millions and millions of people on this earth *are waiting* to be saved at the time of death? How many will be disappointed? *Practically all!* Yes, it is very rare to leave this plane. These words are so disturbing; this type of talk is so disturbing: We have seen people after a few minutes of this talk, immediately get up and leave. They cannot tolerate it. They say it is a terrible thing that is going on here. But what is going on? What are we saying that is so horrible? *"Give up. Let go! See the illusion for what it is, let go of it, and leave this plane of illusion!"*

One who is leaving this plane must be prepared to tolerate a great deal of difficulty. It is not easy. So how does one tolerate? They tolerate because their desire is strong. So no matter how difficult it becomes, their desire will see them through. They will *not* give up; *the only way you will fail is if you give up. As long as you continue, you will succeed.*

Of course, "giving up" also means that you come to something that you need to let go of, but you will not let go; you will not give up. That is the same practically as stopping. This We have also seen. Sometimes specific things were requested where it was obvious that the individual needed to stop something or give up something, and they would not do that – so they stopped. It is very hard to continue to hold on to something and come here. Generally when they do not wish to let go, they simply stop coming, because if they continue to come, they will be disturbed too much, and they fear that eventually they will have to let go.

Try to understand what this means. *Each of you* has to ask yourself if you are serious *now*, because now is all there is. You may even say that you wish to leave, but will you leave *now?* Will you let go of everything *now?* Your body? Everything? Just see what "to leave everything now" means: your family, your relations, all of your attachments, all the activities you will never engage in again. Of course, it is a miserable existence, and what you think is pleasurable is not. The things you think are pleasurable are truly pitiful. *What is waiting is everything!*

If you are not ready to leave *now*, then you need to look and ask, why not? What is it that you are staying for? Why will you not let go of this illusion? Once you are free from illusion, it is not something *you miss*. Illusion means just that. Just as a child has certain illusions, and as they mature, those illusions are gone and other illusions take their place, you no longer have the same illusions as when you were a child. There is no so-called "pleasure" for you any more in certain activities of a child. Why? Because the illusion is gone, and once it is gone, you do not miss it. So you really are not giving up anything. It is nothing tangible, it is just an illusion. And when the illusion is gone, you will not understand how you could engage in that activity and find any pleasure. As you advance, you no longer can take pleasure in activities *that used* to bring you pleasure, because the illusion is dissipating. Though you may try, the pleasure is going.

If one comes, and they are not ready to let go and give up, that is all right. But then they should at least take up a serious process that will take them to the point of letting go and giving up. It may not be possible for some to enter into this stage, because this is a stage of moving very quickly and giving up a great deal in a short period of time. It may be too much. And if you find that this is happening, rather than running the other way and totally losing yourself in illusion again, better to maintain the awareness you have, acknowledge the illusion that you are in, acknowledge that you still desire these things, and take up a process that is not so disturbing, one that you can execute. Once that process has taken you to a point where you *can* let go, then you can come.

Ultimately it all comes to this point: Are you ready to leave? Are you ready to give up? So many have come who have been in *serious* processes of yoga, totally dedicating their life for years to serious processes of yoga, and they are not at all ready to give up or let go. So it may appear that the process failed, yet they just came to a point where it was time to let go of the process and move further. But they would not do that, because there were too many things they were clinging on to. Then they simply go through the motions of religion, but their heart is no longer in it, because the process has taken them as far as it will, and they will not acknowledge the point of surrender. So they are stagnant, and they are trapped.

So for those that are in processes, who have become attached to processes, and are lost in those processes and cannot see any light or a way to get out – then they *should* come here if they truly wish to leave, *if they truly wish to get out* – because here they can receive guidance on how to do that. Here, their illusions will be exposed. They may stay in the religions and no one will ever see their illusions, because their leaders *are not aware*, but here their illusions are exposed. As we have seen with so many that have come, once their illusions are exposed, they never come again, because they refuse to give up. They refuse to let go.

Are there any questions? Last time no one would ask any questions. When they are alone with Me, in one minute they are asking so many questions that everyone can benefit from, but no one will ask in the group. Yet everyone is suffering from the same problems. Everyone is haunted by the same illusions.

Person Three: Gourasana, could you talk to us about attachment in the area of sex?

Gourasana: This is something that must be dealt with very carefully. It is so highly individualized. Each individual has to understand for *themselves*, and if it is something that is plaguing them, then they can discuss privately with Me. Because general instructions mean "general," they cannot apply equally to everyone. This is why the processes are so faulty. They have blanket rules, they have blanket instructions, yet everyone is an individual – highly individualized. So in the processes, for some (a very small percentage), the process may be very good or even ideal; then for so many, not be so ideal, but still beneficial. And then for some, not beneficial at all because the blanket rules do not fit their situation. That is one point that is important to understand. Any instruction that I give generally, has to be taken as that. It is a suggestion, and you must decide what to do. Sometimes there is someone who is specifically in an illusion, and I may directly point it out and tell them they must give it up.

But an area such as sex requires a great deal of awareness. The only way you will be able to deal with this sex drive is to increase your awareness, understand it, and then deal with it with awareness. To artificially stop, when you are deeply attached, very frequently produces a type of insanity, and not that much benefit is gained (other than the practice of austerity, which is beneficial). But because the attachment is still there, eventually the attachment to sex is there again, because it really has not been dealt with properly.

In order to deal with this issue, first one must learn – not only in this case, but in all situations where the senses must be controlled – one must learn the difference *between repression and control.* Just as where there is a dam and water, and to control the reservoir, water must be released at certain times, otherwise the dam will burst. And if one is so foolish as to repress and not use all intelligence, then there will be a failure that can be harmful. There *is* a question of control, but it must be *control, not repression. Repression does not work.* It aggravates the problem, and can produce such a tremendous discouragement and disturbance in the mind that one *gives up* the idea. Yet if it is approached with control and increased awareness, then one can gradually see practical results, practical steps forward, practical *advancement* in the area, and they will become *detached* from sex. They will no longer have the *need*. Even if some urge arises, they will be able to control it. But they will control it with awareness, and because they are approaching it with awareness, will know their limitations. When it is getting to the limit that they can tolerate, then they can engage in some sex, some release.

Cindy: Gourasana, can you talk more about the physiological changes that go on in a person's body as a person's awareness increases?

Gourasana: One thing is, I do not wish to name so much the different things that happen, because I do not want to put another conception into the minds of those that have not had so much *physical* experience yet. The physical transformation is certain, but again, it is so highly individualized. Look at this group that has been coming and compare the difference to what has happened with you. What are the symptoms? Pain in the heart, pressure and pain in the head, so much difficulty in the body. Of course with David, he has had so much trouble for so long now. Constant trouble, similar to you. Also others have had some disturbances. Basically, if one is having these problems, they should discuss them if they need to. But this is where trust is important, because things will not stay the same. They will not stay the same in any way. You will be entering into other states of awareness and having experiences not normal for you. They will vary so greatly. Some have many visual things. Or one may have what they consider to be a dream, yet the real meaning behind the dream, what is really going on, is another thing. Yet they may remember certain interactions in the dreams; but those interactions are not the point. There is transformation going on, which is the point. One cannot be too caught up in the imagery. Then sometimes there is not imagery, but seeing.

Person One: Gourasana, why is it necessary for these people to feel this pain in their bodies? It seems that if it were from a pure light source, it would be a healing energy going through the body and not a destructive one.

Gourasana: It is not destructive. Generally, you have associated pain with destruction. This is not destructive; *this is healing*. Just as when a part of your body "falls asleep" because the blood has been cut off, and then when it is allowed to flow, there is pain, because life is flowing into that area. But this is not destructive; it is giving life. So this pain of the transformational process is not destructive. It is giving life. It is opening channels of energy. Again, this varies. Several people have experienced actual pain, but it is *not* destructive. They have not shown signs of damage in the areas where they have felt pain.

Of course, it is different with different people. Occasionally, with some it can go on practically constantly, because there is so much transformation going on physically. The pain of the transformational process can be verified, not of course just by Me, but also by study of great masters and saints. They went through physical difficulties and agony in their transformation. This is not some new concept; it is very old. It is unavoidable. With some it is far worse than for others. So again, trust must be there. We have at least three here who came to a point where they thought their hearts would fail, and they would die. Yet, nobody died. And others have experienced the pain in the heart.

The body is like dead, like the leg that "falls asleep" and is cut off from certain energy. So the body in illusion is cut off from certain energies, and once the transformation begins, then to different degrees you will feel that energy in your body. In many cases it is piercing and painful. Just like in the case of this one woman, Cindy. Before the transformational process began, she did not have these difficulties. Now they are constantly plaguing her. But because she has trusted, she has moved *so far!* Trust and faith must be there; and because others have gone through before you, this will help. Of course, David was the first in this group to go through the pain and suffering and he is doing well. Those that know of the history – the *terrible pain* he experienced.

What will you do to leave this plane of illusion? What will you go through? Will you give up everything? Even your so-called happiness? But you do it with awareness, with as much consciousness as you can, with as much intelligence as you can muster. Not that mindlessly you do something and suffer *like a fool* needlessly, as so many processes have you do. So-called austerities help only in that they can help you to develop tolerance, but all too frequently austerities *ruin the ability to tolerate anything.* Since people are not using their intelligence, they go beyond just developing tolerance, and they hurt their nervous systems until they cannot tolerate any suffering. So they take drugs because they cannot tolerate any suffering or face even a little pain. There are so many histories of this; for centuries this mistake has been going on.

Here, in this group, even if you are not using your intelligence, it will be pointed out to you, *but you must communicate what is going on with you.* The reason we discourage entering into irrelevant philosophical discussions *is because there are so many pertinent important matters at hand that need to be discussed.* Each and every one of you needs to discuss your particular problems and your progress *at this moment.* What mistakes are you making *now!* What could you do to further your advancement *now!* What are the areas where you are not applying any intelligence, and you are going on mindlessly, foolishly, doing unnecessary things *that are not helping your advancement at all!* This is the case in most processes, because their leaders not only do not give time to this, but do not have the awareness or intelligence to see.

If you ask your question and I do not want to answer it, do not be offended. It is just that time is so short, and certain things could be discussed endlessly. The illusion is so complicated and diverse. There are so many ways you could be bound by the illusion. We wish only to discuss those that are binding you *now.* So do not think of these sessions as some philosophical discussions. Think of these sessions as a time to receive help and practical direction. *Ask a question that you can personally apply to your life so that you can go faster and further.*

Jim: Gourasana, you said on more than one occasion that each of us needs to find our own way of going within, that it's highly individualized, and that it might change from time to time. When I find myself doing this, quite often I find that those around me may have a different idea of what's going on or what I should be doing. This concerns me, because these people are people that I respect and care a great deal for. When this kind of thing happens, I'm often reminded of my weakness in being influenced by other people. This is something I am really anxious to resolve, because it sometimes causes tension that I don't really want to be there. I get feeling kind of stuck; I don't quite know how to deal with that.

Gourasana: First, self-awareness means just that. You become aware of yourself and what you need. You cannot expect those around you to be aware of *your* consciousness. That is not possible. *I* am aware of your consciousness, but they cannot be. Even if they mean well or they have benefited by a certain practice, a certain way of endeavoring, they are only speaking from their experience – *what helped them.* You understand? It is pertinent for them, and they may try to influence you, because they feel it is applicable to all. *So! – you are correct; one must resist influence in an area they know is not true for them.* They must resist it. Everyone in this group is so serious; I do not think that if you openly expressed what you feel, anyone would be offended. After all, everyone is approaching their awareness differently – you can see. No one is doing the same thing. We are not trying to create a dogmatic system here, *not at all*, just the opposite. Not one system, but an *ever-changing system* that changes even day to day, even hour to hour. We are not saying, "You do this one thing and then you will become realized." *That is not possible. That is how you become lost!* Yes, you may do one thing with awareness, and it will help you evolve, and when it is no longer of use to you, *you stop it and you do something else.* Do not be influenced by those around you.

Jim: Sometimes it's hard for me to keep up with the changes and what I should be doing, because it does seem to change from hour to hour.

Gourasana: If one can create a situation of isolation when there is so much going on, then that is ideal. If you are too easily influenced, then create more of an isolated situation. Again, this is not a social group, as you well know, and no one will be offended if you wish to be alone. As you know, David had a problem with this, and at one point in his life, things became *very* confusing and the problem of the influence of others on him became severe. Whereupon, he went by himself for a period of one year to the woods, so there was no other influence at all. Of course, he had a great many things to work out. You can arrange your situation where no one is influencing you. There are ways to do it, and if you desire it enough, you can create practically the same situation as if you were alone. No one will suffer so much without social interaction with you. Even when you are around others, you can maintain silence except when discussing practical matters, thereby avoiding social interaction that is a way to become distracted from what you should be doing. At one point in your day, social interaction may be correct. Let us say in the evening at six o'clock, for one hour your consciousness is such that social interaction, discussing consciousness, will benefit you and be good for you. Then at seven o'clock it should stop, and you should be entirely by yourself.

But you become lost during the social interaction, because you are not doing it with awareness. You become trapped and *caught up* in the social interaction; then another hour goes by and another hour goes by, and you begin to have unhappiness and frustration take you over. Why? Because you are not doing what you should be doing. You are doing *what you have been persuaded to do*, but you *have allowed* yourself to become persuaded. *This is true for everyone.* Until you are stronger in this area and can do it with more awareness, if you find yourself day after day trapped by social interactions, wasting hours that you would rather be meditating, then, artificially for some time, you can avoid so many social interactions. Simply let those around you know what is going on.

Very frequently, people are socially offended by this group, because the important thing is *not* social interaction. The rules of social behavior are *not* only not mandatory, but they are not even required. As may be in your case, they are very detrimental *and should not be observed at all.* So one may come and think you very rude because you will not sit and socially interact with them. They will say that, "This is not good; they are not socially polite people." But that is not the intention. The intention is to become free in this lifetime, and there are so many obstacles to overcome in order to achieve this end *that nothing can stand in the way.* Social obligations are *the least thing* that should stand in the way. The social manners of society are mainly there to arrange many rules to make a happy situation in society. So certain rules of politeness and behavior are expected of society in general. Here it is not necessary to observe so many rules. Only when you interfere with *another's* consciousness are rules needed. Rules like that are another thing.

It is a very good thing that you have raised this point, as the lives of people are often lost because they are distracted from what they should be doing, and they cannot take the steps necessary to create a circumstance where they will not be distracted, or where they can confine their distraction. Just as in marriage, there may naturally be a demand for interaction, but this could be confined to a period of time, and a time of isolation can also be arranged. There is no excuse. There is no circumstance in which one cannot grow or manage to expand their awareness.

Person Four: Gourasana, I hear you saying that our consciousness can be suppressed by someone else, but we have to give them our power to have them do it; so there's no excuse for allowing this to happen?

Gourasana: No. There is no excuse. There is no excuse not to become fully aware. *There are only reasons why you will not do what you need to do:* "It is too hard. I do not want to do it. It creates disturbance. I just want to be peaceful and have all love and light constantly; *so I will not do what is necessary to do.*" There are only reasons; there are only excuses for what you will not do. But they are just that. Yes, if you allow someone to repress you to the point that you cannot become fully aware, then you will not succeed. Where is your determination? Your desire to leave this plane of illusion must take you over. *It must become the dominant desire.* You may be engaged in so many activities and desiring so many other things, but this must become *the dominant desire.* If you make this your dominant desire, then you will see how to deal with every other desire in a way that it can be confined and controlled, and not interfere with steady progress. It is not that you try to repress all of your desires; that is not how you will succeed. But you can begin to control them, or you begin with what you *can* control.

Person One: Gourasana, one of my biggest illusions is that I feel the path to God should be a joyous, glorious, peaceful way and that God would want us to enjoy the abundance of this earth that He created. This is standing in my way. Can you shed some light on that?

Gourasana: First, it is an illusion. So all the things you have stated, while you may still have some desire for them, you need to see (at least theoretically in the beginning, to understand) that they *are* an illusion, and begin to look at them and *see how* they are an illusion. The path of awareness is the same, in many respects, for everyone in the world. You talk of a joyous life of peace and abundance, but for the majority of the world this is not even possible, so-called peace. So many countries are engaged in war; at any time people may die; so many countries have continuous disasters – as this country will in the future – and they do not know when they will die from these disasters. There are so many plagues of diseases; there are shortages of food so people are very hungry or starving. There is no abundance. There is not even enough to maintain the body – so they are dying. And there is little peace, because they are riddled with disease and so many can die at any time. In this country, there is very *tight* control over the people; there is so much money going into enforcing the law. But in most countries the law is not so rigid, so the law is easier to break without repercussions. In many countries, even though there may be a law to not kill someone, there is so much killing going on privately, and the law is not enforced. They do not care enough. They may condemn it verbally, but they do not take the practical steps to stop it.

So at this moment in this country, you could be in this illusion of joy and abundance, but when that changes, what then? You understand, it is *a desire* that is temporary and may or may not be fulfilled? You *may* desire peace, but if there is a war going on, then that peace will not be possible – at any time you may die. A life of abundance may be here now, but at any time it may be taken away and you will have a life of deprivation. These desires are at one end of the spectrum of duality. Of course, everyone wants abundance; everyone wants peace; everyone wants just to feel happy and joyful. That is the desire. That is one end of the spectrum of the duality of this plane. But at any time the spectrum can swing and the other end becomes the reality. Instead of joy, there is terror; instead of peace, there is total disturbance of the mind; instead of abundance, there is deprivation to the point of starvation and death.

So it is an obstacle, because it is a desire *that is binding you*. If you make a condition on how you want it to be, then you are stifling your advancement. You must give up *how you want it to be because it will not be how you will want it to be. Not at all! Never!* It just is not possible. This is what *true* surrender means. This is what *true* letting go means – that you give up even these *basic* desires. You are not talking so much about extravagant things, but even these basic desires can hold you back; because when the abundance is gone, when things are not peaceful, when there is no joy, then you will be disturbed. These things are part of the duality of illusion. That is why they must be let go of. That does not mean that you need to stop the abundance and live in deprivation because this could possibly happen. It simply means you need to give up *your attachment* to abundance. If you become truly detached, if the abundance is taken away, if there *is* deprivation, *your consciousness will not be disturbed* – but if you are *attached* to your abundance, if you are *attached* to a state of peacefulness, then your consciousness *will be so disturbed, and you can become so lost.*

This is why it is so critical to give up things as you want them to be, because you have no idea what is waiting; you have no idea what is going to happen. There is more of an illusion of stability in this country than in other countries, but in other countries, instability is the norm – where you do not know from day to day what your existence will be: changing government, changing laws, changing environment. So you must be detached from whatever happens; you must see everything as illusion, and be detached from it, be it happiness or suffering. You must be the same toward both, because both are the duality, and both will be there. You must not be disturbed by happiness nor by suffering. And if you put a condition on how you want your life to be, then you are doomed, because it will not be that way.

If you want to succeed, the only criterion should be to create an environment that is *conducive* to advancement. What is conducive, generally, is less abundance, more simplicity, more austerity. This produces more of a peaceful state, because you do not want to be working madly, or giving your life just to earn so much money to live at a standard you have set. But again, you must deal with your limitations. You do not want to press yourself too far.

With as much money as an average person makes in this country, you could go to another country, and with one year's savings, live for the rest of your life. But it would be very difficult. You would have sufficient food, sufficient clothing, but it would be the minimum. It would be very hard, especially for people *from this country* who are used to so many comforts. So you must know your limitations. Still, while striving for simplicity, you must still have a situation you can deal with and stay relatively sane.

Everyone must become fixed on their goal. In everyone, the desire to leave must be dominant; therefore it will follow that your activities will be conducive to reach that goal. That will be the criterion for what you do, not other things. These other things can sidetrack you. If you make abundance mandatory, then it can be a great distraction from the path. This is the difference, and this is why you need to look at this.

But you will see things along the way that are far greater than the things you are clinging on to. It is not that first you stop all of your desires, and then you get something in the future. As you let go, you will have experiences, maybe short, but you will begin to see. You will begin to have glimpses of what it is like to be free from the illusion. The reason they are only glimpses is because you are still hanging on to something. So even though you may go to the light and experience so much light and love, you come back because of your attachments. You must give up your attachments, then you can have the most satisfying, the most rewarding experiences. Not the temporary ones, which can be upset at any time. So you give up your material desires and you increase your spiritual desires. When those are satisfied, no matter what happens you will be fine. If there is disease, if there is death, if there is deprivation, you will be fine. The conditions of this world will not influence you, at least not to the degree that they will disturb your consciousness. That does not mean that there will not be some suffering if you starve to death, but it means that it will not disturb your consciousness. You will see yourself as separate, not theoretically, but you will see it through awareness. You will be able to tolerate the circumstance, and leave the body with a state of presence and control rather than in a panic – hysterical – lost.

Person One: Gourasana, what you just said made me realize that I'm attached to my feelings because they make me feel alive. I feel if I give them up, there will be this empty void , like a mindless clone or something. I know it's irrational but it's a real fear. What can I do to help release it more?

Gourasana: Begin to let go and see that there is not a void. As you let go, you will see there is no void: your awareness increases, and you can begin to appreciate how you are advancing, how you are moving forward. This will help you to let go more, but you must begin to let go and test it. This does not mean that where so-called happiness was, there will be more happiness. There will be no void, but there may be great difficulty. So you cannot have a condition on how it will be. If you stay aware, you will see that you are growing. You will appreciate changes in your consciousness, which are very rare. Generally, one's consciousness stays basically the same throughout their whole life. Their personality stays the same; their consciousness stays the same. They change some, but not much. In this process your personality will change *a great deal*, as will your consciousness.

You Must Have One Purpose in Life

February 18, 1989, Pacific Beach, CA

(The first part of this talk has the feeling of a meditation and has music ["The Fairy Ring"] playing in the background while it is spoken. The talk concludes with a short guided meditation.)

This must become everything in your life.

You must have one purpose in your life, and that is to find the truth. Though you may be involved in other activities along the way, your central focus is always on going toward the light, on finding the truth. You must become *obsessed* with it. It must become *everything*. There is only what you can cling on to on this plane of illusion and the truth. For you it is like that, the duality. And you must let go of everything on this plane of illusion. *Everything. And want nothing else but the truth.* If you do not come to this state of mentality, of consciousness, then you will not succeed.

Your interest cannot be divided. Your purpose cannot be divided. This does not mean that you cannot fulfill certain responsibilities in your life, but gradually everything must be changed. Your life must be arranged in such a way that all of your efforts somehow or other are focused on finding the truth.

You should not lie down to sleep at night when your consciousness is not absorbed in this – so that while you sleep you will move toward the light. And when you rise, it should be your first thought. Go to sleep with a prayer and rise with a prayer. It must become everything. To have your attention divided means you have it divided between finding the truth and fulfilling some illusory thing. And as long as you are seeking after some illusory thing, then you will not succeed in this lifetime. Because a part of you is still desiring, is still seeking after the illusion – just as everyone is. You must give all of this up.

You must see it all as illusion, because it is just illusion. Within a matter of a few years, all of the personalities in this room, the personalities of illusion, will cease to exist. They will have no more existence. The illusion will be over anyway.

Try to understand: It is your desire that carries you from place to place. It is your desire that will carry you out of this plane of illusion, and it is your desire *that keeps you* in this plane of illusion. So what is your desire?

The things of illusion: just begin to let go of them more. There are so many opportunities to let go of some aspect of your illusion, to finally be finished with some area by which you have always been trapped, to finally come to a point where you say, "No. I will no longer be in illusion in this area, at least." And gradually, you go from one area of your illusion to another, until there is no illusion left.

But while it's important to avoid the pitfalls of illusion as much as possible, the main emphasis should always be on finding the truth, going to the light. Not that you are constantly looking at your illusions and just trying to get away and solve those problems by themselves. *The truth* will solve the problems of the illusion. So at the very least, you do not want to be taking on any more illusion. Be careful what you choose to do with your life. Be careful what steps you take. Is it something that's going to increase your illusion, or is it something that's going to decrease your illusion?

What will you do to leave in this lifetime? What difficulties will you undertake? As it is a place that becomes increasingly difficult to live in as the illusion lifts, because it is only by the illusion that this place is tolerable – for those that consider it tolerable, which many do not. But without the illusion, the horrible nature of this place becomes clearer and clearer, and it becomes harder and harder to live in many respects. So there is a tendency to be in illusion, because it makes it easier to stay here – to accept enough illusion where it becomes bearable to stay in this place. But you see, you must come to a point where you give up all the illusion. This is not through some method of repression, but a gradual change in consciousness: that you just see the illusion more and more for what it is, that you see more and more clearly, even though that seeing may not be pleasant.

There is a natural tendency to bring with you those that are close to you, that are dear to you, but most will not go. So you will have to give up your attachment to those that will not go, that are not ready to leave, that wish to stay in illusion. Your temporary illusory relationship with them must be given up. And when this is done, *real* love for them will increase – not this pretense of love that is going on, that you generally call love. The thing that you call love here is such a pretense. It is so conditional, so dependent upon the relationship – the behavior of those around you. Real love is unconditional. So while you are becoming detached from the illusory aspect of your relationships, your real love for them is increasing – your unconditional love. You love them, even though they are going to stay and they turn against you and become like your enemy.

You must see the thing in perspective. This is such a tiny period of time, and all of these personalities are such illusion. They are doomed to end so shortly at any rate, between family members: husband/wife, father/mother, brother/sister, children. But never does this mean that love decreases; it means that love increases. Though you may not be able to perceive it at first, the real love is increasing. The real love, love that is not covered by illusion, love that is not contaminated by illusion, controlled by illusion. Not like the love of this plane – which you call love – that comes and goes: one day there is love and the next day there is hate. Not like that.

Once you have entered into a state of full awareness, you will have a love for everyone that you have never had before – and it will be unconditional love. Even though they may hate you and what you are doing, you will not hate them. You will have compassion for them, and you will love them, just as the Lord Jesus loved even those that nailed Him to the cross, that crucified Him, that sent Him to His death. He did not love them any less than He loved His own disciples. This is the nature of real love.

So husbands and wives that are on this path together, their love changes from the illusory love of this plane to the real love – unconditional love. There is more acceptance, more openness. But one who is serious, one who wants to succeed in this lifetime, will let *nothing* stop them. *Nothing!* And if there is a mate or some other person that somehow is influencing them or harming them on their path, then they will give that up. They will give everything up. And if you cannot yet give it up, you will come to a point of awareness when you see the temporary illusion of it all, and you will be able to give it up. Not out of some repression or artificial renunciation, but out of awareness. After all, who your daughter is now, in one hundred years from now will be an entirely different personality, and who your daughter is now will no longer exist. Who your parents are now will no longer exist. Who your brothers and sisters are now will no longer exist. All of your relations will no longer exist. They will become someone else's brother, sister, husband, or wife.

You must let go of what is illusion. If you know that something is illusion and you are hanging on to it, just understand you are keeping yourself in the illusion. It is up to you to let go. You are not alone. As much assistance as you could ever need is here. But it is up to each of you individually to let go, because if you will not let go, then you cannot be taken against your will. So if you insist on clinging to the things of illusion and you will not let go, and you continue in your life and you do not let go at the time of death, you will come back again, because of what you would not let go of.

That does not mean that everything that you can see now is illusion, and you just have to artificially stop it – that is not the way to approach this. That is a type of insanity. You *move* according to your awareness.

But I can tell you one thing: There is always movement that goes on if you are properly on the path. There is always some change that is going on in your life – *some change.* Your relationship with others is changing. The way you think, the way you do things, your desires: all are changing.

You must see that there is change. No one stays the same, day after day, year after year, with little change. You should be able to observe the changes, and you should be ready to *make* them when it is time.

When you have come to a state of awareness and you see something for the illusion that it is, then you must have the courage to act. Once you *know* that something is an illusion and you are ready to give it up, as hard as it is, then you must act. If you do not act, then you just prolong, and you can prolong for lifetimes. But We are speaking here mainly of leaving *in this lifetime*. Though We will help others to advance in their lives, now We are concentrating on those that want to leave in this lifetime, exclusively. Has it become everything to you? And when you ask that, if it has not, then what has meaning for you? If this has not become everything, then what is holding you? Where is your consciousness being directed that is illusory? If you are unsure, then you must begin a self-examination and find the areas of darkness in your life. And begin to do something about them.

The way to approach it is not through sudden repression and denial, but through gradual changing of it through awareness. Just like a husband and wife who have some love for each other that is founded on illusion should not suddenly stop even the illusory love and just sit coldly together expecting some real love to come. You *gradually* change; you *gradually* transform. You gradually let go of the illusory love, and simultaneously as you truly do this in your heart, the real love will take place. So you change the relationship from husband and wife into one of two pure spirits with a pure love for each other that is not based upon the temporary illusion of the circumstance of "husband and wife," a circumstance which will be over in a short time.

And there may be loss to some of those around you, to family members, as you will not be facilitating their happiness in illusion, because you will not be playing your part anymore. You will not be giving so much to the illusion where you used to. You will give less and less to the illusion, so some will become unhappy with you, because you will not support their illusion. *But you must not let anything stop you.*

You must remember that who you think you are is just an illusion. You do not know who you are. Everything that makes up your personality is just an illusion: whether you are male or female, whatever qualities you have good or bad, they are both illusion. If you are moral or immoral, it is just all part of the illusion, and it must all be given up. If you think you are a very *good* person, or if you think you are a very *bad* person, or something in between, it is all just illusion and must go, because you are neither very good or very bad. You are something beyond good and bad, you are something beyond duality, you are something beyond illusion. You have to try to understand this: Who you think you are is just an illusion, as are the relationships between your illusory personality and other illusory personalities.

It is like you are in a play and you have adopted a role, and the play is about to end. And most cast members are just going to enter into another part and enter another play, but you are desiring to leave this cycle. So you must stop taking part in the play. You must step back and see yourself separate from this play. Step back even to see that you are just a character in the play, and that this character is just an illusion and will be gone. You will no longer be a man because you will no longer have a male body. You will no longer be a woman because you will no longer have a woman's body. You will no longer be old; you will no longer be young; you will no longer be any age because you are ageless. For you, there really is no birth or death, except that *you allow yourself* to be in illusion. You ask for it, you desire it. And because all your desires are fulfilled, *it is done.*

You must become obsessed with wanting the truth. There must be nothing else. You must want nothing else. To want nothing else means you *only* want the truth; you *only* want the light. And you want no darkness; you want no more illusion. It seems so simple, yet is the key. The key is that you go where you desire to go. You become what you desire to become; you get what you desire to get. If you desire to come to a full state of awareness in this life, if this is your *only* desire and you will let go of everything else in order to achieve this, then you will succeed. But if you say, "I want the light," but you continue to hang on and will not let go of your illusions, then it will take longer, then more births.

Is there any question about this? Anything that needs to be discussed in order that you may understand better? If there is anything?

(Meditation music stops playing.)

Person One: Gourasana, how can we make this our one and only desire when we are always having so many desires? It seems difficult to make this our one and only desire. Sometimes it seems almost impossible.

Gourasana: It seems impossible to the conscious mind, because the conscious mind does not understand how things are working, so people give up in frustration. They misunderstand the teachings. But you see, there are two things going on. There is your real self and there is your illusory self. And you can bring your true self to a point

– your spiritual self – to a point where you want nothing else, where it is time for you to leave this plane of illusion.

How do you do this? You do this by desire, through prayer. But do not be confused by the conscious mind or your illusory personality. Because as you go on, you should be able to see that there is a distinction between the two. In other words, even while you are engaged in other activities, so many other activities, in your heart you can be continually in a state of prayer and desiring to leave this plane of illusion – even while you are fully engaged in other activities, such as working or other responsibilities, taking care of your family members, whatever responsibilities you have taken on in this plane.

It is not recommended to become irresponsible; that is not helpful. But if you – who you really are – desire to leave, then even certain activities that are considered to be illusory will not stop you, because they are separate from you and they are not your true desire (though they go on because of the body). For instance, you may have the desire to eat, but does this mean that your desire for the truth has stopped, it has ceased? No. It is because of the body that certain desires are naturally there. Certain needs come into the mind, but the mind also is not you. The mind also is temporary and illusory. And even while the mind is going on and involved in so many other things, still, who you really are can be moving and advancing and going toward the light.

It is just a question of your desire.

Person One: So through desiring, prayer, and going within, you'll ultimately come to this point where this is your only desire in life?

Gourasana: Yes. You *must* come to that point, but it has to be your desire to even want that – you see. You have to understand that there is a purpose to this existence and that there are some people ready to leave, and everyone that is ready to leave needs a special assistance. And with that special assistance they can leave.

But most are going to continue on; it is not their desire to leave. So they have no *true* desire to even begin the process. They have no desire to even change their desire, or to begin to truly let go of the illusion. They have nothing to really motivate them on a serious path, because they wish to stay in illusion. And that is all right, because there is a purpose to that also.

It is just that what We are doing here is assisting those who wish to leave in this lifetime. If you truly wish to leave in this lifetime, it is possible. The assistance is there. And as I have taught, there are things you must do. It is *assistance* after all. It cannot be done for you. You must make the effort. But if you make the effort and you have the desire, the desire will grow, the desire will increase.

Do not become discouraged by the more obvious desires. One may have, for instance, sexual drive, and they may even be engaged in sex due to the body and due to illusion that's still going on. But even while engaged in the act of sex, one's true self can be desiring to be freed from the illusion they are bound by, even while they are engaging in the illusion. It need not be *binding* them. Even while they are engaging in the act, they can become free from the illusion.

This is the way to become free, to see something for the illusion it is, not to repress it and to try to pretend that it is not there. Like someone who wants to eat, so they always remain hungry. In other words, you will still desire to eat and you may take pleasure in eating, but this does not mean that you will be taking away necessarily from your path, although, as you advance in years, the illusion of the eating will begin to lift. You will not become so enamored by the illusion of it. You will become less concerned with, for instance, the taste, and you will go through less time and effort to produce varieties of taste and enjoyment in the eating. But it will *come naturally* from your desire – you see. So even while you are desiring and you are *in* the state of going through so much trouble to have something that is very tasteful, even in that state, you can be evolving and growing. Or while you are engaged in sex, and you do not see any end to it, do not become discouraged. This is the number one thing that you must remember: you do not give up; you do not become discouraged and stop. The only way you will fail is if you stop. And that is what the illusion wants you to do.

The illusion wants you to believe that: "As long as you have an attraction for sex, you will not be able to get out. As long as you have an attraction for these things in illusion, you will not be able to get out. First these things must stop, and then you will get out." This is the mistake of so many processes. And in all your religions you have your moral codes, and so many of them are doing so much damage. They are missing the point of how it should be.

It is true that as you approach death, as you come nearer to the end of your life, you must finally be beyond the illusion of these things. But people's bodies, the body itself, has its own consciousness, you may say, its own memory banks, and it is used to certain types of food; it's used to a certain amount of sex; it is used to a certain environment – so many things. So it is not bad to cater to the illusory parts of the body to some extent. For example, it is not that you just suddenly pretend or suddenly repress whatever is there between husband and wife and just say, "Oh, it is just illusion. You are not really my wife; you are not really my husband. You will just be somebody else, so now I don't have that particular attraction." The mind cannot suddenly change; the body cannot suddenly change. Everything must gradually change from a *state of awareness*. But as you become aware of something, then you can help yourself and work in the area.

Like for instance, sexual energy. It is good to control this, but there is a difference between controlling and repressing. It is one thing if you can control it, sublimate this energy in a proper way, then you can be fine and sane about it. But to repress it and just deny it can create another set of problems, like a demented state that creates havoc.

So *how* you become detached, *how* you become free from the illusion must be gradual. Yes, there is a letting go that must be going on. When you begin this process in earnest, you will begin to let go and it is simply that. You just *begin* to let go. That does not mean that one night you have sex and you begin to let go, and the next day it will be gone. It is not possible, practically speaking.

In some cases, things can just be stopped due to a change of heart, a change in your mind and your heart – where you, within a very brief period, suddenly feel entirely different about something and then it can be stopped. And this can happen on your path. And this *does* happen in many ways. People who have been coming notice personality changes. How they deal with others is different, how they feel is different, how they see things is different. Not that they artificially are *trying* to see, but they are just observing and they are just truly seeing. But when the illusory part comes up, do not become discouraged because it is still there. Until you come to a full state of awareness, it will still be there. It is to be expected, so you must not become discouraged.

To come to a full state of awareness is a very rare thing, a very precious thing, not easily achieved. So why become discouraged when some illusion comes up? It doesn't matter what that illusion is; it doesn't matter what society has said; or if you are condemned by society or your friends because of an activity – whatever. It has no meaning; it has no bearing, because it is all illusion. What is very good here and what is very bad here are the same, because they are both illusion. So you may be a humanitarian helping so many people, or you may be a thief and hurting so many people, but as far as coming to a state of full realization, both have the same equal opportunity. *They both* have to let go of their illusions. They are *both* just in an illusion – good or bad it is an illusion and must be stopped. So do not be so concerned if the activities are good or bad, because they are just illusion and have to be given up.

But when I say they have to be given up, it does not mean that tomorrow you will just stop all your illusions and you will just be in a full state of awareness. It does not work like that, it is not possible; and you will only create such havoc in your mind that you will ultimately end up in confusion and frustration and discouragement – and fail. Some people have understood that ultimately, when one comes to a full state of awareness, that one is more or less beyond what you call "the gratifications of the body" – sex and eating (not that one does not need to eat, but one is not bound by eating).

This could be gone into for some length of time; there are so many examples. But generally people have some idea; they know that certain things have to stop. So artificially they just stop all of the things that ultimately will be stopped, and they think that by stopping those things, by just stopping sex now, by just stopping everything that is illusion now, that it is suddenly somehow going to speed up the letting go. In some respects it is true, but *only* if it is stopped from control or from a change of heart. It must be something real; it must be something true. Not just some repression. If it comes from repression, then you are just prolonging something. You still want it, but you are just pretending, practically speaking, you are just pretending that you do not – and that is not aware. Like those that artificially stop sex, and the entire time they have stopped sex, they are desiring sex. The true way to awareness is that you come to a point where you see *the illusion* of sex. And you also have to simultaneously begin training the body, because the energy is used to flowing in a certain direction, and the energy must be changed and transformed, and this takes time. So you must not become frustrated. So the energy and the body must change and be adapted; the mind must change and become adapted, and ultimately through awareness you must *see* the illusion of it. *Then* you will be able to give it up and you will not be hankering. Why? Because you will see the illusion of it. But those that repress and stop something are just prolonging the problem. It does not help.

But you can begin controlling things to some extent. You can begin *practicing* control. Practicing control is good, but you should not become discouraged or distraught when you lose control or when you again engage in an activity, like sex, which you are trying to control. You control it for longer and then longer periods of time, if one is working on that area.

But you see, behind all of this is the desire. In other words, you must decide: Do you want to leave in this lifetime? And if you really do, then all of your activities will change and will start to direct you in a way that you will be able to leave in this lifetime. You will start planning and seeing things in that light. You will start focusing more and more and understanding what it is that you need, what facility you need, what arrangements you need in order to succeed – and you will execute those things. For instance, if someone is in a job where there is no peace and there is so much distress and tension that they cannot focus, and it is never going to be better, and as long as they are involved in it, it is going to be their ruination, then they must begin making an alternative plan: living more simply, making a change where they can do something where there is not that stress, where they can be more aware, they can be more conscious. But right now they may continue the activity. But it is a question of what their desire is now. If you have that desire now, then all of the things you are involved in now can begin to change, slowly. Your relationship with others, how you spend your time, everything can gradually start taking on another slant. Everything in your life will become *influenced* by this desire.

But first, try to see yourself separate from these illusory desires. These desires are not you. See them more as part of your illusory personality, who you think you are. Who you think you are is the personality that is desiring all these different things, and granted, these things will have to be changed, but see that as a separate thing. That is not you. And it is not easy to break free from this illusory personality. So you must be patient, and you must not become confused when the illusory personality exerts itself and becomes dominant, or appears to be controlling or running your life. Because even while you seem to be giving in to the whims of your illusory personality, you can be simultaneously desiring and praying for the truth even *while* you are engaged *deeply* in the illusory activities. That is what I mean by "desiring." So you may desire to have sex, but even while engaging in the act of sex, you can simultaneously be praying and desiring the truth. So the desires of the illusory personality do not stop the *true desire*.

Now of course, We are speaking of those who are sincere. Anyone can use the excuse and say, "Oh, no, I really just desire the truth," and be all in illusion, and not really desiring the truth and just not really changing. That is another thing. But as We have said before, those that do not wish to leave will not leave. It is that simple. And those that wish to leave will leave – *in spite* of these things. If you desire to leave, *you will leave*; and if you do not desire to leave, *then you will not leave*.

But these desires, these illusory desires – no matter how strong they are, no matter how much they seem to be controlling your life – do not have to stop your advancement on this path. And if you think that they do, and you let that stop you, then you have been tricked by the illusion. That is why I say, the main thing to remember is you must never give up. *You must never stop!* Because *only by that* can you fail. If you think, "I am too much in illusion. I have been trying for so long and I still have so many desires, so I will give up," then you will fail, and only then will you fail. Otherwise you will not fail. And you will see, if you practice sincerely, if you pray sincerely, if it is your desire, you will begin to notice this part that I speak of. You will begin to notice that there are two parts of you. There is one part, which you could say is your illusory self, and there is another part that is not bound by the illusion, that wants the truth.

And your advancement is going on continuously no matter what your outward activities are. There are so many examples. Just like when the Lord Jesus came, one of His main disciples was a woman who was a prostitute, which by normal moral standards is not considered to be a good position for advancement. But she suddenly had a change of heart and was able to totally surrender and become His disciple, and truly give up her desires. This is because of her true desire. So even though her outward activities were activities that are traditionally considered to be totally against the truth, totally against awareness, she was one of the most aware people. So this is an excellent example of the two personalities that I am speaking of: your *real* self, your *real* desire, and then whatever the illusory external self is involved in. They are like two separate things going on. This is particularly the case in this path, and you will begin to notice that there is a difference. And you will know when something is your illusory self and something is your true self. There is a difference.

Your conscious mind will understand very little. That is where faith and trust come. They are so important. You must have the faith and the trust in the Lord that even though you cannot understand what is going on with your conscious mind, still you continue and you have faith. Because your conscious mind can understand very little, and indeed, it can be very confusing, because what is going on frequently will appear to be, again by standards you have learned, against normal spiritual progress, you might say.

Guided Meditation

(Often when Gourasana spoke to a group, He would lead a guided meditation after His talk. All of Gourasana's speaking will take you deeper inside, but the guided meditations are specifically designed for this purpose.)

The important thing is, what is your desire now? Now, let go of your illusory personalities. Let go of who you think you are and go within and find that truth – now. Let go beyond the words.

(Meditation music starts playing in the background: "The Fairy Ring.")

How strong is your desire now? And if you cannot find that much, if you cannot feel that much, then you can pray.

There is no reason, there is no excuse to not move. There comes a point where you must let go of trying to understand with your conscious mind, and that point is *now*. Trying to understand it, trying to figure it out, you must let go of these things. The conscious mind will *never* understand. You must let something else take over, but you must *trust* in that something else. You must let it take you over. You must trust that the energy is benevolent.

Then increase your desire. Increase your effort; increase your longing. What is waiting is everything. So you must desire everything: no more illusion, but the truth. You must give yourself over to the truth; you must do *anything* for the truth.

So let yourself go. Whatever comes, let it come. You let the energy move you as you feel. The energy may move you in a way that you sit just perfectly still in silence. Or it could move you to much physical extravagance. So do not judge how the energy moves you, but just ask for it, pray for it, and let it move you. *Feel* the energy that is here.

And don't let anything stop you and never give up. Don't let your misconceptions stop you. There is no reason you cannot succeed. You can succeed. Everything is waiting for you.

The Force that Is Controlling Everything Is Not Chaotic

April 22, 1989, Pacific Beach, CA

(Meditation music ["The Fairy Ring"] is playing softly in the background during this talk.)

Sometimes it may appear as one goes through life that a force that is chaotic and irrational is controlling what is going on. Especially in times of suffering; there does not seem to be any apparent motive or need for such a thing as suffering. But need or no need, who can deny the existence of suffering and that it is going on so rampantly? The force that is controlling everything is not chaotic; it is in perfect order. The chaos only lies with you.

You are being guided. You are being taken to different places, put into different situations by your desire. And by the same desire you can become free of so many traps and illusions.

Most of you have been coming now for some time and have seen that people are placed in their life by their desire, by what it is that they want. Although to one who wants nothing but the truth, it may seem like insanity to want anything else; still, the reality is that most everybody wants the illusion. So you observe those around you, and you see how they are choosing the illusion. More often than not, they will clearly come out and state that they have no business with finding the truth – or very little. They will state that they are happy here on this plane of illusion and are not afraid to come back, and are looking forward to coming back. They have no plan for leaving.

Now leaving this plane of illusion is one of the *hardest* things to do. It requires the complete focus of every individual who wishes to leave. It must become *everything* in order to leave. But you see, with most people, they are not even serious about spiritual life. And then, even amongst those who are serious, there are so many things that they will not let go of; so many concepts that they have formed that they will not let go of. They cling on to them, and therefore they stay locked into a belief system.

So many belief systems, yet there is only one God. And the truths that are written seem to be contradictory preaching – talking about *different* Gods. Yet there is only one. So when one begins searching, immediately they can become trapped in so many processes, paths, so many variations. Just like what you call the New Age process; they become involved in so many things. And some of the things are so impotent against the illusion that one who knows, one who desires to leave, can see clearly that they will not become free by the processes others are taking up, nor are the others taking them up to become free.

But here we only have one focus, and that focus is to become free from the illusion – *completely* free from the illusion in this lifetime. And the reason that this is almost unheard of is because there are almost no individuals that are willing to pay the price to leave. It is rare to find someone who is even interested or willing to begin to pay the price, what to speak of finding someone who will go all the way, all the way out of this illusion.

Now I have not come for a while, and when I have come I have hardly spoken at all, and yet, look at the meditations of everyone. Look at the consciousness of everyone, and how it is changing. How it has been changing so rapidly. *Overwhelming energy*. This is how you find the truth – from direct experience, not from some scripture, not from some words. It is not the words that I am speaking now that are critical. It is not the words that I am speaking now that will save you. They merely are a direction for you to go in, to give you some hint, some idea.

Where is the faith coming from? Where is the faith coming from of the few members who have stayed and who have continued this *very* difficult process? The faith is coming from the experience. And I have shown, more or less, that My being in this body makes no difference. This is just a manifestation to guide and to help, to assist. But the Lord is everywhere; so wherever you are, whatever circumstance you end up in, in your life, you can come to a state of full awareness.

It is not that there is not some benefit to these processes that others are practicing, but the illusion is so strong that there is no time to waste with weak or impotent processes.

Another thing that is unique about this group is the individuality that is maintained. In organized religions especially, there is literally a force pulling everyone to become alike, to become the same, but here there is such a diversification of personalities and life styles. So you need to be tolerant and understanding. You cannot understand another's reality. It is so complex; it is built upon lifetimes. The psychologists think they know how much your life is affected just by the past of this life, your childhood; what to speak of how your life is affected by so many other lifetimes. So every individual is so complex and literally is formed by such a wide variety of factors that it makes understanding them practically impossible – practically – to understand them completely and their behavior.

Actually, individuality is good. If it is there, it is a good sign, because there is not some trap being formed of some way that you should behave if you are involved in this. There should not be a set of concepts, a set of behavioral rules that everyone will act the same and look the same and fit into a certain mold – which is emphasized in the organized religions. Not just religions, but society itself is dictating conformity all the time. So do not try to change what is not possible to change, what there is no reason to change, and that is the highly unique characteristics that each of you has as individuals. You can see an individual's personality as an interesting aspect of them. This is for practically dealing with each other. Ultimately, even the personality will go. Someone does not need to behave like you in order to advance. This we have seen from the wide varieties of behavior in the people that have come – some from far away, some close, different problems and yet the same end result is being achieved. The same faith is increasing. You see? Some come more; some come less; still the same connection is there. You cannot say that one must come a certain amount and then they will achieve consciousness, and if they don't, then they will not. That is not true. It is your desire that will decide whether you succeed or not. So if someone is not coming and they are not concerned, then they will not leave the illusion, and that will be according to their desire. And that will be perfect.

If someone truly wishes to leave this plane of illusion in this lifetime, you do not need to be their guardian because *they* will see to it that they leave.

Check your heart now. Is there anyone who does not want to leave this plane of illusion? Is there anyone? Is there anyone who wishes to stay here for another life? That desire must grow; to leave this plane of illusion must become *everything*. And if that isn't planted in somebody's heart, you do not need to govern them at all so that they may succeed. This is not a process. This is not an organized religion where there are leaders to see that the followers are following the rules properly, executing the dogma properly, and seeing that the words are repeated properly – and where what the leaders consider to be "proper changes" ends up perverting the truth.

I'm mentioning this because there must be a certain freedom, a certain license to move in whatever direction you need to, at whatever speed you need to, in order to succeed; and that is going to *vary widely* from individual to individual. One person may be building a foundation upon which to act, but they may not act for several years, whereas another person is all ready to act and is acting, fully, one hundred percent all of the time. This does not mean that one is succeeding and one is failing. They are just approaching the same problem from different places.

So you as individuals also must have faith in yourself. If it is in your heart to leave here, then the way will be shown *how* to leave here. You do not have to behave like everyone else. Or more frequently, people think certain things are *misbehaviors* that are holding them back. You do not need to be concerned so much about these things, behaving or misbehaving, behaving "good" or behaving "bad." It is all an illusion. So if you are involved in a so-called bad illusion or if you are involved in a good illusion, it is the same problem. It is just an illusion that needs to be cleaned up. So what is considered immoral or wrong against this society's standards or other societies' standards is not so critical, it is not so important. But I want to emphasize: for an individual who is involved in activities that are frowned upon by maybe husband or wife or other friends, that nothing is going to stop you if you want to leave this plane of illusion. *Nothing is going to stop you!*

So We try to talk a little bit. We try to have some understanding through speaking, but it only helps a little bit. If everyone who has been coming were to say at this point what is the philosophy, what is going on, there would be such variation; so many different slants on the same thing. Some very wrong. Some opinions and concepts are strongly controlling, that you can be certain of. The concepts are so ingrained. They are ingrained not just from this lifetime, but from so many lifetimes. Society, in order to go on as a society, has to have certain rules and standards. But those rules and standards are just that – for society's functioning. And one need not feel bound by these things, because you are not bound by them. You are only as bound as you choose to be.

So from the beginning, I have said that here we want to move very quickly. And there are those who perhaps one year ago were doubting their movement, and now there is no doubt; who one year ago did not understand the movement that was taking place at the time, were practically not even aware of it, and are now overwhelmed by it. But one year is not such a long time.

The true understanding will come from your heart. The true understanding will come beyond the words. During the meditation when you let go, something takes you over and moves you. That something cannot be explained by words. You cannot find that place by words. That is the real communication.

Now we are talking, so are there any questions? Is there any discussion that anyone would like to have, to try to understand?

Person One: Gourasana, when you talk about us moving, this movement that's going on, how can one understand this? Is there something physical that is taking place? Just a feeling, a knowing that things are changing in our lives? There's been a lot of changes in my life since I've been coming here and not all of them seem good. I'm just trying to understand this word "movement."

Gourasana: Yes. Well, one good point in the question is that frequently it does not feel good. Again, because of previous concepts, some people have difficulty in this area. They think if they are going toward God, then it should be all happiness and joy and love and light. But this is not supported *anywhere*. If you study all of the great yogis, all of the great teachers, all of the great masters, you will know they went through *so much* suffering and difficulty. Not just suffering physically, but suffering that they went through in their minds: mental anguish, the doubt, the fears. Their situation is not so different from your situation. So anyway, that is one thing – because something does not feel good, do not misinterpret and think that you are going in the wrong direction, because as some have seen, sometimes it feels very bad, because who you think you are is beginning to die, is beginning to disappear, to lose its hold.

Things to detect in movement are difficult. This is one area that you *can* detect sometimes. It is a possible area to detect, and that is when you look at how you feel, at who you are; if you have some clear idea of that, you will see that it is changing, because as you change, as you go nearer to the light, then your personality, who you think you are, is going to change. Also, your awareness of what is going on around you is going to change. You're no longer going to have the same perspective. Even if you've been involved in spiritual life, even if you've looked at the world as illusion before, still it is not going to be the same, because you are going to be seeing it more and more through realization. So you will *just see.*

But it is a basic thing to practice seeing the illusion. You *must* be able to see the illusion. You *must* be able to see what is light and what is dark. So as you move, as you advance more, it should be clearer to you what is light and what is dark. And this will be there in observing other's lives. You will see their darkness. You will see where they are holding on, what they are clinging on to, what they will not let go of. You will see why they are in that situation – because they will not hear, because they will not change. They have an idea, they have a desire, but that is not to leave. They have *another* desire, another idea, and they are fulfilling that. So what can be expected but that their desire is fulfilled, or at least their endeavor to fulfill that desire is there.

Yet there's also movement that you can feel. It is just a motion that even when sitting perfectly still, you can feel. Not a motion of the heart beating or the lungs expanding, or other organs functioning, but a motion that is moving the entire body. It is a slow powerful motion, but it is so subtle that one has to come to a certain point of awareness *to feel it.* But even then, you have to remember these are words, and how one perceives it can be entirely different than the words used to describe it.

The thing is, if your desire is to leave, and you will not be changed, you will not give up that idea no matter what; if that is in your heart, then you will move. If you are making an endeavor with an end result, or a conclusion in mind by a certain point, even though you may not have a conscious figure – but in your heart you are going to try something for so long, one or two years, and then if it doesn't work you are just going to stop – then it will not happen. This change, this momentum, will only take place when one is ready to give up everything.

This does not mean that you can give up everything at this moment, but it means that *you are willing to give up everything.* And this means *everything*, because everything here is an illusion. So even though you cannot see how you will do something, you must *be open* to doing it. If you are not open to doing it, then you are closing a door on the truth.

One may have to give up family. One may have to give up a husband or wife or lover or friend. *May* have to. Eventually you will give up everything. *But what giving up everything means is you give up the illusion of it.* So one may give up their illusory relationship with another living entity, but once the illusion is gone from the relationship, then the relationship becomes something so great, so different. So you cannot understand how things can be, but one who wishes to leave will not let *any* thought stop them. They will not think, "I cannot go through the suffering, the pain, the separation from someone that I love, someone that I care for. So I will not do that."

I'm just giving examples. The changes that everyone needs to make are as individualized as the people – *highly individualized.* What everyone needs to do is very different. What everyone needs to let go of is different. But in one sense, it is all the same, and that is, it is all just illusion. You just have to let go of the illusion.

You can tell you are moving. Why? Because certain illusions will begin to lift. But even while certain illusions are lifting and practically disappearing, there still may be certain illusions that are holding on, that are strong; and you must not let these discourage you. You must not make the mistake of thinking that the level you are at depends on the degree to which all your illusions are gone, because everyone has the hard illusions – the last few illusions that they need to face and let go of, and they may not do this until the last few years of their life. Maybe even the last few months of their life, there just may be something they're holding onto until the very end. There are illusions that are more directly related to cycles of the body and bodily functions, and they may tend to control you more than other illusions. But in any case you will see illusions disappearing; you will see your consciousness changing; you will see your view on things changing.

But you cannot judge accurately your advancement – although it is necessary to evaluate and to constantly be doing the best that you can and constantly analyzing and thinking how you can do better. That is a part that is going to be there if your desire is there. But you cannot, you should not, make the mistake the illusion wants you to make – and that is to judge yourself so harshly that you believe that you cannot make it because of some imperfection, because you have a concept. Everyone has so many concepts of what it is to be a saint or a sage or a yogi or a self-realized person – whatever you want to call it. And of course, the societies that are controlling the literature are tainting everything with their moralistic versions. You may be led to believe that all saints and yogis have a certain moral standard and they all have that, and if you do not have that, then you cannot be in the same category. This just comes from a moralistic society. So many that have died fully aware have not been considered saints, because they did not fit the picture that society has painted of what a man or woman should be like if they are with God.

Even if you cannot detect movement, movement is going on. That is one thing you should try to remember. Even those that are *not* endeavoring are moving; everyone is evolving. There is no one that is not evolving. Just through their normal existence, everyone is evolving (although someone who is endeavoring is moving at a faster rate). And in that evolving there is a certain motion, a certain movement that is taking place.

So again, what others are doing, what experiences others are having, this is not you. This has to be remembered by everyone. You cannot tell from the outside. You cannot tell; your awareness is not great enough to tell where another is, what their consciousness is. They might be *so* very sincere to a point, and then suddenly they are against it, as we have seen. We have seen some come who appeared to be *so sincere, so deeply sincere*. They verbally made statements dedicating their lives to this. And now they are in total darkness and illusion; now when they speak, they say their goals are illusion, and they state what their goals are. And the goal of leaving this plane of illusion no longer exists for them.

So the key will be if you cannot understand clearly, if you cannot measure motion properly, if you become discouraged at all – the main thing is that you do not give up. If you do not give up, then you will succeed. Why do so few make it? The ones that begin do not continue properly. They do not maintain the intensity necessary to succeed.

So where you end up, what you do in life is going to depend upon your desire. Everything is dependent upon your desire. If your desire is for a little light, a little awareness, then there are so many organizations; there are so many things you can do. You can go and receive advice from beings that are coming through, channeling, as you call it. They can give good advice on how to be happy on this plane of illusion. As this is what everyone is trying to do, naturally they are very popular.

As I have said, to leave the plane of illusion frequently means entering into a state that is not so pleasant – that requires, unfortunately, more difficulty than if you did not do it. So where everyone is looking for less, here, you may find more difficulty. But that is the way of the path. I can tell you no one has ever come to a state of full awareness easily. It is very, very difficult – and it is based upon your desire, and it is beyond the words. Though the words may be helpful, just see how little *need* there is for talking amongst the group. Although I'm here to answer questions, the need, the pressing need is not in this area, because already most have come to the point of understanding it is beyond the words. There is just very little to talk about. Mainly it is a time to move.

And if you cannot understand when the movement isn't there and you need to know why, then there is prayer. Always one can pray. One can pray constantly to know the truth, to find the truth. But who will seek the help? So few now will even seek the help. How many will pray to the Lord and ask for His help? The popular groups mostly turn away from this direction: "You find your own power." But you *will* find your own power if you find the Lord. But you will *never* know your power unless *you do* find the Lord. Do not waste time with these things; they are of practically no benefit. Use some discrimination in what you do, in what your activities are. *See* if they actually are moving you. *See* if they actually are helping you. Use discrimination; do not just do anything.

So. Before we go on, are there any more questions?

Person Two: I have a question. This is my first meeting, and it's a very exhilarating concept to liberate from the mundane, a very interesting concept to embrace God. Can you explain that experience?

Gourasana: This is not clear, what it is you need to know.

Person Two: A person can liberate himself from the mundane and feel that liberated movement, the throbbing of the heart. But even in that space it seems that there's further to go – a personal relationship with God has to be there. How do you embrace that concept?

Gourasana: You speak of concept but it is not a concept, it is a reality. The Lord is a reality. And one will come to that point through desire. Because to be free from the illusion means that you are with the Lord. You cannot truly be free from illusion and not have a connection with the Lord – although there are different degrees in the relationship along the way. Once one comes to a full state of awareness, then they are fully aware of the Lord. Some people do not even recognize it is the Lord in the beginning of their meditations (as the word "the Lord" is not used). It is an energy that is felt; still, it is coming from the Lord. That is why the only test of what is going on here, the only test of what is being said, is your own direct experience. Not that some words or some belief system is formed and everyone believes and acts the same. Those that are here, are here because they have had an experience and are continuing on in that experience. And what they are finding in their experience is a more personal connection with the Lord.

When We speak of letting go, or moving, automatically that connection with the Lord will begin to come. But again, depending upon the individual, the emphasis upon the personality of God is more or less the emphasis. So one may use silent meditation and just move without any words or thoughts. Or one may devote the majority of their time to prayer and seeking help and assistance. Or of course, then the combination of different ways of achieving this. But whatever way one approaches the Supreme, they are going to begin to feel that personal relationship; though they may not understand what is going on, they are beginning to feel it.

And because of the overwhelming nature of the energy of the Lord, it may come as fear; it may come and it may feel like the worst thing you have ever felt, because it is a total threat to your illusory self and it is coming like death. Because serious progress in the spirit means that the material is going to die. So this is one reason it does not feel very good at times, because always there is something that is dying. The illusion is dying; you're letting go of it and it is dying. But you cannot avoid your connection with the Lord. If you are moving, you cannot avoid that.

But again, depending upon the individual, the personal feelings, the personal exchange that is there with the Lord will vary. And one cannot judge themselves too harshly because they do not have some feelings like that. And by the same token, if someone does have these feelings of love, or even what they consider to be love, they should never be complacent. One should never become complacent in spiritual life. Never satisfied. Never satisfied until a full state of awareness has been reached: no matter how many realizations, no matter how many experiences, no matter how far you've come, no matter how much you are removed from the illusion – *you never stop*. And hopefully you do not slacken, you continue.

Person Three: Gourasana, when I experience this overwhelming love, when I have that personal connection, it's difficult not to be attached to it being like that all the time. When I come the next time, I try to get that same experience to happen again and it's never the same twice. But still because it was such an overwhelming experience, I want it to be the same. It is very difficult to get beyond that, or if I don't get that experience, to not get discouraged.

Gourasana: Yes, it will never be the same, because you are always changing. The circumstances are always changing. Whenever you go into a meditation, you must always remain open to how it's going to be, because it can be so entirely different every time. And though certain experiences may come, generally there is just work and endeavoring that has to go on, and this may not be pleasant – the work and endeavor that has to go on to become free. And if you become caught by only the pleasurable aspects, then it is indeed a trap. You must be willing to accept *everything* that is going to aid you to move forward. The focus must be in becoming free from illusion. That must be the focus, not the experience. The experiences will come by the way and they will go – good *and* bad experiences. You must not become attached to the experiences. Of course I say you must not, so if you are, then it is something you need to let go of, because it is indeed something that holds you back. It is indeed something that you must let go of.

To let go of an area of your illusion could be the most excruciatingly painful thing that you have experienced; but you should welcome that just as much as you welcome ecstatic experiences, because that experience which feels bad may be moving you forward further than the other experience. So again, the concept of how it should be spiritually. . . . You must welcome however it comes and move however is profitable at the time. And that will come from your knowing.

When someone is in illusion, their illusion is always very clear. It is not something very vague and subtle that is hard to perceive. There is something always there that makes it very clear why that person is in illusion, why they are not moving, what it is they will not let go of.

This is a common problem. I am not saying this is your problem, but this is one of the foundations for what you call the New Age thinking or philosophy: They want everything to be the positive side. When they meditate, they want to experience only joy, only love, only laughter, only happiness, what they consider these things should be like. And if something else comes, then they have labeled it as bad and do different exercises and things to remove the bad feelings so they will only feel good. But this is self-defeating if they truly want to advance spiritually, because as I have said, the movement frequently feels bad. It does not feel good.

So don't become trapped in this like so many of the New Age people, because it is a terrible trap. Be grateful for when those ecstatic times come, and immerse yourself into those experiences that you do have. That is nice. They can be appreciated, certainly. You want to appreciate *any* experiences you have. But not only do you not want to seek for those same experiences, you want to be open to anything that comes. Just as you have seen in spiritual life, and others here have also seen, experiences may be there of the positive nature, but generally they are in the minority; and it is generally very hard, very hard work. So you have to give up that it is going to be easy and that it is going to be ecstatic. You have to become open to however it *should* be at the time – not how you *want* it to be. This is very important in meditation.

So I think that is enough talking for tonight. So now everyone should get ready to begin working. Whatever is necessary.

Acknowledgments

Enormous thanks to everyone who helped produce this book of Gourasana's words.

I have been closely supported in all aspects of this project by Ed Jerum.

Special thanks go to Tamara La Toto, Nan Inglis, Nancy Coleman, Maha Swanson, and Ian Ross for their review and editing help. Much thanks to Jennifer Luth for cover design and art direction, Edwin Mossop and Andra Joyce-Higa for copyediting, Leslie McDonald for production and proofreading, Claus Pfitzner for layout design, and Nate Scoble for layout. And my great appreciation for those who pitched in to help with all the final checking and proofing of the book: Marlowe Kayce, Shelley Geffen, Deborah Byers, Terrie Clark, Selia Trujillo, Sonja Dehm, Christine Vlachos, and Mark Christie.

THE LADY

About Miracle of Love

Miracle of Love is a nondenominational church offering a path to spiritual freedom. It was founded by Gourasana in 1991 and is now led by His successors, Kalindi and The Lady. Kalindi was given the special destiny to personally present spiritual truth as the living Voice of God. As such, she provides the spiritual direction for Miracle of Love and has been guiding thousands to their spiritual freedom. Anyone, anywhere in the world can become a student or disciple of Kalindi.

Miracle of Love has a worldwide network of centers and communities, and offers programs, books, lectures, DVD's, and Internet classes to assist people traveling the path Home. A highlight of all Miracle of Love programs is the close personal and individual support given to participants.

One of the main offerings is the ***Miracle of Love Seminar,*** which is held throughout the world. This is a profound six-day experience guiding people within to wake up their consciousness and discover the truth of who they are. The Seminar helps people come to a place where they experience unconditional love and a personal, undeniable connection to God. Participants are led within to release the pain, fear, guilt, shame, anger, and heartbreak inside of themselves.

In the Seminar, participants learn the ***Modern-Day Meditation***, a unique meditation practice that provides direction for achieving both spiritual and material success. This meditation was developed by Gourasana to help with all aspects of modern living, including the needs of body, mind, heart, and spirit.

More Information

Websites about Miracle of Love and Gourasana

www.miracle.org
www.gourasana.org
www.miracleofloveseminar.org
www.theladyinprayer.org

Audio versions of Gourasana's talks are available for purchase at www.bookstore.miracle.org.

Contact Numbers for Miracle of Love

US main number
(800) 338-3788

Los Angeles
(866) 922-3366

Asheville, NC
(888) 250-8115

Germany
++49 [0]180-Kalindi
++49 [0]180-5254634

Holland
++31 [0]88-Miracle
++31 [0]88-6472253

Switzerland
044 586 07 30

Australia
+61 8 9284 5104

Argentina
00 54 11 5983 0981

Made in the USA
Middletown, DE
28 October 2023